D0883065

History Shock

History Shock

When History Collides with

Foreign Relations

John Dickson

UNIVERSITY PRESS OF KANSAS

© 2021 by the University Press of Kansas

All rights reserved

Published by the University Press of Kansas (Lawrence, Kansas 66045), which was organized by the Kansas Board of Regents and is operated and funded by Emporia State University, Fort Hays State University, Kansas State University, Pittsburg State University, the University of Kansas, and Wichita State University

Library of Congress Cataloging-in-Publication Data

Names: Dickson, John S. (John Shields), author.

Title: History shock : when history collides with foreign relations / John Dickson.

Other titles: When history collides with foreign relations

Description: Lawrence : University Press of Kansas, 2021 | Includes bibliographical references and index.

Identifiers: LCCN 2020040365

ISBN 9780700632022 (cloth)

ISBN 9780700632039 (epub)

Subjects: LCSH: Dickson, John S. (John Shields) | United States. Foreign Service—Officials and employees—Biography. | Diplomats—United States—Biography. | United States—Foreign relations—1989– | United States—Foreign relations. | Diplomatic and consular service—United States—History—20th century. | Diplomatic and consular service—United States—History—21st century.

Classification: LCC E840.8.D477 A3 2021 | DDC 327.2092 [B]—dc23

LC record available at https://lccn.loc.gov/2020040365.

British Library Cataloguing-in-Publication Data is available.

Printed in the United States of America

10 9 8 7 6 5 4 3 2 1

The paper used in this publication is acid free and meets the minimum requirements of the American National Standard for Permanence of Paper for Printed Library Materials Z39.48-1992.

To Joe, Margaret, and Annie.

"People are trapped in history, and history is trapped in them," Baldwin wrote. But it is also true that the little pieces of history move around at a tremendous speed, settling with a not-always-clear logic, and rarely settling for long.

—Teju Cole, "Black Body: Rereading James Baldwin's 'Stranger in the Village,'" *New Yorker*, August 19, 2014

Contents

Preface and Acknowledgments

One of the reasons I look back fondly on a career in the Foreign Service was that it afforded me an unending opportunity to learn. The sense of wonder upon arriving in a foreign culture and taking in the new and different sights, sounds, and smells always invigorated me. After three days, I found myself an "expert," only to spend the next couple of years peeling back the layers of complexity and nuance in each foreign environment. The realization would emerge that I could never truly become an expert, but the ability to keep learning lasted until the day I left, making for rich, fulfilling, and intense experiences.

For these reasons, international travel continues to take up too much of my annual calendar and budget, but there are always more places than either time or money will permit. I used to refer to getting bitten by the "international bug" that won't let go and will return once the pandemic eases.

Early on, I found that in the process of learning about the foreign culture, I was also gaining insight into my own. Sometimes this happened as I interacted with people whose views about the United States ranged from the comical to the infuriating. One university professor in South Africa, for example, wanted to know why he couldn't vote in US elections since our decisions would impact his own life. Conspiracies about the role of the United States in seemingly every single mishap or views gleaned from the American television shows seeped into foreign perceptions of home.

Seeing different ways of life also made me look at the environment I grew up in and took for granted. Like the fish who doesn't understand water until forced out of it, I was able to see those areas that the United States had in common with or where we stood apart from other societies. These ranged from the mundane, such as the hours for work or meals and the high walls surrounding our homes, to the more profound, including the decidedly more visible complexity of race relations and tensions in the United States. I suspect I am not alone in this aspect of foreign travel or living. Not only do we learn the foreign culture, but the opportunity to take in that environment causes us to learn and for the most part appreciate our home culture.

Over the course of my career, I began to notice a history gap: my foreign counterparts were drawing on a history that I never learned, either because I had a competing version or because I was simply unaware of any version at all. Even though I had studied history in college and continued to read almost exclusively nonfiction histories and biographies, I grew increasingly aware of these differences in historical understanding. Furthermore, I also found myself more and more at a disadvantage in my professional endeavors to advocate for and defend US interests and policies, as I was starting out with a different base of knowledge than my counterparts. Pushback from my exchanges would occur with a lesson in history that, because of my own ignorance, was hard to counter.

As I reflected on my career, I noticed that this historical gap manifested itself differently in the various countries where I served. In South Africa, for example, I tended to graft my history onto theirs. In Canada, I accepted that I simply did not know. In Mexico, the resentment against the history of American involvement was as fresh to Mexicans as it was shocking to me to learn.

In order to delve more deeply into this phenomenon, I resolved to pursue an advanced degree in history. I applied to the graduate history program at the University of Massachusetts Amherst, which has a focus on public history, that niche of academic history concerned with conveying historical knowledge to a broad public. The areas of concentration in writing, preservation, museums, digital history, and archives paralleled traditional academic classwork and research.

When David Glassberg introduced the interplay between memory and history through the alluringly different lenses of *Remembering Ahanagran* by Richard White and *Confederates in the Attic* by Tony Horowitz, I knew I had found the path to unearthing my puzzling experiences with history abroad. John Higginson expanded this with the reading of *Silencing History,* Michel-Rolph Trouillot's analysis of history denial in Haiti. The idea of a book came in a writing class with Marla Miller, and my two workshop colleagues, Amy Braimeier and Trent Masiki, gave the first real encouragement to going through with the whole project. What follows bears the prints of other UMass academics, including the immigration and colonization research of José Hernández, the study of the foreign interventions of the United States under the tutelage of Chris Appy, and the careful mentoring of Mark Hamin on my thesis.

The case studies from my twenty-six years in the Foreign Service flowed easily. Harder, but more rewarding, was delving into the histories that I ought to have known as I maneuvered through these foreign interactions years earlier. Studying the history after the fact helped me appreciate what I had missed. I was not alone, though. The veteran career diplomat Bill Burns, who retired as deputy secretary of the State Department, noted in his memoir: "There is no playbook or operating manual in the Foreign Service, and the absence of diplomatic doctrine, or even systematic case studies, has been a long-standing weakness of the State Department."[1]

The case studies selected here are not the highlights of a career, of meetings with foreign leaders or diplomatic breakthroughs. They represent examples meant to highlight this interaction between history and foreign relations.

- Two separate chapters on Mexico demonstrate the presence of the past, of (1) a war fought over 170 years ago and (2) the impact of a long history of border crossings on immigration policies in the United States.
- Not knowing, or, unfortunately, even caring about Canada's history limits the prospects of what ought to be the closest, most mutually beneficial partnership the United States could enjoy.

- The difficult, painful history of race relations in the United States is no less complicated in the two cases presented here. Domestic racial tensions and crises play out on a world stage and detract from our ability to hold up American values in our relations overseas. At the same time, our own history clouds our ability to see the realities of race, as seen in the case study on Nigeria and South Africa.
- When Venezuelan president Hugo Chávez gave the newly inaugurated Barack Obama a book at the Summit of the Americas in 2009, he overshadowed all other outcomes from Obama's entry onto the world stage, by showcasing a competing version of the history of the United States in Latin America.
- The example of not knowing the history of American interventions in Haiti diminished what should have been a diplomatic victory in leading a surge of humanitarian support in the aftermath of the devastating earthquake in 2010.
- In Peru, I lay out a case where we actually employed history to our advantage through the State Department program of protecting cultural, archaeological property.
- Cuba presents the starkest example of competing histories, even as those histories are tied to a timeline, where the United States has a history that starts in 1959, while Cuba's extends back to the nineteenth century.
- The last two chapters try to make sense of the reasons why a full historical awareness is important in our relations with other countries, and then why we as a nation are so abysmal at knowing history and using it in our diplomacy.

I am indebted to the many friends and family members who withstood my rambling explanations of what I was proposing and who helped refine and clarify my own thinking. My Foreign Service colleague and historian Peter Samson proved to be a wise sounding board for my ideas and took a critical red pen to my first draft attempt. Two other Foreign Service friends, Jim Dickmeyer and Jim Nealon, have also followed the progress of my writing and helped keep me moving forward when I was close to abandoning the whole project.

A casual conversation with a Dutch friend about the book brought Susan Verhagen, an American expat living in the Netherlands, to my email in-box. Both her lack of firsthand Foreign Service experience and her long exposure to life outside the United States made her perspectives invaluable. A former editor herself, she devoted time to do her own research that resulted in suggested changes related to the historical content.

As a former teacher, I knew that the preparation for teaching is one of the best ways to master a subject. Classes at the Berkshire County Massachusetts chapter of the Osher Lifelong Learning Institute (OLLI) forced me to delve deeply into several of the countries discussed in these pages. Also through OLLI, I was introduced to Alice Heiserman, who took on the thankless duties of acting as my agent and another close editor of the manuscript.

In full disclosure, as a former employee with access to classified information, I had to obtain clearance from the Department of State's National Security Information Office, which made no changes in the manuscript but did ask that I include the disclaimer that "the opinions and characterizations in this pieces are those of the author and do not necessarily represent those of the US government."

None of this would have been possible without the support of my wife and advocate, Mary Boyle Dickson. She too got bit by the same bug, traveled with me to all these same places, withstood the hardships of life abroad, raised our three wonderful children, asked all the right questions about this project, and encouraged me to finish.

1

The Past Is a Foreign Country

When asked in May 2013 why Mexico curtailed cooperation with the United States in combating drug trafficking, *Washington Post* journalist Dana Priest said, "Well, Mexico has had a history of nationalistic dealing and a feeling of resentment towards the United States. We did invade the country a couple times and they haven't forgotten that."[1] She could have just said, "*History*." That single word captures at once how deep the memories lie in Mexico of two centuries of interactions with their northern neighbor, who has practically no memories of the same period.

The interview with Dana Priest appeared on the eve of President Obama's trip to Mexico City that same year. For seven years, under Felipe Calderón, the previous Mexican president, the two countries had enjoyed an unusually high level of cooperation against a backdrop of an enduring, unprecedented level of violence. Helicopters, secure networking equipment, computers, cellphone-tracing technologies, and training formed part of the more than $1 billion package to support Mexico's efforts to reduce violence and crime. Mexican authorities revamped their police forces by supplementing them with military units and set up vetted units to share information with US law enforcement. After six years of determined effort, the Mexican government arrested the heads of the major criminal organizations, and levels of violence started to decline.

The new Mexican president, Enrique Peña Nieto, wanted to reduce the imprint of US law enforcement in this effort. He wanted Mexico to exercise its sovereign rights and responsibilities. The *Post* reporter, though, interpreted this more broadly as *history*. Ignorance of the history of the relationship between the two countries leads to diplomatic missteps, if not disaster.

Her answer took me back about nineteen years to a visit to the National Museum of Interventions in Mexico City, a visit vividly imprinted in my memory. The year was 1999. I had been in Mexico for only a few months. At the start of my assignment to the US Embassy, my job as a public affairs officer dealt with press matters and cultural exchanges. I had gone to the museum on the recommendation of an American businessman. He was a long-time expatriate. We had discussed, on and off, the daily criticisms of the United States in the media that were so often made effortlessly and with such relish. He mentioned the museum and suggested that I might gain useful insights into how the United States was viewed in Mexico. I might begin to understand, he said, how deeply these feelings were rooted in Mexico's identity.

Mexico City was then, and still is now, full of important world-class museums. The Anthropology Museum, with its grand chambers illuminating the pre-Columbian civilizations of Mexico, is a wonder. The National Palace and its two-story Diego Rivera murals offer a vivid and colorful representation of Mexico's rich culture. The murals highlight the history of struggle and conflict in Mexico. Before the businessman mentioned it to me, I had not heard of the Museo Nacional de las Intervenciones (National Museum of the Interventions), in Churubusco in the southern part of the famous sprawl of Mexico City. The name of the museum itself, highlighting *interventions,* prepped me a little for what I might encounter there. I walked up the worn stone path to the entrance of the ancient monastery that had survived the bloody Battle of Churubusco and was now the museum. I braced myself to see how Mexicans viewed the war with the United States in 1848, when they lost half of their territory. The incongruities could not hide in this beautiful old Franciscan monastery built with walls of stone and rounded red clay tile roofs, with flowering bougainvillea gracing its grounds. Serene.

But no amount of bracing prepared me for this state-run museum, opened in 1981 by President José López Portillo, at Churubusco, the site of one of the last battles of the Mexican-American War. Here Mexican forces made a last courageous but vain attempt to defend the city against advancing, overwhelming US forces. In the museum I encountered people and events about which I had known little or nothing: St. Patrick's Battalion, a group of Irish and American deserters fighting side by side with the Mexicans 150 years earlier; Texas's struggle to break away from Mexico; the role of Ambassador Henry Lane Wilson in the overthrow of President Francisco Madero of Mexico, who had launched a revolution to install a democratic alternative to the longtime ruler José Porfirio Díaz in 1910; the siege of Veracruz and General Pershing's Punitive Expedition in 1916–1917, crossing the border into Chihuahua and trying to hunt down Pancho Villa, who had raided Columbus, New Mexico. The impact was not just the panels or the artifacts. It was the very notion of an entire museum dedicated to memorializing all the slights the United States had inflicted on Mexico, all the aggression, in one place, sanctioned by the government. I was shocked.

My instincts led me to argue with what I was seeing in the exhibits. The United States won the Battle of Churubusco, even though Mexico had St. Patrick's Battalion of deserters on their side, paving the way for the takeover of Mexico City. In 1916, General Pershing stopped the pursuit of Pancho Villa only because the United States entered World War I to help save the rest of the world! Where was the display on the massacre at the Alamo? Texas remembers the Alamo.

I latched onto and wouldn't let go of a few displays that strained credibility, as my way to deny the uncomfortable Mexican points of view on the events conveyed in the other exhibits. Only a small corner was given over to the mid-nineteenth-century moment in Mexican history when French emperor Napoleon III installed his Austrian cousin Maximilian as emperor of Mexico. The bullying role of the United States in Mexican affairs dominated the museum's interpretive themes, but France, in cahoots with Spain and Britain at the time, actually installing an Austrian as emperor in Mexico merited only a corner? And furthermore, the United States could not escape

blame even in this display. One of the placards in the exhibit casti-
gated the northern neighbor in this instance for *not* intervening over
France's Mexican machinations. Here the Museum of Interventions
seemed to imply that in this case Mexico wanted the United States
to intervene, but only on Mexico's terms, and that the United States
apparently selfishly refused. The label on the placard also omitted any
mention that Mexico's American neighbors to the north were thor-
oughly distracted by and immersed in their own Civil War! Further
still, the last exhibit, chronologically arranged, was dedicated to the
most recent intervention: NAFTA. The free trade pact, which had
been first posited by Mexico's President Carlos Salinas in the late
1980s, was here portrayed as a US economic intervention.[2] NAFTA
was official government policy in Mexico, the United States, and
Canada, and here was a Mexican government museum decrying the
free trade pact as yet another US intervention. I was surprised, angry,
and argumentative.

I was still arguing lividly in my head when I went to the exit. I
noticed two girls there, in school uniforms, looking at the first display,
which showed just a few maps and charts of Mexico before 1846 and
after. "No es justo," one said to the other, pointing to the obvious
discrepancy in size of territory. "It's just not fair."

My only consolation on leaving the museum was that there were
very few visitors, in contrast to the constant heavy traffic in other museums across the city. Perhaps not many people would see what was
going on here. At this beautiful Spanish colonial ex-convent, there
were signs of disrepair, even neglect. I thought hopefully that these
signs meant that the intensity of feeling toward the events depicted
in exhibits inside did not reflect the feeling of real Mexican people
outside. I was wrong. What led me past the anger to a more troubling,
lingering angst was the realization that it was hard, if not impossible,
to argue with the simplicity of the conclusion of the two girls. It *was*
just not fair. They echoed Carlos Fuentes in his novel *Gringo Viejo:*
"Haven't you ever thought, you gringos, that all this land was once
ours? Ah, our resentment and our memory go hand in hand."[3]

In sharp contrast, much of the American public hardly remembers its role in Mexico, or even the Mexican origins of the southwestern United States. A survey team sponsored by the Lincoln and Mexico Project in San Diego in 2014 traveled the length of the border marking the original boundaries. They encountered "only a few people . . . [who] barely seemed to grasp that Mexico once encompassed all of present-day Arizona, California, Nevada, New Mexico, Utah, Texas, more than half of Colorado, and smaller portions of Wyoming, Kansas, and Oklahoma."[4]

While the Museum of Interventions may have lost the immediacy of its hold over the collective Mexican memory, as witnessed by low visitor turnout, the interventions themselves have not. These events form an enduring part of Mexican identity. They are the *history* that Dana Priest of the *Washington Post* referred to when describing the reluctance of Mexican president Enrique Peña Nieto to continue working as closely with US law enforcement as his predecessor had. They are what gave me History Shock.

History shock is like culture shock in describing the sense of strangeness in engaging the ways of a foreign land. History shock is like future shock in that it causes a similar kind of surprise. But history shock looks backward and sees the present anew through a past differently constructed. The museum was not my first experience with the shock of confronting competing understandings of a shared history, but it starkly captured the notion of history in foreign relations. It clarified my own memories of prior personal encounters with the shock of competing histories; it helped prepare me for subsequent encounters.

I had come to the Foreign Service as an educator. I was a public school social studies teacher. But I had grown up with foreign encounters at a young age, from a summer camp in New Brunswick, Canada, to three years of teaching in the Peace Corps in Gabon, Central Africa. This teaching background led me to self-select the press and cultural track in the Foreign Service, known under the rubric of public diplomacy for its role of engaging foreign publics, in contrast to foreign governments. Initial assignments in Nigeria and South Africa led to more experiences on other continents as I moved to Peru and Mexico before closing out my career in Canada. Full circle.

Like many in the Foreign Service at the time, I felt this was a front-row seat on history. I started in 1984, when there was no certainty as to the outcome of the Cold War. Moving on, I then watched the ripple effects of the fall of the Berlin Wall from as far away as South Africa, which used that opening to launch its transition away from apartheid, again with no certainty as to its outcome. Countries from Rwanda to Somalia, Afghanistan to Yugoslavia, or even Peru and Mexico had not heard of the *end of history*, as the political scientist Francis Fukuyama proclaimed at the end of the Cold War. Events in those countries and elsewhere quickly filled the void left by the end of US rivalry with the Soviet Union, demanding sustained US engagement. The September 11, 2001, attacks drove that lesson home more starkly, but even our closest partners questioned the extent of the US response to those attacks. Finally, what seemed like a collective sigh of relief around the world, if not embrace, followed the election in the United States of Barack Obama. A country with its troubled history of race relations that could elect as president an African American, who had spent part of his youth overseas, had seemingly put behind its darker adventurism in the world. But then the subsequent rise of the turbulence of Donald Trump and his appeal to nationalist, xenophobic sentiments promised to nullify much of what Obama stood for in the eyes of the world.

Throughout, I knew that of course nations have different histories, which stress their own collective experiences, commemorations of their heroes, and dates of their decisive events in building their identities. Out of these, nations become *"imagined communities,"* to use the term that the political scientist Benedict Anderson coined in his influential book by the same name. Taken a step further, using the language of social constructivist theory, these identities, composed over time through social interaction, influence how nations define, pursue, and defend their national interests.

History shock grows out of these constructed identities, particularly when nations look at the same event differently. Nations arrive at their own collective understandings through debate and struggle over what the past means. Citizens use those understandings to determine a current course of action. These debates take place in schools and textbooks, in museums and monuments, newspapers, television, and movies, in parades, stamps, and coins. They unfold with little reference to the same struggles taking place in other countries, which have their own sets of issues to grapple with as they create a past to move forward. In such ways, countries pursue their own distinct understandings of events that spill across national boundaries. And in recent times no country seems to spill across its national boundaries as easily as the United States.

The front lines of these misunderstandings occur within the large diplomatic presence of the United States around the world. As diplomats approach their daily routines—processing visas, managing foreign assistance or cultural programs, preparing political or economic reports, advocating to advance and protect US interests, however they define them—they come face to face with history shock. That kind of daily conduct only rarely rises to the level of national import, since many of these interactions are small encounters. Still, a small decision to open the door to protesters outside the gate in Teheran, or a benign press statement from the US Embassy in Cairo, can ripple out and affect long-term policies and even presidential elections.[5] Moreover, these small human encounters can and should inform the larger issues at stake, and help determine how to approach those larger issues.

History shock occurs when these competing histories obstruct or color present-day events. From a foreign relations perspective, history shock can obstruct efforts to cooperate and engage on issues of mutual interest. In the extreme, it can lead to a total breakdown of diplomatic relations. Perhaps the most striking example was the 1979 takeover of the US Embassy in Iran. In deciding to allow the ailing shah, Reza Pahlavi, to enter the United States on humanitarian grounds, the country misread the depth of resentment in Iran for the US role in overthrowing Prime Minister Mohammad Mosaddegh and restoring the shah to power in 1953. So too, though, can the small interactions, repeated over time, have a longer impact. The single denial of a visa to an AIDS activist or a pattern of repeated visa denials from targeted countries have affected US foreign relations. Likewise, the offer of an exchange program to the man who would oversee South Africa's apartheid government transition or the accumulation of exchange opportunities for young democratic activists can have long-term, unforeseen consequences.

This book is, on the one hand, a personal memoir of isolated, seemingly unconnected incidents during my twenty-six-year career as a Foreign Service officer. Personal experience becomes the vehicle to shed light on the intersection of national memory and history with foreign relations. The personal memoir taps into and alternates with historic analysis that helps explain the personal experience.

It may be an overgeneralization to say that the conduct of US foreign policy has favored a pragmatic, power-relations approach. The United States brings to bear its full power—economic, military, political—as it seeks to exert its influence on events outside its borders. That approach, though, is rarely seen at the individual level. The exceptions are glaring, such as when a US corporate lawyer told his Canadian counterparts that they should seek a settlement of a softwood lumber trade dispute because "we have more lawyers than you do," just to keep it in front of the courts indefinitely.

Much of that power projection comes in the size of the US footprint overseas. The Foreign Service consists of a relatively small corps by US agency standards. Roughly eleven thousand officers fill in the organizational chart by functions: political, economic, management, consular, agricultural, commercial, and public diplomacy. Within that number are specialists (such as computer technicians, office managers, doctors and nurses, or budget officers) who keep the 265 overseas embassies and consulates operating. Some four thousand work as part-time or family-member appointments, given to working spouses and dependents. That's not all; there are at any given overseas post about two to three times the number of locally employed foreigners, adding another thirty-seven thousand employees to the total. Furthermore, within each embassy employees from other government agencies also pursue their unique missions. For example, in the US

Embassy in Mexico, employees from thirty different US agencies were represented, from the American Battlefields Monuments Commission (there is a US cemetery in Mexico City) to the FBI and the Defense Department. In Mexico, a total of 1,700 employees across the embassy and nine consulates has grown to 2,000 since I left in 2004. Those kinds of numbers translate into embassies that in some cases are almost the size of the foreign ministry.[6]

It is at the individual, personal level of each member of the Foreign Service where the United States can wield a different kind of power. My own bias shows preference for "soft power" (as elaborated by Joseph Nye in his book *Soft Power*). In contrast to hard, coercive power, Nye refers to the "attraction to the U.S." that helps to expand US influence. In this formulation, the world looks to US democratic values and defining achievements in science, technology, higher education, economic growth, and even entertainment for inspiration. Nye's view is that these serve to attract and convince rather than compel and coerce as the United States seeks to influence. With an eye to the politics of language, Hillary Clinton found the phrase "soft power" insufficient, so she coined "smart power" as a similar contrast to military muscle in the way the United States projects itself and seeks cooperation. The durability of Nye's formulation continues as scholars currently refer to the recent spate of information cyber attacks as "sharp power."

Face-to-face meetings with government officials, legislators, journalists, academics, business leaders, or visa seekers are still how most US diplomats assigned overseas engage. These are inherently soft power exercises. This approach of attraction rather than coercion ought to take into account the history of conduct between the United States and other nations. Our predilection is naturally to remember a foreign policy replete with Washington's Farewell Address warning about foreign entanglements in contrast to an internationalism highlighted with Woodrow Wilson's Fourteen Points, the Marshall Plan, or Jimmy Carter's emphasis on human rights. We tend to overlook our aggressive military or economic power behavior. Many other parts of the world well remember invasions, such as in Mexico, Cuba, and

Iraq, overthrows of governments in Iran or Guatemala, and assassinations of leaders in Congo or Chile.

The reality is that this kind of grand, sweeping history is only superficially available to most diplomats, at least on the US side. While a minority may have studied international relations at university, most arrive at a specific new post with an uneven mix of knowledge, experience, and background on the country. Once in country, they then set out to absorb as quickly as they can information about those individuals and events that have shaped that country's history and its relationship with the United States. Or, more starkly, in the words of one colleague: "History starts the minute the officer arrives at post."

Historians who seek to uncover the struggle over competing histories take into account, for example, in the US case, perspectives of previously marginalized groups. That contest similarly occurs between the United States and other nations over the arc of events they have shared. This book will offer examples where these competing histories influence the way the United States conducts its foreign relations. The competing histories include (1) different versions of the same history, (2) total ignorance of either history, either our own or the foreign version, and (3) misunderstandings arising from the different histories. This lack of historical awareness means, of course, the need to arm those representing the United States with history, both officially and informally. In this way, our representatives overseas can appreciate and overcome those encounters with history shock. More than that, though, it also means confronting history as elaborated by other countries and finding a place for it within our own history.

After the attacks of September 11, 2001, the question many in the United States asked was "Why do they hate us?" It was a natural question, which did not seek to excuse, explain, or apologize for that horror, but instead came from an honest confusion over a different image of ourselves as a nation. When Americans looked in the mirror, we saw ourselves as a generous nation, concerned with the plight of peoples around the world. Why didn't others see this? Confronting the realities of how the country has projected itself beyond its borders may be uncomfortable, may at times conflict with that image in the mirror. It should, though, be faced, not overlooked, not Photoshopped with an image imposed on other nations. If we face it squarely, relations the United States does seek around the world might actually improve. They will not get worse.

Suggested Further Reading

Many books provide background into the US Foreign Service and foreign affairs. The American Foreign Service Association published a compilation of officers telling stories that reflect the range of functions in US embassies: *Inside a U.S. Embassy: Diplomacy at Work* (Washington, DC: Foreign Service Books, American Foreign Service Association, 2011). Robert Moskin provides a more detailed, chronological narrative history of the Foreign Service in *American Statecraft: The Story of the American Foreign Service* (New York: Thomas Dunne Books, 2013). In his memoir of life in the Foreign Service, William J. Burns narrates his experiences on the front lines of policy making: *The Back Channel: A Memoir of American Diplomacy and the Case for Its Renewal* (New York: Random House, 2019). Richard J. W. Harker offers an excellent comparison of public history and public diplomacy in his *Museum Diplomacy: Transnational Public History and the U.S. Department of State* (Amherst: University of Massachusetts Press, 2020). Two critiques of American foreign policy are Michael Hunt's *Ideology and U.S. Foreign Policy* (New Haven, CT: Yale University Press, 1987) and William Appleman Williams's *The Tragedy of American Diplomacy* (New York: W. W. Norton, 2009). Walter Russell Mead outlines US foreign policy traditions in *Special Providence: American Foreign Policy and How It Changed the World* (New York: Knopf, 2001). Finally, I need to credit David Lowenthal's *The Past Is a Foreign Country* (Cambridge, UK: Cambridge University Press, 1985) for the title of this opening chapter, for its play on history as foreign relations, and for its wide-ranging exploration of the impact of the past on our present.

Mexico: The Impact of the Forgotten War

Madeleine Albright did not want to be photographed climbing up and down the pyramids in a floppy sun hat, comfortable frock, and sneakers. We were planning her visit to Monte Albán, the pre-Columbian archaeological site in Oaxaca, Mexico. Frumpy photos would not do. At least that is what her advance staff told us. Secretary Albright was coming for a one-day meeting with her counterpart, Rosario Green, as part of a three-day tour of Latin America. She had accepted an invitation from Foreign Secretary Green for an early Sunday morning private tour of Monte Albán before the site opened to the general public. Albright's staff insisted that the walk around the site take place outside of the view of the press. She wanted to dress casually. She did not want unflattering pictures of herself managing the uneven steps of the pyramids.

That changed late Saturday night, when the positive chemistry between the two foreign ministers during the day lowered either Secretary Albright's or her staff's guard. We had only a short time to get word to the press that they were welcome to come along. Unfortunately, not all the Mexican reporters learned of the change in time to catch the bus out to the site early the next day. By the time some of them arrived, the site was closed for security reasons. No more journalists could enter. Their prolonged protestations eventually led to permission to enter, but it was too late. The damage had been done.

Rather than frame this problem as a technical glitch, the journalists left outside saw this through the lens of the United States "taking over" a site of Mexico's heritage. "Monte Albán, Bajo el control de EU"

(Monte Albán, under US control) was the headline in the leading Mexico City paper *El Universal*.[1] For a week following the event, editorials and related stories decried the US "takeover." The Mexican press reports overshadowed the substance of the bilateral meetings on immigration, counternarcotics cooperation, migrant worker protection, NAFTA, and corruption. The US papers that covered Albright's trip carried nothing of this flap. Some just quoted her impressions of the visit to Monte Albán: "'No setting has been more inspiring than this one,' said Albright, speaking to reporters after her return to Oaxaca."[2] The United States believed it was a good trip and did not think any more about it.

That Madeleine Albright's early morning visit took on the trappings of controlling Mexican territory speaks to how close to the surface earlier interventions are in Mexico's collective memory. The incident exemplifies, in miniature, Mexico's zealous protection of its national sovereignty and patrimony. It is a story whose threads extend back to the war in 1846–1848. In the US-Mexican War, Mexico lost what is now Texas, California, Utah, almost all of New Mexico, Arizona, and large tracts of Colorado and Wyoming to the United States. It was a little over one-half of Mexico's territory at the time. Not surprisingly, Mexico's memory of that war is different than what the United States remembers, if we remember it at all.

Even the name of that war reflects competing interpretations of a common history. In Mexico it is called the War of North American Intervention. It is a name replete with implications of naked aggression. In the United States, calling it either the Mexican-American War or the US-Mexican War makes the conflict sound more balanced between two nations.[3]

Beyond just the name, each country entered the conflict with its own internal and heated political struggles that threatened to divide their new nations. In the United States, the issues were slavery and expansionism. In his campaign for the presidency in 1844, the Democratic candidate, James Polk, made expansion of US territory a priority theme, reviving the polarizing debate whether new states would be slave or free. Texas had proclaimed independence from Mexico nine years earlier, and the prospects of its statehood dominated the campaign. The likely prospect that it would enter the union as a slave state threatened a regional split in the country as a whole and within each of the two major political parties. Democrats generally tolerated slavery at that time. The Whigs were divided, with Cotton Whigs supporting slavery and Conscience Whigs in opposition.

Polk, as a candidate and later as newly elected president, was able to avoid a confrontation over slavery by drawing on nationalist sentiments of expansionism. It was a newspaper columnist, John O'Sullivan, who best captured the prevailing mood. In a July 1845 article, O'Sullivan coined the phrase "Manifest Destiny," which defined and inspired the self-described, very special virtues of the American people as a confident nation, with new industrial power, advancing rapidly to its preordained, natural boundaries. Factions in both parties and regions could rally around this shared glory, as long as they could sidestep the slavery issue. The irony is that while avoiding the racism inherent in the slavery implications of expansion, Polk embraced the racism inherent in Manifest Destiny: by the grace of a God-given right, Anglo-Saxon civilization had a duty to extend all of its advantages to everyone living between the two shining seas and, in turn, would reap the rewards.

In his first year in office, Polk was able to acquire Oregon from the British via the Oregon Treaty. Texas proved messier. Mexico had never recognized Texan independence and still considered it part of Mexican territory. Unmoved, the debate over statehood during the election campaign had raised the issue to such an extent that the lame duck president, John Tyler, and Congress felt compelled to act. Knowing that they would not get the two-thirds majority approval for a treaty with the independent Texas, Congress, by simple majority vote, approved an agreement to send a delegation to Texas to negotiate terms of annexation. President Tyler signed the agreement four days before Polk's inauguration, clearing the way for Texas to become a state.

In contrast, Mexico was still finding its footing as a new nation. Mexico declared independence from Spain in 1810 but did not gain it until 1828. However, Spain's and other European countries' political and economic influences were still strongly present in Mexico. Their impact continued across the racial, political, and economic fissures between criollos (Mexican Spaniards) and Indians, rich and poor, monarchists and republicans, federal and regional authority, which led to a series of unstable governments in its early years.[4]

By the time the war began, Mexico had had three different constitutions, and Antonio López de Santa Anna, who led the Mexican army in the war, had been president ten different times. Texas was not alone among Mexican regional entities in attempting to secede, but only Texas was successful. New Mexico and the Yucatan had strong independence movements of their own. Other regions openly defied call-ups to fight in the national army.

Perhaps it is unlikely that the journalists at Monte Albán specifically recalled the outbreak of the fighting in the war in 1846 when they wrote 155 years later that Madeleine Albright took control of Monte Albán wearing her floppy hat, comfortable frock, and sneakers. But the war could very well have been on their minds, since the first shots fired took place in territory that both sides claimed as their own. (Coincidentally, General Zachary Taylor was known to wear comfortable clothing and a wide straw hat that President Polk sent.) That territory lay between the Rio Grande (or Rio Bravo in Mexico) and the Nueces River several hundred miles to the east. It came under dispute following the ousting of General Santa Anna and his army from Texas in 1836. Santa Anna's forces were defeated decisively at the Battle of San Jacinto. He signed the Treaty of Guadalupe Hidalgo, recognizing Texan independence, at the border on the Rio Grande, not at the traditional boundary of Texas at the Nueces. Almost immediately, however, Mexico and Santa Anna repudiated the treaty and refused to recognize Texan independence or the extended boundary.[5] This type of indecisive behavior reflected a Mexico without an organized national mindset that would give her citizens and governments reason to stand united against foreign influence. As a result, they were unable to defend themselves effectively against these foreign intruders from the north and Europe.

Diplomatic efforts between Mexico and the Polk administration over the status of Texas failed due to their half-hearted pursuit, the changes in government in Mexico, and US overconfidence that war would achieve the same territorial goals, and perhaps even more land than they envisioned. Polk decided to push the boundary issue by extending the United States even further into Mexican territory, as he saw its destiny. He ordered General Zachary Taylor and his forces into the disputed territory between the two rivers. It was a deliberate act to provoke the desired outbreak to declare war. It worked.

The internal dynamics in each country and the outbreak of the war played into early remembrances of the war's outcome. Initially, it was Mexico, suffering from political instability, that wanted to forget the defeat and the loss of territory. Santa Anna was labeled a traitor and banished yet again. The army fell into disrepute for suffering the ignominy of defeat. For a period lasting into the early 1870s, Mexico deliberately tried to forget this war. It reverted back to its own civil war between advocates of conservative and liberal political organizations in Mexico. Initially, the liberals, who wished to broaden democracy to all Mexico's peoples, were predominant. That did not last. Conservative monarchists forged alliances with the French to install their leader, Emperor Maximilian, the Austrian cousin of Napoleon III. Maximilian's was a troubled reign that ended in his execution. President Benito Juárez restored the Mexican Republic, but not for long. Porfirio Díaz finally captured the presidency and served eight terms. These internal political dynamics may have clouded Mexican memory of the war with the United States, overshadowed by the efforts to stabilize its government.

By contrast, the United States initially remembered the war, but it was a conflicted memory, mixing victory with shame. As the war progressed, antiwar sentiments grew and expanded from the early opposition centered in New England around the question of the expansion of slave territories. Reports of the volume of casualties and the conduct of the war, including several highly publicized atrocities committed by US troops, led to broader doubts beyond just the New England states. Still, once the war ended, celebrations greeted the return of the victorious troops. Paintings and lithographs in the pages of the newspapers highlighted the bravery of the troops. Parades in cities around the country welcomed the soldiers home, and the government erected memorial statues.

Zachary Taylor emerged as the war's hero. He rode this reputation to the presidency in 1848. Ironically, Taylor ran as a candidate for the Whig Party, which had opposed the war because they saw it as a pretext to expand slavery into new territories. As anticipated, the issue of slavery in the new territories arose immediately. Political incorporation of these new territories necessitated a temporary resolution, with a compromise in 1850. This compromise brought California in as a free state, leaving undetermined the outcomes in New Mexico, Arizona, and Utah.

How and why the war started and how it was conducted led to lasting implications for the way the United States remembered it. The slavery issue, Manifest Destiny, and the atrocities committed by US soldiers were, at least initially, the focus of US remembrance. It took only a matter of decades for the war to recede into a state of amnesia for many in the United States. By contrast, Mexicans would seize on memories highlighting the bravery of their soldiers against the US onslaught. In addition, they would hold on to the bitterness engendered by the territory they lost, not how the war started or ended.

"They actually interrupted the funeral? They will not let you leave?" I asked for clarification from Jim Dickmeyer, the embassy's press attaché. He had just finished telling me over the phone that he and other embassy officers were in a stand-off with a unit from the Mexican army at a funeral where a young Mexican soldier, killed in service in Iraq, received his US citizenship. In service to the United States. A funeral in Guanajuato, Mexico. A US military funeral. Posthumous citizenship. On July 4. So many elements of those five incomplete sentences touched so many of the wrong nerves in Mexico. I should not have been shocked.

On many levels, Americans' contentious interactions with Mexicans inside government, at universities, with journalists or artists or people at church ran counter to Mexicans' reputation for warmth and fun, civility and politeness. Not far beneath the surface lies their collective memory of American intervention and loss. The result is an ingrained instinct to protect sovereignty. Such instinct led one former US ambassador to Mexico, Jeffrey Davidow, to refer to the relationship between the United States and Mexico in the title of his book as *The Bear and the Porcupine*, with the United States as the clumsy bear and Mexico crouched in a sharp-quilled defensive posture.

The funeral on the weekend of July 4, 2004, brought these sentiments of Mexican sovereignty face to face with contemporary issues of immigration and reaction to 9/11 and the resulting wars in Afghanistan and Iraq.

As the war in Afghanistan moved to a looming war in Iraq, Mexico, serving on the UN National Security Council, was increasingly reluctant to cast its vote to authorize the invasion of Iraq. Likely, the US case for Iraqi possession of weapons of mass destruction did not convince the Mexicans, especially in light of the failure of UN inspectors to turn up any evidence of such weapons. More likely, the foreign policy principle of nonintervention in the affairs of other countries played a decisive role in Mexico's decision. Theirs was a defensive foreign policy, growing out of their experience with the United States. Sanctioning an intervention on the far side of the world could set a precedent for similar action closer to home. Mexico had a long track record of defending the principle, proudly pointing to its objections to US interventions in Nicaragua and El Salvador in the 1980s. Mexico, of course, was not alone on the Security Council in expressing its reluctance. Despite relentless efforts to persuade Mexico's president Vicente Fox to cast his lot with the United States in the Security Council, he paused long enough for his decision to become moot. President Bush decided that he had legal grounds to invade without UN approval. He based his interpretation on the notion that since Iraq refused to live up to the terms of the ceasefire ending the first Iraq war a decade earlier, the 1990 Security Council resolution authorizing force was still valid.

Opposition in Mexico was sharp and unanimous. Or at least that's what their media and political circles conveyed.

As the war proceeded, stories filtered out in Mexico not only of Mexican Americans serving in the US armed forces but also of Mexicans enlisting in the US military. You could almost hear the head-scratching. How could a Mexican, raised on the history of American trampling on Mexican sovereignty, possibly enlist on the side of the great invader? How could a Mexican participate in and support yet another invasion of some other country?

It was only a matter of time before the first Mexican and Mexican American casualties occurred. Lance Corporal Juan López Rangel was killed in action in Iraq. His parents wanted their son buried in their hometown, San Luis de la Paz in Guanajuato in Mexico. They did not want to bury him in their adopted home in Georgia. Further, the parents wanted a US military funeral, which fell to the US Embassy to support. That should have been the exclusive purview of the defense attaché's office. But as they began their preparations to receive the casket with an accompanying color guard, coordinating with their Mexican counterparts, one issue quickly became a stumbling block: the color guard carried weapons. When officials in both the defense and foreign relations ministries opposed the idea of a twenty-one-gun salute, the marines opted for ceremonial rifles, which could not even fire blanks.

Thus, in the days before the funeral, other offices in the embassy became involved. As the deputy chief of mission, I called my counterparts at the foreign relations secretariat (SRE) to ask for their help in intervening with Mexican military authorities so that this soldier's parents could give their son the military funeral he earned through his sacrifice. I received a hearing, but despite multiple conversations, I received no firm assurances that the funeral could proceed without incident.

Calls from both Mexican and international media demonstrated enough interest in the funeral to convince our press officer to accompany the group of marines and defense attachés from the embassy to Guanajuato. Sure enough, as the color guard marched away from the site, Mexican soldiers approached them demanding the rifles. With the funeral interrupted, a press frenzy ensued, prompting a flurry of phone calls from US ambassador Tony Garza and many others from the embassy to our counterparts in the foreign and defense ministries. After forty-five minutes, the Mexican soldiers departed, without the ceremonial rifles, allowing the funeral to proceed. The dignity of the funeral, however, was tainted.

We later heard that this was a Mexican unit acting on its own authority. It was unclear whether that information was encouraging, because it could reflect either deeply engrained attitudes regardless of a command structure or simple miscommunication. The incident did reveal sensitivities that comingled the history of US soldiers with rifles on Mexican soil and two contemporary foreign policy issues: First, Mexico resisted supporting the Iraqi invasion. Second, while continuing to seek protection of their nationals in the United States, Mexico had to come to terms with the fact that their nationals had dual allegiances and might feel a strong enough allegiance to enlist in the US military.

This small incident passed quickly, but it did underscore the coolness in our military relationship, which manifested itself in the stiff formality of interactions between our militaries.[6] It was an especially rigid relationship with the Mexican army, which is a different cabinet department than the navy. We worked quite well with the Mexican navy, especially in areas of drug interdiction and immigrant rescues at sea.

It was the image of US soldiers on Mexican soil carrying weapons, even if they could not shoot, that brought 1848 to the surface. The small unit interrupting the funeral, on orders or not, was motivated by a desire to defend the national sovereignty to the point of sacrifice. The idea of sacrifice for the nation runs deep in Mexican memory. Everyone learns at a very young age and relearns through annual commemorations, the story of the Niños Héroes.

These "boy heroes" are the six young military cadets who were defending the final bastion of Mexico City, Chapultepec Castle, as the US Marines advanced on the capital in 1847. With marines scaling the walls of the castle, the young, untested cadets fought back fiercely, but ultimately proved no match for the overwhelming numbers and superior weaponry of the marines. The story emerged through the memories of veterans of the battle that six of the cadets hurled themselves over the walls of the castle, sacrificing themselves, like the Jews at Masada, rather than risk capture. One of them, Mexicans learn, wrapped himself in a flag before leaping over the wall to ensure it did not fall into the hands of the aggressor.

The fighting at Chapultepec, while not the final battle in the war, was the culminating engagement in a month-long siege of the capital. The final battle took place after General Santa Anna retreated from the capital, and his army quickly dissolved at Puebla, southeast of Mexico City. His weakened, ill-equipped, and hastily recruited army, despite its numerical advantages, had started its campaign months earlier marching first north, then east, and finally to the capital to attempt to repel, unsuccessfully, invaders approaching from the two fronts. Zachary Taylor led his troops south from Texas, and Winfield Scott had advanced on the capital city from the east after landing his troops at the port of Veracruz. Two other US forces went directly west to seize and control California.

Taylor had already won a string of early victories that enabled him to cross the Rio Grande and capture both Matamoros and Monterrey. As a result, General Santa Anna came out of exile to take control of the military. Despite assembling twenty thousand troops to engage Taylor's army of five thousand, Santa Anna lost almost half that force during his march north and later at the Battle at Buena Vista. The loss of so many soldiers in the face of superior US cannons at Buena Vista led Santa Anna to retreat—even though he had pushed back Taylor's army and might have prevailed if he continued.

However, Santa Anna retreated, and his forced march of troops to the other front coming from the Gulf of Mexico further depleted the size of his army. It also allowed for President Polk to redirect many under Taylor's command to Winfield Scott, who had landed at Veracruz on the gulf and planned to push for Mexico City. Scott had surrounded the port city and laid siege to it, killing hundreds of civilians with a sustained fierce bombardment. When Veracruz fell, undisciplined troops entered the city; it didn't take long for reports of rape and plunder to make their way into US newspapers. Outside of Veracruz, several hundred miles inland at Cerro Gordo, Santa Anna's hastily prepared, ill-equipped, and worn-out troops proved no match for a fresh army with superior training and weapons with longer range. By August 1847, forces under both Taylor and Scott were on the outskirts of the capital and began their advance.

South of the city, at the Franciscan convent of Churubusco, Mexican units, composed of civilian soldiers and a smaller brigade, the St. Patrick's Battalion, gathered to defend the entry to the city. This small group of foreign fighters earned its name from the mostly Irish soldiers in its ranks. More than just foreign soldiers, though, the roughly 175 men were foreigners who had deserted from the American fighting forces. The 40 percent of Zachary Taylor's army composed of recent immigrants, many of whom were Catholic, were the target of an aggressive propaganda effort from the Mexicans to appeal to their shared faith and doubts about the war aims of American expansion. Setting up their defenses at the Churubusco convent, at the entry to the city, the St. Patrick's Battalion reinforced the civilian guards and engaged in some of the war's fiercest fighting, including hand-to-hand combat inside the walls of the convent, to repel the American advance to the heart of the city at Chapultepec Castle. The Irish deserters were especially tenacious since they knew the fate that awaited them if they failed. With both sides suffering heavy casualties in a seesaw battle, the Mexican units eventually gave way to the superior numbers of their American foes. The fall of Churubusco allowed the Americans to push on to the final battle at Chapultepec.

Such a brief account of the war does not do justice to the complexities of military history over the two years of the war. What matters here is that, in the years immediately following the end of fighting, an ashamed population in Mexico sought to erase the memories of defeat. Then, gradually, a new narrative emerged that glorified the sacrifice of the soldiers defending the city, especially the Niños Héroes, but also the St. Patrick's Battalion.

Initially, Mexican remembrance of the war focused on the heroic defense at Churubusco, since the units protecting the entry to the city were not the disgraced regular army with its corps of officers drawn from the conservative elites of society. Rather, they were composed of national guard citizen-soldiers and the St. Patrick's Battalion. The Mexicans chose the August 20 date of the Battle at Churubusco as a national day of remembrance for the defense of the city. The commemoration found support not only among liberal political elements but also from anticlericists who wished to see the former convent converted into a secular monument to heroic defense.

Such was the dispute between political rivals in the country that when Santa Anna incredibly returned to power in 1853, he forbade recognition of the August 20 national remembrance. After all, his actions led to the loss that day. Churubusco's day of remembrance returned after he left power again just three years later and was resurrected yet again in the 1870s. The symbol of this convent that saw such fierce fighting would solidify later in the 1980s, after the site became home to the Museum of Interventions. There I got my first lesson in history shock.

It took years for the stories of the young soldiers throwing themselves over the walls of Chapultepec Castle to emerge as a parallel, and ultimately more searing, remembrance than the defense of Churubusco. Accounts written in the immediate aftermath of the war had the boy soldiers heroically defending the castle to the end, when they "were hurled over the rocks by the bayonets or taken prisoners."[7] Following the death of Maximilian in 1867 and the expulsion of the French forces that installed the emperor, a newly confident nation was better disposed to find elements in the earlier war against the United States to remember. It was not until 1871 that commemorations honoring both the army and the national guard took place at Chapultepec Castle, with veterans recalling the bravery of the six young soldiers' sacrifice to the nation. What emerged was an account that the young soldiers, rather than being taken captive by American forces, chose death by jumping from the walls of the castle high above the rocky surface below. No one recorded the flag-wrapped young cadet's story until a veteran told the story at the 1878 annual ceremony. Three years later, the government unveiled the first monument honoring the six Niños Héroes in Chapultepec Park, below the castle, and the spot became the site of annual ceremonies after that.

The story of the young heroes had become a fixed part of Mexican historical myth, a symbol of the broader sacrifice made by so many Mexican soldiers who were attempting to repel the invasion and preserve their territory. Each generation of Mexican leaders sought to preserve the Niños Héroes as a memory to unite a divided country, an example for the young of heroic sacrifice to the nation.

During this same period, on the other side of the border, the United States reversed its earlier remembrances and embarked on the long journey of collective forgetting. The intervening years of the Civil War, with veterans from the war with Mexico serving on both sides, and its unexpectedly destructive toll on the nation, overshadowed any memory of the earlier war. It took twenty-one years after the fighting ended for a Republican-dominated Congress to enact pensions for veterans of the Mexican-American war. Many of these same congressmen had opposed the start of the war as members of the Whig Party. Their reluctance to remember that earlier conflict is perhaps best explained by Ulysses Grant, a lieutenant during the war, who wrote in his 1884 memoirs, "We were sent to provoke a fight. . . . I was bitterly opposed to the measure, and to this day regard the war which resulted as one of the most unjust ever waged by a stronger against a weaker nation."[8]

The divisive start of the war has continued to play into its contested memories. In Texas, attention to its fight for independence from Mexico looms larger than the subsequent war a decade later. Efforts in the twentieth century to establish a national park reflect the dissonance in remembering the conflict. The Palo Alto Battlefield National Historic Site in Texas, commemorating one of the earliest battles, was finally established in 1978 after years of lobbying by the Brownsville, Texas, community and business leaders. Still, it took fourteen more years to convince Congress to allocate funding to staff it. Another ten years passed before the site was able to open a visitors' center, with language written into the bill to take into account the perspective of Mexico. Park Service staff ended up portraying the multiplicity of viewpoints, to provoke more questions and discussion rather than to settle on one official account.

The congressional mandate to portray Mexico's perspective aligned with an overall approach to the relationship with Mexico to seek and build cooperation, as neither government could address many of the cross-border issues emerging in the two countries in isolation, without the support of the other neighbor. Cooperation was hardest to forge in the realm of military relations, undoubtedly due to the historical remembrance of conflict.

It's a remembrance that we sometimes, inadvertently, stoke. Each year, US embassies around the world hold Marine Corps Balls, which are timed around the November Veteran's Day holiday and are an expression of gratitude for the detachments of marines who guard each embassy. In these events organized by the detachment and the embassy defense attaché's office, ranking host-country military officers are invited to the gala dinner and dance. The first Marine Corps Ball that I attended in Mexico City was held at a restaurant in the sprawling Chapultepec Park, one of the largest urban parks in the world. It wasn't until Ambassador Jeffrey Davidow rose to speak that I made the historical connection, almost certainly made earlier by invited members of the Mexican military. He cited the US Marine Corps hymn ("from the halls of Moctezuma . . .") and pointed to the illuminated Chapultepec Castle through the glass enclosing one side of the banquet hall. Davidow made the point that the two countries had come a long way since that battle, but I studied our invited guests to get any sense of how they viewed the selection of the site. No one walked out, but my suspicions of their discomfort were confirmed when we chose other venues for subsequent Marine Corps Balls.

Mexico's remembrances of conflict with the United States did not end with the war in 1848. Two more incursions took place in the early years of the twentieth century during Mexico's decade-long revolution. One was a US naval occupation at Veracruz in retaliation for the detention of several US sailors and the discovery of German arms shipments to Mexico in violation of a US embargo. The 1914 occupation lasted only eight months, but, according to Mexican historian Enrique Krauze, the resistance of ordinary citizens to the American forces led to "the renewal of rancor among Mexicans."[9] The second incursion took place from 1916 to 1917, hundreds of miles away in the northern Mexican desert. General John Pershing led an unsuccessful eleven-month expedition in search of Pancho Villa, another contestant in Mexico's brutal civil war. Villa had earlier conducted his cross-border raid, attacking an army outpost in the town of Columbus, New Mexico, in search of military supplies. Villa successfully eluded Pershing, whose extended stay in Mexico stoked more anti-American sentiment, unifying a bitterly divided populace during the civil war.

With these memories overshadowing the United States–Mexico military relationship, the reality in 2002 was that interactions between the two militaries rarely ventured beyond Marine Corps Balls, protocol visits, and meetings. Thus, misunderstandings arose quickly and persisted when, in the aftermath of 9/11, the United States announced the creation of a new command structure for North America and the Caribbean. This reorganization would replicate a command similar to those we have in the Middle East and Central Asia (Central Command), Latin America (Southern Command), and Asia (Pacific Command) and would allow for coordination with foreign militaries on developments in the geographic region of North America. No such bureaucratic structure had existed, and Mexican and Canadian military officials had been able to conduct their business with officials at the embassies and directly with the Pentagon in Washington.

The language the United States uses in its geographic command structure includes phrases such as "command and control" and "area of responsibility." Thus, the US military staff assigned to the newly established Northern Command, or NorthCom, would exercise control over an area of responsibility that included the United States, Canada, Mexico, and parts of the Caribbean. By that, the United States meant the staff would be responsible for that geographic region, coordinating whatever military responses would be required and working, advising, communicating, and even planning, where possible, with foreign counterparts.

It didn't take long for Mexicans to consider those words quite differently. In its extreme manifestation, in the media and the Mexican Congress, people saw this as the United States preparing for the possibility of military incursions into Mexico. Others wildly interpreted it as the United States trying to assume control over Mexico's military. Even the most responsible voices, such as the secretary of national defense, decried that his channel directly to the Joint Chiefs and the Pentagon would be cut, requiring him to communicate through NorthCom in Colorado.

It took a long time to unravel these perceptions, involving an extended campaign of direct engagement with journalists, with members of Mexico's Congress, and with the Mexican military. Once NorthCom was established, the US Embassy organized trips to Colorado for Mexicans to meet with officials there. Communications were rewritten, dropping terms such as "control" and "area of responsibility," in favor of "internal bureaucratic re-organization."

Despite the distance coloring military relations since 1846, it is surprising to learn that for some time during and immediately following the Second World War, the two militaries aligned closely. Mexico abruptly broke off diplomatic relations with Germany and Japan after Pearl Harbor. In early 1942, in the face of such a pervasive global threat, Presidents Roosevelt and Ávila Camacho established the Joint Mexican–United States Defense Commission to protect the continent. Later that year, Mexico formally declared war and committed its troops to fight on the same side as the United States for the first time.

The United States also enlisted Mexicans to provide labor in its fields and factories by establishing the Bracero program—allowing more than three hundred thousand Mexicans entry for work purposes. A Mexican air force squadron fought in the Pacific, closely coordinating with US forces. The two presidents signed another agreement allowing Mexicans to enlist in the US military, in exchange for citizenship following the war. More than fifteen thousand Mexicans volunteered and fought in US units.

This period of cooperation was lost on both Mexicans and Americans in the funeral of the Mexican who fought in Iraq, sixty years later. Initially, the era of good feelings continued after Roosevelt's death and into Truman's presidency, but relations soured with US interventions in other Latin American countries through the 1980s. Differences with the US policy in Cuba and over the rise of the Sandinistas in Nicaragua were the backdrop to the inauguration in 1981 of the National Museum of Interventions at the convent in Churubusco. Then President José López Portillo, a supporter of Nicaragua's territorial sovereignty, may well have assumed that by shining light on the record of US interventions in Mexico, he could shame the United States and preempt contemporary interventions in and around the hemisphere.

Despite the almost century-long effort to construct and sustain remembrances of the sacrifices to the nation of the Niños Héroes and the St. Patrick's Battalion in the face of the loss of large swaths of their territory, Mexico showed in 1940 a willingness and ability to set aside differences to face a global crisis with the United States. The question remains under what other circumstances this type of military cooperation could take place. When Mexico was reaching out to the United States and Canada to form a free trading zone in the early 1990s, the minister of education and later president, Ernesto Zedillo, embarked on an effort to downplay the War of North American Intervention and the Niños Heroés in school textbooks, perhaps to reflect an era where greater cooperation would be needed. However, those memories had formed an indelible part of Mexican identity, prompting an outcry across the country. The government scrapped the new textbooks and restored the older version of memory.

The outcome of the free-trade discussions and the subsequent aid to help Mexico weather its peso crisis did end up pushing down those seared memories of US interventions. Beyond just a spur for economic growth, the North American Free Trade Agreement served to bring the three countries closer together, tying the economic well-being of each nation together with the other two. Flows of trade between the three nations very quickly made this the second largest trading block in the world, after the EU. Economic integration certainly brought about closer political, social, and cultural links as well.[10]

Such was not the environment, though, as I looked out my window from the fourth floor of the embassy in December 2002 and saw thousands of protesters march by in the lead-up to the tenth anniversary of NAFTA. Walking, driving tractors, and even riding horses, protesters carried signs in Spanish that read "NAFTA means Death." The crowds were larger than any of the protests focusing on the wars in Afghanistan or Iraq, which were taking place at the same time.

We didn't need to read history to appreciate opposition in the United States to NAFTA, mostly associated with the potential for loss of jobs. Each of us had personally absorbed presidential candidate Ross Perot's quip about the "giant sucking sound" of jobs moving to Mexico. What we quickly got, though, in 2002 was a lesson in Mexican history and identity. For most Mexicans, corn or maize is more than just its principal staple crop; it is very much linked to its identity. With evidence dating back over seven thousand years, Mexico can legitimately claim its territory to be the origin of corn.

Maize was the lifeblood of the small Mexican farmer, who would grow for himself and sell locally whatever small surplus remained. The withdrawal of tariffs from corn coming from the United States meant an influx of imported corn that could drive down prices for this large group of small and subsistence farmers. Further, it was a different type of corn grown in the United States that would flood the Mexican market. Imported corn seed would drive out the local variety, leaving Mexican consumers with a taste and texture that was foreign. For all these reasons, the original NAFTA provisions kept tariffs on maize at a whopping 200 percent, before gradual reductions over the next twelve years.

For months, the embassy's agricultural attaché, Bill Brandt, warned of the potential for political opposition to the trade pact's phasing out tariffs at the ten-year mark on twenty-one food items, particularly on corn. The looming deadline opened up opportunities for opposition politicians, even those from the PRI, the party of Salinas and Zedillo that had originally supported the pact. With Bill sounding the call inside the embassy amid growing media attention, we watched the mounting opposition to NAFTA. Then came the calls from the Mexican Congress to renegotiate the trade pact.

Sensing a political crisis affecting the overall relationship, the US Embassy mounted a comprehensive campaign to prevent renegotiations. We met with congressional leaders to remind them that there were provisions that Canada would want to renegotiate as well as others that the United States wanted to include. We used all the public media to argue for the overall benefits of NAFTA and the uncertainty that reopening the agreement might bring. It took several weeks of effort, along with the intervening extended December holidays, to push the notion of renegotiating NAFTA off the political calendar.[11]

There's no question that the original NAFTA negotiators on all sides were aware of the sensitivities of eliminating tariffs on agricultural products since they incorporated within the text the gradual phasing out of these trade barriers. However, not even ten years later, those of us in the embassy were surprised by the intensity of the opposition to NAFTA. We thought we were facing a straightforward trade issue, but the Mexicans were looking at this not just as economic survival for a beleaguered population, but as a threat to their heritage and identity. We received a hard-earned lesson in history shock.

In his excellent history of the construction of collective memories and amnesia on each side of the border, Michael Van Wagenen correctly concludes that decisions to remember and forget weigh heavily on the conduct of relations between the two countries.[12] I saw it firsthand in the accounts noted here, but also in dozens of other daily interactions. My original question, upon exiting the Museum of Interventions at Churubusco, is whether it is possible to overcome these memories and build a more durable relationship of cooperation, despite this shock of history.

Two realities emerge from such hope. First, it may be as unfair as it is unrealistic to expect Mexico to erase its memory of the loss of half of its territory. Second, though, it remains the case that these memories have changed over time; they are altered and even repressed, at times to gain political advantage. In a relationship with such interconnections as cross-border trafficking in drugs and other contraband, immigration, and major commercial trade, it may require more remembering on the part of the United States to heal Mexican scars.

Suggested Further Reading

As noted, Michael Scott Van Wagenen's *Remembering the Forgotten War* (Amherst: University of Massachusetts Press, 2012) traces and contrasts the way the two countries remember the US-Mexican War, with well-researched documentation of the emergence of the Niños Héroes narrative in Mexico. Timothy Henderson in *A Glorious Defeat: Mexico and Its War with the United States* (West Sussex, UK: Wiley-Blackwell, 1988) offers an excellent account of the war, while Amy Greenberg provides insights into the politics leading up to the war in *A Wicked War: Polk, Clay, Lincoln and the 1846 U.S. Invasion of Mexico* (New York: Alfred A. Knopf, 2012). Sean Wilentz adds details of prevailing domestic politics in chapter 18 of his *The Rise of American Democracy* (New York: Norton, 2005). Three books I read while assigned in Mexico helped fill in the gaps in my ignorance of Mexican history: Enrique Krauze's *Mexico: Biography of Power* (New York: HarperCollins, 1997), T. R. Fehrenbach's *Fire and Blood* (New York: Da Capo Press, 1995), and John Ross's *The Annexation of Mexico* (Monroe, ME: Common Courage Press, 1998).

3

Canada: The Other Forgotten War

After a long pause, way too long, uncomfortably so, I asked my friend, a senior Canadian government official, if he could remember a time when the United States had helped Canada. Ultimately, he gave up, empty. He could not recall one time when the United States reached out to its close ally in a time of need.

My question came in the course of a conversation where this official repeated what had by then become a national lament: President George W. Bush omitted Canada in the list of global friends he mentioned and thanked in his speech to a joint session of Congress on September 20, 2001, days after the attacks on the World Trade Center and the Pentagon. Bush had cited Paris and Berlin, prayers in South Korea and Cairo, mourning in Australia, Africa, and Latin America. He said, "America has no truer friend than Great Britain." It was not the only time during my three years that the Bush omission came up, but it was the only time I dared ask the question whether anyone remembered the United States helping Canada. Ever.

Certainly, there were times when the United States had singled out Canada for special treatment. During the evacuation of Lebanon in the summer of 2006, I was on conference calls with the Canadian Foreign Affairs Department and consular officers in Lebanon to invoke a mutual assistance agreement that allowed the use of US military assets to repatriate Canadians along with Americans in the event of disasters overseas. The joint air patrols of the Arctic by the binational air force units under NORAD (North American Aerospace Defense Command) was another example. Cross-border emergency support going in both directions was yet another. Each year, the people of

Nova Scotia send a Christmas tree to the people of Boston for the latter's support following the massive Halifax munitions explosion in 1917, which proved more devastating than any human-made explosive device before the atomic bomb. The best example I witnessed came at a meeting between Secretary of Homeland Security Tom Ridge and his Canadian counterpart. In approving the establishment of a preclearance facility in Halifax so that Canadians could go through US immigration before arriving in the United States, Ridge said, "It doesn't make financial sense to us, but this is important to you, so it's important to us." Halifax became the eighth Canadian airport to accommodate US customs and immigration officers, who would do all the intake processing, so that on arrival at US airports, travelers from Canada enter the country as domestic passengers.

Examples of US aid did not come to mind as readily as the spontaneous outpouring of aid across Canada in the days after September 11. As the United States grounded planes across North America, passengers were stranded in major airports in Vancouver and Toronto, but also in smaller ones such as Halifax, Nova Scotia, and Gander, Newfoundland. Canadians took in the passengers from around the world, but mostly from the United States, and put them up, often in their homes, for days before airports opened and planes were allowed to resume flying. Mourners besieged the US Embassy in Ottawa, stuffing flowers through the iron railing of the fence along its entire length. Thousands crowded on Parliament Hill, outside the seat of government, for a memorial service the Friday after September 11.

One way history shock influences the conduct of US foreign policy in Canada is through this issue of recognition or attention. Simply put, the United States overlooks Canada; it takes the country for granted. On the other hand, Canada cannot escape the shadow of its southern neighbor. This asymmetry was reflected most vividly in the geographic organization of Canada's Department of Foreign Affairs, with two different divisions. During my tenure in Canada, one assistant deputy minister ran an office focusing on North America (the United States and Mexico). The other dealt with the rest of the world. In the US State Department, for many years Canada was placed in the Bureau of European Affairs. Not simply overlooked, but lost! This unconscious disregard led one historian to a far-reaching conclusion (probably too far) that "Canada has not been simply overlooked; it has been repressed."[1]

The strength of the Canadian desire for attention may also lie in their determination to be recognized as something different than the United States. Often, *different* meant *better*. At both the personal and official levels, Canadians bristled at the slightest hint of similarity with the United States. There was embarrassment all around when a guest from South Carolina at a Fourth of July dinner at the US ambassador's house in Ottawa asked the president of the iconic Hudson Bay Company why Canada wouldn't want to be a part of the United States. She must have forgotten her junior high school history class on the War of 1812. The roots of both features in the United States–Canada relationship, recognition and difference, go back as far as, and even farther than, that forgotten War of 1812.

Google the "Forgotten War," and not only does the war with Mexico appear, but so do references to the War of 1812 and the Korean War. Why are we so apt to forget some wars?

I certainly needed a crash course in history when invited to participate in the unveiling of a plaque at Deadman's Island in Halifax, Nova Scotia. At this site, 195 US soldiers were buried. They died at Melville Island, a nearby prison, which housed thousands of soldiers captured in the fighting near the Great Lakes. They became pawns in the war, pieces to argue over concerning the treatment of prisoners on both sides. Long since forgotten were those who died, imprisoned there while awaiting transfer to England. Forgetting our fallen soldiers seemed unusual for the US military, which goes to such incredible lengths on the battlefield to leave no one behind and which maintains cemeteries from Normandy to Mexico City. It took an unusual assortment of organizations—the War of 1812 Society in the state of Ohio, a couple of determined US current and retired military officers, and the Halifax Regional Municipality—to forestall the construction of luxury condominiums on Deadman's Island and push for the installation of a plaque commemorating these fallen soldiers.

I traveled to Halifax in June 2005 to attend the unveiling of that plaque. Cold and damp as June can be on the coast of Canada, it was easy to see why soldiers died. And this was June, not January. The vestiges of Britain were apparent: the forlorn tones of a bagpiper opened and closed the ceremony; speaking for Canada was the lieutenant governor, the Queen's representative to the province; reenactors in the red uniforms of the British army fired the less than twenty-one-gun salute. My remarks from the podium that day imagined the prisoners looking down on the United States–Canada relationship in 2005, seeing distinctly unhostile cooperation, so totally foreign to their own experience. They might have agreed with the historian Barbara Tuchman on the folly of war in general or with Harry Truman, whose oft-repeated quote probably best captured the mood in the United States toward the War of 1812: "It was the silliest damn war we ever had."

Silly. Truman remained true to his reputation for speaking plainly. Apart from the tragic loss of life and destruction, this war was silly in the mistakes made repeatedly by both sides, but particularly by the United States. With an unprepared and underresourced military led by officers chosen politically, President Madison and War Hawk Republicans such as Henry Clay saw the war against Britain as a way to capture the glory of their founding fathers on the battlefield. They likely desired to extend their way of government north and remove the British from all of North America. The stated war aims were to provide security in the western frontier north of the Ohio River and to end the British practice of impressments, seizing American sailors and forcing them into the Royal Navy during the war against Napoleon raging in Europe. That they did not achieve those initial war aims added to the folly.

Political infighting between the Republicans in national power, who argued for war, and the Federalists in control of New York and New England further contributed to a lack of unified purpose. Politics infused the leadership and the ranks of the troops from the United States so much that Federalist generals were accused of treason by the rank and file for not prosecuting the war vigorously enough. Federalists seemed bent on preserving commercial benefits that the war had disrupted and sought to protect their property, which explains why the United States never sought to cut off the St. Lawrence River and isolate the British at the Great Lakes.

The soldiers fought the battles around the Great Lakes in miserable conditions. Temporary exchanges of territory occurred, but the war ended with no land gained or lost by either side. More signs of folly stemmed from the ego of the commanders, selected for their political connections and not for their military acumen.

Errors abounded, from the start. The American commander, William Hull, persuaded Madison to invade Canada from the west at Detroit and then cross the expanse of territory to Montreal, rather than take a direct route. The British learned of the American declaration of war before Hull did and seized a ship with plans for the initial invasion of Canada at Fort Amherstburg, across the river from Detroit. Hull at first tried to convince the opposing soldiers to defect, promising them protection. He did not pursue enemy forces after small land gains from initial skirmishes, leaving the British confident that they faced ineptitude. His promises of protection were belied by his failure to stop the plundering of farms and shops by the American troops.

Finally, General Isaac Brock decided to attack Detroit and mustered a force, about half of whom were Indians. The presence of war-painted Indians surrounding the fort at Detroit caused desertion in the American ranks and a premature surrender of the fort despite Hull's larger and better-equipped defending army.

Both sides engaged in folly. Flush with a victory that contributed to invincible confidence, General Brock met his fate in the next major skirmish of the war. An American shot Brock in the chest as he led his forces in a charge to retake the Queenston Heights to the east near Niagara. American militia had briefly captured the town and the high ground across from a fort at the strategic inlet to Lake Ontario, but relinquished it shortly after Brock's demise, again terrorized by the sound of the Indian war screams. The advancing British, under Brock's replacement, opted for a truce and prisoner exchange instead of crossing the Niagara River to pursue the fleeing and demoralized US troops.

So began the war, which continued with similar accounts of land seized on both sides of the border, but never held for long. Battles at York (Toronto) and Buffalo, Plattsburgh, and Ogdensburg (all in New York) were replete with missed opportunities and lack of preparations, which led to extreme hardships during the winter months, made worse by a perennial low state of provisions. The subsequent plunder and looting enraged citizens on both sides of the border, including some potential allies in Upper Canada, who had initially sympathized with the Americans.

Two years later, the war ended much as it started, when one side did not know the war was declared. This time, neither side in New Orleans knew that the war had officially ended with the signing of a peace treaty in Ghent, Belgium, two weeks earlier. This last battle went ahead, and General Andrew Jackson delivered perhaps the most resounding victory in the entire two years of fighting, which gave him status as a war hero and helped him secure the presidency years later. The actual exchange of ratifications of the Treaty of Ghent formally ending hostilities took place after the battle.

The border over which the British/Canadians and the Americans fought and the territory they exchanged would be understandably unrecognizable to them today. Even in the early 1800s, crossings were fluid and uninterrupted, mixing both personal and commercial connections across political and natural barriers. Take away the modern technology and it would be the sheer volume of crossings now that marks the most striking contrast along the three-thousand-mile border. It is the longest border shared by any two countries in the world. The interdependence between the two countries—energy and manufacturing, tourism, and agriculture, emergency response, and education—is deep, enduring, and busy. Roughly three hundred thousand people cross every day. Canadians take nearly forty million trips to the United States each year; Americans take twenty million trips to Canada.

At the end of 1999, Ahmed Ressam, an Algerian who had received al-Qaeda training in Afghanistan, sought to use that number of three hundred thousand crossings as cover and attempted to enter Washington State. An alert, suspicious immigration officer stopped him there before he could reach Los Angeles where he planned to bomb the airport on New Year's Eve, earning him the name, the Millennium Bomber. None of the 9/11 terrorists came into the United States from Canada. That fact did not stop the persistent allegations that they crossed the border on their way to hijack the airplanes. Despite the 9/11 Commission laying to rest that rumor and Canadian efforts to dispel those rumors each time they surfaced, prominent Americans from former presidential candidate John McCain to Secretary of Homeland Security Janet Napolitano continued to make such an assertion.[2] Still, after 9/11, it was the border that became one of the principal arenas for action. Initial difficulties in reaching any significant achievement on border security either with Canada or with both Canada and Mexico fed the eagerness of the United States to act unilaterally. The byword of the aftermath of 9/11 was action. Do something and anything and everything—at the same time. Now.

Canada was then reluctant to agree to the United States proposed strategy of *perimeter security,* where both countries would jointly protect the North America perimeter. So, the United States acted on its own and beefed up security at the border between the two countries. This border was the one over which we fought in 1812; it had seen strict enforcement in the immediate aftermath of the war. Over the years, though, it had evolved into more of a dotted line that, while not porous, was fluid and easy. At some border checkpoints, an orange cone in the middle of the road was the only indication that the border crossing happened to be closed at that moment. (When I mentioned this at trilateral meetings with Mexican officials and academics, it was hard not to notice their jaws gaping in disbelief as they considered the fences and armed patrols at their northern border.)

The unilateral upgrades to border security following 9/11 looked to the Canadians as though we were hearkening back to the War of 1812. We had put aside hostilities long ago, and we had decades of fluid, frequent, and incident-free crossing into each other's countries behind us. For them, this history mattered. For us, hardly.

"Three words: border, border, and border." That was the comprehensive conclusion offered by George Shultz, the former secretary of state, still unfailingly sharp and persuasive. He was summing up the challenges facing the three countries of North America at a meeting of government officials, academics, and private individuals from all three countries in Banff, Alberta. It was 2006, and the policies to strengthen the US borders following 9/11 were taking effect and causing delays and annoyances at both the southern and northern borders, reducing the economic advantages of proximity to market and production.

Shultz's mantra of priorities pushed me to assess firsthand the impact on the border myself. Most of the security upgrades dealt with new procedures taking advantage of new technologies to provide precise information to border officials on who and what was coming across. New documents were required, and the implementation of the requirement that all overland passengers carry passports was still more than two years away. But the Canadians were overwrought. The free and easy flow back and forth across the border that they had grown up with was giving way to a complicated, time-intensive obstruction. With 90 percent of Canadians living within one hundred miles of the US border, it's understandable why they attached such importance to easy passage.

Stories spread of towns bisected by the border, including one place where the border even runs through a library on the Vermont/Quebec border. Media and government officials drew on these stories as case studies in explaining why the new requirements were impractical. It was difficult to sort out the causes of long delays at the border: were they the impact of the new procedures or just the old infrastructure of too few lanes and inspection booths?

So I made arrangements to sit in the cab of a semitruck hauling a load across the border at the busiest of crossings, that between Detroit, Michigan, and Windsor, Ontario. I knew it was a little bit of a gimmick, but I also felt, that after months of reading policy papers and attending logistics meetings, it was long past time to see what crossing the border looked like in practice. Fortunately, it was spring, so the snow had melted. At least we did not have to contend with the impact of weather conditions on cross-border trade. Another example of good fortune was that my contacts at the trucking association seemed to have chosen the most organized driver in their ranks to drive me through the gauntlet of fourteen miles of city traffic in Windsor, between the highway and the border.

We met at a coffee truck stop at the start of the city streets. I was early and was wandering around the large parking area full of idling trucks, wondering where to find my volunteer. "Out of place" was an understatement for me in my coat and tie, so I figured he would find me first. Cellphones were just becoming widespread, but for some reason we weren't connecting. A few minutes late, though, he drove up and quickly sized up who his guest passenger was going to be. The driver, whose name I unfortunately no longer remember, looked like he had walked off a golf course, dressed in a polo shirt and cargo shorts. Hopping in his cab, the first thing I noticed was a computer screen that connected him to his dispatcher. His documents were printed out neatly on a clipboard but had already been transferred to US customs. Both he and his truck were part of the precleared program for frequent crossers, having completed a lengthy process of background checks. As we drove through the traffic, with fourteen lights to navigate, he explained his route on the other side of the border and talked about his family life.

It was midmorning, so traffic was past the rush hour and well before the peak truck-crossing time later in the afternoon. The approach to the bridge was a bit of a spaghetti bowl, circling and seemingly backtracking. The driver had done this before, and the signage was sufficient. Only a couple of trucks were ahead of us, so the wait was minimal. When we pulled up to the inspector, he was already able to scan the license plate and see who was approaching. He took the paperwork, checked it against his computer, and then asked a few questions before addressing the only anomaly. "Who are you?" he said pointing at me.

I explained what I was doing, hopped out of the cab, and thanked the driver, who proceeded on his way. The whole trip, including getting through the border, had taken only thirty minutes. I knew this was the way it was intended to be, the best-case scenario. I also knew that this was not the way it would be later that day or for those trucks that had not been precleared. Still, it was a sign of what could be, with more enrollment in the program and with more and regular use of the technology. The argument I would use in the coming months was that the technology was supposed to ease the delays at the border, providing the inspectors with more information, so they wouldn't be wasting their time trying to look over the myriad forms of documentation to determine who and what was in front of them.

The Canadians were not convinced. They had enjoyed, for well over a hundred years, easy access to the United States for traveling, shopping, and enjoyment. They had benefited from the millions of travelers coming to Canada to enjoy the beauty of their country, a more rugged and rural natural setting than one finds in parts of a crowded United States. If they were honest, they would say, but never publicly, that they did not want to be treated like the Mexicans with border walls, visa requirements, and constant patrols. Canadians wanted to maintain a different border. For many years, Americans had almost forgotten there was a border between the two countries. Until 9/11. Only then did we seek to re-create the border with Canada to resemble the one in the immediate aftermath of 1812, the one that looked like most other borders in the world, outside the EU.

Truman's characterization of the War of 1812 as "silly" even seemed to haunt the commemorations of the bicentennial of that conflict, which offered a vivid current example of how nations remember and choose to remember differently. Canadian commemorations revolved around a search for a national identity, which was a constant backdrop during my assignment there, immediately after leaving Mexico. Americans living or traveling north of the border experience this quickly in the fierce Canadian desire to distinguish themselves from their only neighbors, whose proximity and size are as present in Canada as Canada is absent in the United States.

The Canadian government of Conservative prime minister Stephen Harper took the opportunity of the bicentennial to put an estimated $50 million of federal funding behind promotional efforts. The goal was to remind Canadians of the importance of the War of 1812 in forming their nation. This action quickly spawned a controversy, partly because of ongoing fiscal cutbacks in other social arenas and partly because many, even in Canada, looked at this war with a collective shrug of the shoulders.

Both timelines and geography worked against Harper. First, critics pointed out that there was no Canada at the time, so there was no nation to be "formed." Canada did not achieve nationhood until 1867. Second, the fighting principally took place in the Great Lakes and upper St. Lawrence regions, barely touching Quebec, the Atlantic Provinces, and western Canada. At best, when they looked back to the War of 1812, Canadians in all their geographic and linguistic diversity could find common ground in what sets Canada apart from the United States. They considered how Canada, even before it became an independent nation, resisted American expansion, to develop a distinct nation later on. At worst, Canadians criticized the effort as a political attempt to strengthen Harper's Conservative Party, more comfortable with supporting Canada's military past. In this way, Conservatives were seen as shoring up Canada's present military, in the face of political opposition that wanted to use the armed forces only in peacekeeping capacities.

Canadian funding supported a television advertising campaign, a slick website produced by Heritage Canada, a federal ministry, and a series of provincial and local government events commemorating various slices of the war. Museums applied for funding to support their exhibitions, and groups received funding for reenactments and artistic installations, including one at the site of York (present-day Toronto), where artists set up hundreds of small tents, each housing a different artist's representation. At night, the lighted tents, aligned in symmetric rows, transformed into a stunning collective work of art against the backdrop of the modern Toronto skyline.

The logo for the promotional campaign speaks best to its purposes. Portraits of four heroes are featured: Laura Secord, Sir Isaac Brock, Tecumseh, and Charles de Salaberry. A woman, a British general, a First Nations chief, and a French Canadian. Outside of Tecumseh, these names probably are not familiar to those south of the border. Laura Secord warned the British troops of an American invasion, earning her the sobriquet of "Canada's Paul Revere." British general Isaac Brock led troops to an early, decisive victory at Detroit, but just two months later died at Queenston. Tecumseh, a Shawnee chief, forged an alliance with the British in hopes of keeping Americans from settling north of the Ohio River. And Charles de Salaberry, a Quebecois officer, led a small force to repulse a much larger American contingent advancing toward Montreal. Despite their genuine claim to national recognition, their inclusion on the official logo reflected as much their present-day diversity and the commemoration's purpose to find unity in Canada's distinctive lack of national unity.[3]

Conversely, New York governor Andrew Cuomo's decision to veto spending for his state's commemorative projects epitomized the disinterest south of the border. It fell to the US Postal Service, museums, private individuals, and allocations by a handful of states to underwrite commemorative stamps, exhibits, and events such as reenactments and the visit of tall ships in the United States. As a result, the bicentennial passed relatively unnoticed in the United States, despite the war's contributions to the national memory, from the "Star Spangled Banner" to the burning of the White House and Andrew Jackson's victory at the Battle of New Orleans. Americans remember the British attacking Washington, DC, but few know of the earlier incident of Americans looting and burning York, the capital of Upper Canada, present-day Toronto.

On both sides of the border, commemorations focused on what

happened locally, with scant reference to the broader national narratives of the war. Halifax remembered the prison at Melville Island. Western Canada remembered the sale of Fort Astoria in current Oregon and the Peace Arch at the border commemorating the Treaty of Ghent. Baltimore remembered the attack on Fort McHenry. Toronto remembered the assault on York (Toronto). Plattsburgh, New York, remembered the failed attempt to attack Montreal. Toronto did not know about the "Star Spangled Banner" and Fort McHenry. Likewise, Maryland did not learn about the razing of York. Few of the commemorations saw the war through the lens of a single, comprehensive narrative, even though Canadian commemorations sought to highlight the national formation angle. It was almost as if three or four separate wars took place with little connection between them.

Seen from the Canadian side, this was a war to remain separate and distinct from the United States, and only perhaps secondarily to maintain loyalty to the British monarchy. As strong as the links between the United States and Canada were then and remain, the desire to forge an identity, distinct and unique, may be even stronger. If sweeping generalizations are allowed, Canada was and is not anti-American. However, Canada is proudly, fiercely, not America.

Well before 1812, settlers north of the boundary, set by the Treaty of Paris following the Revolutionary War, sought to highlight differences from their neighbors south of the border. Initial distinctions emerged based on political lines and attitudes toward Native Americans and slavery.

As far back as the 1600s, when Samuel de Champlain explored the St. Lawrence River and the Atlantic Coast of North America, he pursued a policy of cooperation with the tribes he encountered. He practiced restraint in responding to Indian hostility, in contrast to patterns of revenge and retaliation in settlements further south. Champlain, on a voyage along the Atlantic Coast as far south as Massachusetts, became aware of the British settlers' more confrontational approach toward the original inhabitants.

The story is well known of the Loyalists who favored the monarchy and English rule and fled north to what became Canada, in the tumultuous years of the American Revolution. An estimated 50,000 left the colonies, most of whom landed in the current Nova Scotia and then moved on to New Brunswick. About 10,000 ended up in Quebec, in what was called "Lower Canada" at the time. There were even an estimated 3,000 Black people among the Loyalist emigrants, most escaping slavery, who also made their way north to Nova Scotia. While some Loyalists did eventually return to the newly independent United States, most did not. About 1,200 of the Black Loyalists opted to leave Nova Scotia in 1792 and sailed to the newly established colony of Sierra Leone on the west coast of Africa. Those Loyalists who decided to stay in the British colonies of Canada continued to harbor ill will toward those who they thought forced them to leave and lose much of what they had worked to build for their families and communities.

To continue to maintain a distinct identity required a population, and ironically, the easiest way to populate the territory came not from recruiting those in Europe or elsewhere, but from the newly independent neighbor. In Upper Canada, further west on the St Lawrence River and the Great Lakes, the population stood at barely 14,000 in the years immediately following the Revolution. This stood in stark contrast to the 340,000 residents across the border in New York alone. The lieutenant governor of Upper Canada, John Simcoe, offered a land grant of up to two hundred acres of land in exchange for small fees and loyalty to the king and Parliament. At six pence per acre, it was considerably cheaper than the two to three dollars charged per acre in the United States. As a result, the population grew in Upper Canada to almost 75,000 by 1812.

This large number from the United States overshadowed both Indigenous and original white settlers and ultimately proved problematic. First, in the lead-up to war, these "late Loyalists" allegiance to British North America came into question. Many remained ambivalent toward the outcome of the war. Some openly preferred assimilation in the new country, seeing economic opportunities in siding with the United States. More, it seemed, just wanted to be left alone. They did not want to be recruited to serve in the British army, but they also wanted to be free from the ravages of the fighting near their homes.

As it turned out, they could accomplish neither end. The Canadian deserters who fled across the lakes and rivers to avoid service in the British army presented a recurring issue throughout the northern theater of the war. Furthermore, the nature of the fighting moved from a case study in lack of preparations and ill-advised military decisions to one fought with scorched-earth techniques. The lack of preparations on the US side led to desperate soldiers raiding and plundering after attacks on civilian areas, most notably in York (present-day Toronto), Fort George, Newark, Dover, Niagara, and Moraviantown.

The "silly" war, as described by Truman, was anything but for those who lived in the theater of fighting around Lakes Erie and Ontario. There, the British looted and burned homes, farms, and barns, not only to offset the lack of preparations, but also to seize provisions to feed their forces. British retaliation also took place through raids on civilians in Buffalo and other towns that left thousands homeless.

The devastation in Upper Canada, from Detroit to Toronto, was widespread, fueling resentment among those settlers who had come north and creating a rift not previously there. When the war started, before surrendering at Detroit, General Hull pursued a strategy of trying to lure the settlers on the other side of the border away from the British sphere, with some luck. By 1814, though, the governor of Michigan, Lewis Cass, pursued the opposite tack and persuaded US forces to destroy all farms from Detroit to Niagara, laying a "desert between us and them."[4]

The rift resulting from this destruction of civilian property and livelihood may be the single most enduring result of the war. Not only had the British prevented absorption of their territory into the United States, but the war also deepened the sentiment for a distinctive Canadian identity, eager to be separate from the United States. In this manner, Stephen Harper's promotion of the bicentennial as formative in Canada's history is accurate, but principally in its desire to be non-American.

Harper was not the first to see the war as a critical turning point in his nation's history. National Public Radio did a segment on how teachers taught about the war in elementary schools in the two countries. In US schools, reference to the war is fleeting, meriting two to three days of study, with an emphasis on impressment; the western frontier; the burning of Washington, DC; the "Star Spangled Banner"; the Battle of New Orleans; and let's move on to the Civil War for weeks and weeks. By contrast, the Canadian teacher interviewed devoted weeks to this war, focusing on the burning of York (Toronto), the repulsing of the Americans around the Great Lakes, and heroes such as Laura Secord, who warned the British/Canadians of an attack at Queenston.

This contrast between the two countries in their awareness of the war was on full display when a headline ran across my *New York Times* feed on June 6, 2018: "No, Mr. Trump, Canada Did Not Burn the White House Down in the War of 1812."[5] It shouldn't have surprised me. Donald Trump had already demonstrated on multiple occasions displays of historical ignorance, from thinking that Frederick Douglass was still alive to being surprised that Abraham Lincoln was a Republican. Trump's views on history seem to be confined only to the history that he thinks he is making.

The *Times* was reporting on a phone call with Canadian prime minister Justin Trudeau over the imposition of tariffs against Canadian steel and aluminum. Trying to force Canada to move more quickly on a new trade agreement to replace NAFTA, Trump had announced the tariffs, but used the excuse of security concerns. The president must have tried to trot out a historical fact to make the case with Trudeau that, in fact, Canada was actually a security threat. It's not hard to imagine before the call a White House aide pointing out that there was historical precedent for viewing Canada as a security threat: the building they were sitting in was actually burned by Canadian troops in the War of 1812. So the president tried to school the prime minister on the War of 1812. The problem was that, like most Canadians, Trudeau knew quite a bit about the war. He must have drawn on the famous Canadian civility when he calmly shot back that those were, in fact, British troops that burned down the White House, as Canada did not exist as a separate nation in 1814. It must have taken even more famous Canadian reserve not to point out that the attack on Washington, DC, was in retaliation for the earlier razing of York (Toronto) by American troops.

Trudeau could have continued, even telling the story known to so many Canadians of the American woman who warned the British of the American threat of invasion. Laura Secord's evolution into achieving national status in Canada took decades, tracking the delayed emergence of the Niños Héroes' story from the war with Mexico in 1848. Secord, a late Loyalist who had moved north with her husband in the years after the Revolutionary War in the United States, tried for years to seek compensation for the risks she took and for the loss of property she incurred during the plunder. She turned in to the British authorities affidavits testifying to her actions, but to no avail, even after her husband died in 1841. Her story first reached the public in 1845, but she still received no compensation. It was only through a visit to Queenston by the Prince of Wales in 1860 that Laura once again pushed her story, this time to a more receptive audience. A history prepared in 1867 and a subsequent play twenty years later began to embellish her efforts and helped lead to the erection of a memorial statue in her honor.

It is easy to see why Canada looks to Secord as an independence hero and this war as a formative event. Canadian historians bemoan the fact that Canada has no founding event such as the American Revolution; it has a Confederation Conference held in Charlottetown, Prince Edward Island, and then the passage of an act in the British Parliament to mark its independence. There is no Declaration of Independence or Constitution and no general like George Washington who was victorious against colonial rulers. Instead, Canada has a war (waged by its mother country) that repulsed American intervention, and it has war heroes who now represent Canada in its diversity, in its struggle to forge a unified identity.

After the issue of recognition, the second way history shock plays into our interactions with our neighbor and partner is grounded in this issue of distinctiveness. Canada, as "not America," was the common thread underlying the discussions between the two countries in the post-9/11 climate. We repeatedly ran into the "differences that don't make a difference" but took a monumental amount of time and effort to unravel in trying to achieve the simultaneous goals of facilitating and strengthening the border. The War of 1812 planted the seeds of these differences, but it was during the war that the roots took a firm hold, deep in the consciousness of Canadians.

Perhaps no group better epitomized Canadian distinctiveness than the Council of Canadians and their outspoken leader, Maude Barlow. When I met her and a few of her colleagues to discuss the goals of a George W. Bush initiative, the Security and Prosperity Partnership, they were skeptical. We were seated in a small conference room in the suite belonging to this left-of-center nationalist nongovernmental organization. I had taken a small group of embassy staff over to see if we could open a line of discussion on a broad range of US-Canadian issues. The council and its executive director, Maude Barlow, could always be counted on to provide an oppositional viewpoint in any media story concerning US relations with Canada. We had heard their views through the media for years, but no one had ever met with them. Their heightened rhetoric made us unsure if they would even meet with anyone from the embassy.

As we went down the list of objectives under the initiative, John Carlyle, the embassy energy officer, touted one of the "major" accomplishments of the new partnership. The two countries, he told them, had reached an agreement to standardize the size of pipelines crossing the border. "That's all there is? It can't be," said one incredulous council member, and repeated, "It can't be." After a year of negotiations, the two countries had, yes, agreed to harmonize government regulations concerning the size of the diameter of pipelines that crossed the border. Unfortunately, that *was* it: a major accomplishment that the two countries would have the same size pipelines that met at the border. There was no agreement on what could flow through the pipelines; that would be years later when one actual pipeline known as Keystone became controversial, not for its diameter, but for the fact that it would carry oil taken by environmentally risky extraction practices.

The council was suspicious of the Security and Prosperity Partnership, or SPP, using the government-speak language of acronyms. Their opposition stemmed from the stated goals of deepening or furthering the integration of the three countries of North America, which was unpopular in all three countries, especially if taken to its logical conclusion of a common market such as the European Union, as only a handful were advocating. Words such as "integration" or "harmonization" set off protests. The Council of Canadians probably was the most vocal of any group in the three countries in its opposition to any current or past plan to integrate; they had even predated the Occupy Wall Street movement with a catchy protest slogan for the SPP: "Integrate This!" The council imagined they were the last bulwark of defense against American efforts to grab Canadian resources (water and oil) and to impose US identity, attitudes, or values on Canada. More than that, though, they saw a distinct Canada, vulnerable in the shadow cast by the United States. Politically, however, the only influence the council could use was through the media. The Harper government could withstand their attacks in the media and move forward to identify areas where integration made sense.

The SPP was a policy wonk's dream come true. This trilateral arrangement between the three countries of North America intended to resolve a host of obstacles related to economic integration and security cooperation. The concept behind this informal project grew out of two separate arrangements the United States had developed with Canada and Mexico after 9/11. Each one, the Smart Border Declaration and Action Plan with Canada and the United States–Mexico Border Partnership Agreement arose from a laudable goal of enhancing security at the borders while limiting any adverse effects on the sizable economic trade relationship. Each had a manageable set of action items that the governments committed to addressing, followed up by regularly scheduled meetings to assess the impact. If these action items were not enough to bring a grin to a policy wonk, then the two separate agreements merged into one for all three countries, and the thirty or more points in the action plan grew to several hundred. There were checklists and color codes to indicate the status of completion; there were lead agencies with supporting casts; there were task forces in each capital responsible for tracking each country's progress; and then there were annual trilateral leaders' meetings and reports set with a deadline to force the bureaucracies to meet and move the plan forward. When we sat down with Maude Barlow and her colleagues, the three countries were busy preparing an annual report, consisting of two hundred pages, in three languages, citing the status of more than three hundred different projects, in twelve different baskets to reduce inefficiencies in the commercial relationship and strengthen our security.

The secret, which we tried to unveil for the council, was that a large number of discrete projects meant, first of all, that it was impossible to do anything major in North American integration. We were only consigned to do what was feasible, and even those steps had to be small. No one wanted any agreement that would invite congressional treaty responsibilities. Still, even those small things were unbearably hard to get done. Skirting a broad goal of accepting one of the other countries' foods or drug scientific testing, thereby reducing repetitive, costly delays in testing, we settled for a large conference of regulators to explain the processes in each country for approving foods or pharmaceuticals for consumer markets. We ran into new terms such as "geographic inhibitors," which were those places along the border where security officers from the United States had to cross into Canada to get to another place in the United States. When that happened, mostly in the Great Lakes, those officers had to put their weapons in a lockbox on board their vessel, even if they were only in the other country's territorial waters for a short period. But unraveling that absurdity proved to be too hard at the time. In the end, the three countries settled on accomplishments such as agreeing on the diameter of pipelines.[6]

After nearly two hours with Maude Barlow and members of the council, I think we successfully convinced them that we were hiding something.

The different reading of the War of 1812 in the two countries underpins the conduct of relations between them. Canada will consciously, vigorously, and controversially place the War of 1812 in front of its peoples. The United States will look past the war and probably even past Canada. Issues of recognition, distinctiveness, and identity, all rooted even before the war, play into Canada as the un-America, like 7UP is the uncola. That *un-America* is one of the strongest ties uniting a country divided by language, region, and ethnicity.

Despite these forces pulling Canada at the seams, Canadians *do* have other distinctive memories that *do* bind them together. Most prominent is a collective appreciation for their origins as a country of the north and the struggles to adapt their lifestyles to a territory reaching to the Arctic Circle, which is apparent in the early contact between English and French settlers and traders. Out of necessity, they forged a coexistence, largely peaceful and cooperative, with the First Nations groups they encountered. It remains apparent in Canada's vigorous defense of its claim to the exclusive right of ownership of the Northwest Passage, in the face of widely held interpretations of the law of the sea conventions. Hockey, curling, ice fishing, skating, skiing, and snowmobiling are their sports, accounting for much of their drive in owning the podium in the winter Olympics. This northern heritage also distinguishes Canada from the United States, even including Alaska. The contradiction is that, in this northern country, 90 percent of the population lives within one hundred miles of its border with the America from which it is trying to distinguish itself.

But we all have our contradictions, and we hate it when a foreigner points them out. Ultimately, Canada's story will continue to be a chronicle of efforts to create an identity from the deep and enduring language and regional divisions. There may be no way to disentangle the United States from those efforts. At the very least, history can help show us a way to recognize them in the conduct of our relations.

Suggested Further Reading

Alan Taylor makes his case for calling the conflict a civil war by describing the similar backgrounds on both sides in *The Civil War of*

1812: American Citizens, British Subjects, Irish Rebels, and Indian Allies (New York: Alfred A. Knopf, 2010). The prolific, popular Canadian historian Pierre Berton offers a fast-paced account of the war in his *Flames across the Border* (Toronto: Anchor Canada, 2010). For a staunch Canadian nationalist perspective on relations between the two countries, Mel Hurtig is unsparing in his fears of influence of the United States on Canada in *The Vanishing Country: Is It Too Late to Save Our Country?* (Toronto: McLelland & Stewart, 2002). David Hackett Fischer explores contacts with First Nations groups in the early settlements of Canada in *Champlain's Dream* (New York: Simon & Schuster, 2008). Two compendiums of Canadian history that I drew on during my time in Canada are Robert Bothwell's *The Penguin History of Canada* (Toronto: Penguin Canada, 2007) and Craig Brown's (ed.) *The Illustrated History of Canada* (Toronto: Key Porter Books, 2002).

4

Nigeria and South Africa: Whose Civil Rights?

In anticipation of the first official Martin Luther King Jr. holiday in the United States in 1986, my colleagues and I in the cultural section at the US Information Service in Lagos decided to mark the event with a major celebratory event in Nigeria. In this, my first tour in the Foreign Service, I was running a small but busy cultural center in the old US Embassy on a busy intersection in the heart of Nigeria's capital. "Busy" would be an understatement. The scene resembled an unorchestrated dance between drivers, laying on their horns in the muggy heat, and pedestrians and hawkers clothed in the bright prints of loose-fitting dress, weaving between and oblivious to the traffic. The noise and heat seemed to reach past our air conditioning directly into our offices. To the simple greeting of "How are you?" a common answer in Lagos would be a stoic "Struggling to survive." It did seem like a struggle every day, but this was also a nation of survivors.

We invited some journalists to the center to discuss our plans for the King celebration, a few days in advance. Midway through the briefing, one of the journalist's questions elicited an awkward pause: "Why do you push Martin Luther King so hard? What about other Black leaders, like Malcolm X?" My two colleagues, both African American women, and I knew that Nigerians followed US political developments closely. Their freewheeling press and the large numbers of Nigerian students attending US universities during the 1970s translated into close attention and scrutiny. More likely, the journalists, and perhaps my colleagues as well, knew that Malcolm X had come to Nigeria in 1964. I did not. Speaking before a university audience in

Ibadan, Malcolm X "gave the true picture of our plight in America, and of the necessity of the independent African nations helping us bring our case before the United Nations."[1] Because I didn't know of this prior visit, I was not expecting this question on Malcolm X.

Maybe the journalist who asked about Malcolm X knew how difficult it had been and how long it had taken to secure national recognition for a King holiday. His conclusion would have been that King and his message of integration were acceptable to a white majority, just as Malcolm X and his rejection of integration in favor of Black nationalism were not. I stumbled on an answer, dealing mostly with the ongoing reappraisal of Malcolm X and his evolving views before his untimely death. The journalist's question, though, revealed how closely Nigerians followed the US history of civil rights, to the extent of appreciating the internal dynamics of the struggles to achieve justice and equality.

The narrative we wanted to promote was part solidarity with the Nigerians, drawing on the same sentiments that Malcom X had found twenty years prior in referring to the "warm reception here in Africa" and the repudiation of the idea that "the black man in Africa is not interested in the plight of the black man in America."[2] However, we also were trying to paint a picture of progress on civil rights in the United States, but Malcolm had anticipated this as well on his 1964 visit, saying that "the U.S. information agencies in Africa create the impression that progress is being made and the problem is being solved."[3]

In 1986, though, we were highlighting progress for two reasons. First, going back to the early years of the Cold War, discrimination against our citizens had lingered as a liability in our foreign relations, especially as we sought to advance our democratic model as an alternative to communism. At the same time, we were trying to distinguish the US experience from the racial impasse on Africa's continent, at its extreme southern tip. South Africa weighed heavily on the minds of Nigerians, who, as the continent's and the broader African diaspora's most populous country, placed themselves in a leadership role in defending the rights of Black people everywhere.[4] This journalist cut through our intent with a simple, straightforward question. He preferred a different history, Malcolm X and Black consciousness, not integration, since Malcolm's story appealed to the raw emotions on the continent toward continued political discrimination in South Africa.

Later in the year, the cultural center was fortunate to host George Foreman, the former heavyweight boxing champion of the world, whose fight with Muhammad Ali in Kinshasa in 1974 made both athletes hugely famous on the continent. More than ten years later, Foreman had long slipped into obscurity, descending from a second defeat into drink and drugs, before hitting bottom and opening a small street-front church in Houston, Texas. We had invited Foreman to Nigeria to run boxing clinics, but also because he articulated so well his personal story that carried an uplifting message about redemption, hope, and hard work for youth everywhere. We were two years beyond an all-out diplomatic effort to convince African countries not to join the Soviet boycott of the 1984 Olympics in Los Angeles after we had led a boycott of the Moscow Olympics over the Soviet invasion of Afghanistan. Our efforts included providing training clinics for African athletes that helped launch a foray into using sports as a tool of diplomacy. Foreman's visit was a high-profile program to reach thousands of youth across the continent; at the same time, we were lobbying the Nigerian Olympic Committee to support US bids to host future Olympics.

As was our practice, we would start such visits with a press conference, which would help introduce a different George Foreman than the boxer and get the word out about his schedule. The auditorium was overflowing with journalists, and we quickly learned they were not all covering a sports beat. It seemed they wanted to lure the former heavyweight into a statement critical of President Reagan's stance toward South Africa. His administration was pursuing a controversial policy toward the country called "constructive engagement," conceived by Chester Crocker, the assistant secretary of state for African affairs and former Georgetown University professor.

The administration claimed it shared with its critics the goal of dismantling South Africa's system of institutionalized racism, *apartheid*, but Crocker geared his policy toward tactics. He envisioned the downfall of apartheid taking place by the United States engaging the white minority government and nudging it down a transitional path. Such an approach ran into opposition from antiapartheid groups in South Africa, in the United States, and elsewhere that were calling for a total boycott of the regime. Further, Crocker's policy of engaging the regime was not producing results, certainly not fast enough for antiapartheid activists around the world, who were stepping up divestment campaigns and protests in front of South African embassies. In this climate, engagement seemed more like an encouragement of this twisted social engineering experiment designed to separate races into neighborhoods and territories, at home, in the workplace, at school, at play, in hospitals—in every facet of life.

I do not recall whether Foreman knew about constructive engagement, but I do remember him stepping politely, even gingerly, around the idea of criticizing the US president, no matter what his views may have been. He kept repeating that he came to Nigeria to conduct boxing clinics, not to talk politics. Still, the same questions kept coming. Finally, his frustration mounted, and he gently launched into his history lesson, talking about how much had improved since he started boxing: new gloves, new techniques, new medicine. What had not changed, he countered, were journalists, always trying to find the wedge. Foreman had hit on a sure way to annoy the press.

And then he dropped the line that was to haunt the rest of his trip in Nigeria when asked how it felt to be a Black man in a country where racism was endemic and that supported racist South Africa. "I am not a black man, nor a white man. I am a hu-man," he declared. It came across as a sound bite that he had used before and that had probably worked before. Here in Nigeria, the press turned that quote into a headline about Foreman turning his back on his race. Foreman reflected his history, one that still held up the goals of equality and integration even if the country still had a long way to move down that path, which was not the narrative that Nigeria saw, or wanted to see. That headline writer wanted Foreman to defend his race and to speak out against the current state, not the idealized state, of race relations in the United States, in South Africa, and in the diaspora.

Ironically, Foreman's comments might have coincided with anti-apartheid views in South Africa, where I took up my next assignment in Durban, South Africa. Before departing, I worked on the South Africa desk in Washington for a few months, and I was there when an invitation came from the South African ambassador to the United States, an Afrikaner named Piet Koornhof. His arrival in Washington coincided with mounting daily protests in front of his embassy and calls for divestment of US companies from a nation still holding fast to its policies of separate development for the races. The event at the ambassador's residence was to see off a group of exchange students, traveling to South Africa at their government's expense. At one point during the dinner, Lulu Koornhof, the wife of the ambassador, leaned over to me. In barely a whisper, she tried to explain her country and its exceptionalism. "You see," she said, "your Blacks are different than ours." She went on to explain how African Americans in the United States with their higher levels of education were more prepared for full participation in society, without appreciating that apartheid may have been responsible for the lack of preparation in *her Blacks*. Her view of African Americans came from the Bill Cosby show, perhaps the most popular show in the United States at the time. Dumbfounded, I had nothing to say. It was one of those moments you want to get back; even as early as the taxi ride home, when I searched for the right response, I finally hit on what I should have said: "So are your whites."

Before departing for the post, I was reminded not to expect any fundamental change in South Africa during my assignment; it would only be an exercise in frustration. On the plane ride into the country, I read the news about South African security forces greeting with water hoses a protest march led by Nobel Peace Prize–laureate Archbishop Desmond Tutu. Change seemed slim and remote. The year before in 1986, Congress had passed, over President Reagan's veto, the Comprehensive Anti-Apartheid Act of 1986, which spelled out a series of sanctions taken against the regime.

To get out ahead of the mounting criticism over his policies toward

South Africa, Reagan appointed Edward Perkins as his new ambassador to the country. Perkins, a career Foreign Service officer, already serving in Liberia as ambassador, would be responsible for implementing the remnants of constructive engagement with the white minority regime. Because he was African American, his selection might also blunt some of the criticism against Reagan for his policy, but at some personal risk. Perkins openly acknowledged this in his memoir, in a conversation he had with President Reagan shortly before he left for South Africa. He told Reagan that African Americans "would not like" his taking the job, a job that meant engaging "constructively" with a racist regime.[5]

The US diplomatic service has a checkered history with diversity, a reflection of the broader society. On the one hand, the first African American diplomat, Ebenezer Bassett, was appointed in 1869, just after the Civil War, and the list of African Americans serving the country includes such renowned figures as Frederick Douglass, W. E. B. Du Bois, and James Weldon Johnson, who went on to head the NAACP. However, the first career African American diplomats did not enter the service until the 1920s, and it took several prominent class action lawsuits in the latter decades of the twentieth century to shed light on discriminatory promotion and hiring practices against racial minorities and women. Perhaps the most shameful blot on the Foreign Service's track record of diversity was its long-standing rule requiring female officers to resign when they married, a rule not eliminated until 1972. That is not a misprint, 1972. It is no wonder that the description of the Foreign Service as "pale, male, and Yale" has persisted.

As a white male with a degree from Princeton, not Yale, I saw firsthand the benefits and advantages of a diverse service, reflecting diversity in the nation, even if still not at the same proportion as the larger society. How many other countries in the world can send representatives abroad whose own heritage traces back to the region or to the nation in which they serve, touching almost every country in the world? Such a situation is especially true in the ability to operate in a foreign language, where the United States can make up for our broader societal monolingual bias with diplomats who grew up hearing and speaking languages other than English.

Admittedly, I stand on shaky ground trying to interpret the experiences of my African American colleagues. I did, however, witness a different dynamic at play in their interactions with Africans, not dissimilar to the ambiguities as related from the earliest days of returning to the continent.[6] The response that the noted African American scholar Henry Louis Gates Jr. described in his essay "Africa, to Me" was one I saw repeated with my African American counterparts, whose presence in Africa elicited curiosity and solidarity. After Gates had introduced himself as an American to a group of people in Sudan, a woman exclaimed, "Africa is on your face."[7] Whether it was Africa on their faces or a familiarity and immediacy that comes with normal family upbringing emphasizing pride in one's heritage, I saw my African American (or for that matter, Hispanic and Asian) colleagues able to cut through the cultural national barriers faster and, I am ashamed to admit, more comfortably than I was. The flip side is that I also felt that expectations ran higher in the diplomatic dialogue between African Americans and Africans. I assumed that access should be easier, understanding would come quickly, persuasions would be more effective, in both directions. When, inevitably, national interests trump ties of heritage, such heightened expectations could turn to disappointment, on both sides.

Further, while minorities in the Foreign Service have gravitated to assignments in countries of their heritage, they also have objected to being typecast as interested or able to serve in only those countries. Terence Todman, an ambassador serving in Denmark when he turned down Reagan's request to serve in South Africa (a post that Perkins accepted) referred to this practice in the State Department as a ghetto mentality: "I resented, and I still resent, the 'ghetto' assignment of blacks to Africa or to Caribbean nations."[8] Todman, an Arabist, pointed out that the strength of reflecting a diverse society in our diplomatic corps allows us to send multiple messages in societies whose populations are more homogenous or rigidly stratified. We have had women representatives in the strongest male-oriented Middle Eastern countries and first generation Mexican Americans from circumstances of poverty in class-bound Latin American societies. Ultimately, though, it is the talent and skills that each officer brings to the representation of the country that matters, regardless of race, gender, and only recently sexual orientation. Not allowing talent in the Foreign Service because a woman gets married or because of heritage or race has diminished the country's abilities to operate beyond our borders. Pigeonholing talent to one region of the world is a disservice to the wide range of our changing needs and requirements in advancing US interests.

There is one more benefit of diversity in the Foreign Service, this one on a personal level. My African American colleagues taught me about race, about the importance of perceptions in a race, and profoundly challenged my perceptions because we both worked *and lived* in closer proximity than we would have in the United States. On multiple occasions, I found out that not only was my version of history different from my foreign counterparts', but also from the views my African American colleagues carried about US history.

Case in point was the five-panel glass display case that hung on the walls of the elevator lobby on the twenty-ninth floor of the highrise in Durban, where the US Consulate General was located. It was an ideal location for visitors to our offices to learn a little more about the United States. Usually, the displays featured what came later to be known as exhibits of "soft power," those features that attract and support ways nations exert their influence, like jazz, sports, entertainment, art, and photography. Historical themes, such as the US civil rights experience, were also recurring staples, especially during Black History Month and around the Martin Luther King Jr. holiday. And occasionally we introduced what I considered to be noncontroversial policy topics, such as drug prevention.

This was still the era of Nancy Reagan's "Just say no" prescription to drug use, even during the Bush administration, which also championed policies aligned with promoting personal responsibility in the African American community. Thus, the focus of the panels on drug prevention centered on communities taking charge and pushing back on drug use in their own neighborhoods. The photos and texts showed success stories, in my eyes, of church leaders and local activists working together to remove the scourge of illicit drugs, one neighborhood at a time.

This was not how one of my consulate colleagues saw it. Of the six Americans working in Durban, two were Black, our consul general, Bismarck Myrick, and a young consular officer, Cyril Sartor, on his first overseas tour. Cyril stopped me in the hall one day and complained about the display on drug prevention. What I saw as success stories, he saw as a negative portrayal of African Americans. "Most of the pictures of these communities affected by drug abuse," he noted, "were of African Americans." Here, against the backdrop of the waning days of apartheid, the raw nerves of US race relations were playing out. Unspoken was how the portrayal might be seen in South Africa, perpetuating racist views in their own situation.

At our next staff meeting, I raised the disagreement with Bismarck, and we talked it through. We ended up allowing the display to stay up. But I kept churning the incident over in my head, quietly pulled the panels out of the case earlier than planned, and sent them back to Washington with a note advising colleagues that the display perpetuated negative stereotypes. This time, though, it was a history shock that was deeply personal, with my unawareness as a white American of perspectives of race developed across the history of my own country.

Edward Perkins came to Durban once during my tour and addressed the consulate staff. After meeting with local officials, he presided over a Black History Month jazz concert at the consul general's residence. Not only was it important to have an African American as our ambassador in what we then did not know were the waning days of apartheid, but it was important to have Edward Perkins as our ambassador. He made it a point to reach out to all communities, engaging not just the government but also all of South Africa. He carefully chose the pace for public comment, adding to his credibility and the moral impact of his messages. He did engage the government, but as he noted, "The president [P. W. Botha] and I were never to have a civil conversation during my entire time there."[9]

Still, in the efforts to reach the goal of supporting the disman-
tlement of apartheid, Americans continually looked at the country
through the prism of our own experience. The speech given by Robert F. Kennedy at the University of Cape Town in 1966 perhaps best
reflects that optic. At the time, Kennedy's visit was well received, and
it continues to be well remembered in that country. He opened with
this:

> I came here because of my deep interest and affection for a land settled
> by the Dutch in the mid-seventeenth century, then taken over by the
> British, and at last independent; a land in which the native inhabitants
> were at first subdued, but relations with whom remain a problem to
> this day; a land which defined itself on a hostile frontier; a land which
> has tamed rich natural resources through the energetic application of
> modern technology; a land which once imported slaves, and now must
> struggle to wipe out the last traces of that former bondage. I refer, of
> course, to the United States of America.[10]

Even Perkins admits to making this comparison in his memoir that
recounts a difficult encounter when he presented his credentials to
President P. W. Botha. When he told Botha, "Our two countries have
a lot in common," he recalled Botha's retort that the US Congress had
just "declared economic warfare" on South Africa.[11]

Beyond a common history of racial prejudice and institutionalized
racism, the two countries' histories of race sharply diverge. It's more
than just the glaringly obvious racial transposition, where a white minority in South Africa denied political rights to its Black majority.
It's also more than the uniqueness of the US "one-drop" definition
identifying African Americans' racial status. Under apartheid, South
Africa divided its society into racial classifications of whites, Indians,
coloreds, and Africans, with subcategories in each grouping.[12] Differ-
ing experiences with slavery were also obvious to everyone. What was
not so obvious were the significant differences in the history of opposition to racial segregation and in the strategies to overcome both it
and its enduring legacy.

In South Africa, or for that matter almost anywhere outside the United States, I never heard the term "civil rights" in the context of removing racial discrimination. It was always "human rights." The distinction implied that addressing the legacy of racism encompassed more than just the political issues of representation or voting or segregated facilities. In South Africa, the history of opposition to racial discrimination was tied intimately to economic issues. Following Ghandian protests against the pass laws at the turn of the last century, the early battlegrounds for protests against racist policies were in the workplace, specifically in the gold and diamond mines that brought so much wealth to the country, to its white elites, and to their foreign investors and participants, among whom were US engineers and bankers.

From the labor unions emerged the concept of "non-racialism," an all-encompassing term not only for the tactics to remove racial distinctions but also for a vaguely defined ideal of what society would look like once they were eliminated. Sowing discrimination in the workplace, employers in the mines attempted to lower the costs of labor, reducing the wages of Africans by half by the end of the Boer War at the turn of the last century. As a result, almost fifty thousand Africans opted to stay away under these conditions, a gap filled by the importation of indentured workers from China.[13] Despite this, with wages for white employees accounting for the largest component of overall labor costs, the mine managers concluded that competition from the Chinese, as well as improved processes in extraction coming from the use of cyanide, would reduce their dependence on white labor. In this climate, it began to dawn on the racially segregated unions that they needed to work together, that they shared disadvantages in the workplace cutting across race.

The first unions to advocate for unity across the races bore both the name of socialism and allegiance to socialist ideals. In a leaflet directed at white workers in 1920, the International Socialist League (ISL) proclaimed, "The native workers are beginning to wake up. They are finding out they are slaves to the big capitalists. . . . White workers! On which side are you? Your interests and theirs are the same as against the Boss."[14] Within a year, the ISL had teamed up with other socialist unions and organizations to join the Communist Party of South Africa (CPSA), the first political organization open to all races, adopting a banner of non-racialism.

This close affiliation with the CPSA tainted non-racialism for African political organizations opposed to the principles and tactics of communism. The African National Congress (ANC), formed in 1912, was an all-African group directing its agenda to the inequities suffered by the African majority. They rejected the idea of violence and revolution, appealing to the influence of Britain to bring about reform within South Africa. Also, the ANC for many years disallowed whites to serve in positions of leadership within the organization; they were suspicious of whites in the CPSA or any organization making decisions or speaking on behalf of the majority population.

It was more than just a failure of the ANC to accomplish any of its goals that moved the organization in the direction of non-racialism. Racial discrimination became more entrenched with the election of the National Party in 1948 that advocated apartheid, a rubric of legal reforms to institutionalize the separation of races, or "national groups" in the language of the newly elected party. The ANC had already signed a pact of cooperation with the Transvaal and Natal Indian Congresses in recognition that they too bore the costs of racial discrimination. The following year, Oliver Tambo and Nelson Mandela assumed leadership roles in the African National Congress, just five years after they had launched the ANC Youth League, and they proceeded further down the path of seeking alliances across the racial divides.

In this way, non-racialism took on other connotations besides those of the workplace. First, non-racialism became the logical counterforce to policies designed to enforce separation of the races. In other words, opposing the new apartheid policies that sought to divide races implied a strategy that would unite the races beyond racial groupings. Also, to have the greatest influence in their campaigns to defy the new laws of apartheid, the ANC and other organizations realized, just as the earlier trade unions had, the value of numbers across the racial divide. There grew as well a recognition that white South Africans had lived in the country for hundreds of years, and, in the words of Walter Sisulu, an ANC Youth League founder and later secretary general of the ANC, the idea of forcing whites to leave was both "futile and reactionary."[15] He went on to lay out how such cross-racial cooperation would work, "on a basis of equality and disinterested adherence to mutual aims."[16]

In this climate, in 1955, the Freedom Charter was drafted, outlining the platform of the African National Congress and its goals of non-racialism, without ever using the term. It was a statement of principles: "South Africa belongs to all who live in it, black and white, and that no government can justly claim authority unless it is based on the will of all the people." Unlike the US Declaration of Independence, it limited its grievances to just one overarching one, that "our people have been robbed of their birthright to land, liberty, and peace by a form of government founded on injustice and inequality." Instead, it laid out a vision for what a postapartheid country would look like, an ideal state to be sure, outlining not only political rights but also economic and social ones, including redividing the land and ensuring free education and health care.[17]

If there is an equivalent seminal document on race in the United States, it would probably be Martin Luther King Jr.'s "I Have a Dream" speech. His remarks in front of the Lincoln Memorial in August 1963 paint his vision of a racially integrated society, almost a postracial state, that moved a nation and continue in the national consciousness today. King's dream of integration differs from the notion of non-racialism, as the latter emphasizes the disintegration of race and racial categories. King's notion of integration led to policies of affirmative action to make up for years of inequality. Affirmative action implies maintaining racial categories, which runs counter to the South African concept of non-racialism, as the Freedom Charter calls for sharing resources and redividing the land.

King's speech also differs from the Freedom Charter as the text of one man, albeit built from his experiences and those of many others over many years battling racial discrimination. The Freedom Charter described non-racialism not only as a goal but as a process. First, a coordinating council of the organizations affiliated with the African National Congress issued a "call [to] all the people of South Africa to prepare for the Congress of People."[18] Then, an estimated fifty thousand people reached out across the country's divides to solicit the input of freedom demands. A smaller group of people edited the document and prepared a draft for the Congress of the People, held in Kliptown on June 26, 1955. There, close to three thousand people of all races, predominantly African, adopted the charter as their platform. This consultative approach linked non-racialism closely with democracy and made leaders accountable. Even in his first remarks upon release from prison, Nelson Mandela made sure that his allies knew that he did not negotiate on his own with the government. He announced that he would have more to say after he had an opportunity to "consult with my colleagues" and that he remained loyal to the ANC and its principles.[19] There was no question that he was their leader, but there might have been challenges to his authority had he presumed to speak for all groups without their concurrence.

Not all in opposition to apartheid agreed with non-racialism, either its principles or its process. Africanists within the ANC and in other organizations continued to express reservation about working with whites, a recurring division in the antiapartheid movement since the adoption of the Freedom Charter. Some, like Robert Sobukwe, the leader of the Pan-African Congress, rejected race altogether, in words surprisingly similar to those George Foreman mouthed in Lagos more than twenty-five years later: "The Africanists take the view there is only one race to which we all belong, and that is the human race."[20] Others, such as Steve Biko, who walked out of the white-led university student organization to form the South African Students' Organisation (SASO), advocating Black Consciousness, complained about whites in leadership roles of Black organizations, knowing "what was good for the blacks."[21] The SASO platform specifically rejected the notion of integration, as one where Blacks would integrate into a "white-type society."[22] Black Consciousness presented the most serious challenge to the concept of non-racialism in the 1970s but lost its most powerful and charismatic advocate when Biko died in police custody in 1977. Advocates of non-racialism felt that adherents of Black Consciousness emphasized race not entirely dissimilar to the way white Afrikaners did, and shifted the focus of opposition away from economics and class.

It was in the early 1960s when the efforts to eliminate institutional racism in the United States and South Africa diverged most sharply. In the United States, pressures from nonviolent protests and revulsion over the tactics used in the Deep South to put down the protests gradually resulted in the passage of the 1964 Civil Rights Act and the 1965 Voting Rights Act, the two landmark pieces of the law outlawing most forms of discrimination.

In South Africa, on the other hand, the government's clampdown on protests caused a different reaction. After police opened fire on unarmed protesters at Sharpeville on March 21, 1960, killing sixty-nine, it took just ten days for the government to declare a state of emergency to quell the ensuing uproar, banning and arresting the leaders of the main antiapartheid political organizations, including the African National Congress and the Pan-African Congress. Many in South Africa realized that nonviolent protest would not achieve the end to racial discrimination. Nelson Mandela explained the transition to the armed struggle during his trial in 1964: "When all channels of peaceful protest had been barred to us, that the decision was made to embark on violent forms of political struggle, and to form Umkhonto We Sizwe,"[23] the Spear of the Nation, the armed wing of the ANC. That summer of 1964, the two countries took sharply different paths. On July 2, in Washington, DC, Congress passed the Civil Rights Act that, among other things, prohibited discrimination in public places; ten days later, Mandela and his seven coaccused were sentenced to life imprisonment in Pretoria for their actions to seek the same removal of legally sanctioned discrimination.[24]

The stance taken by the United States toward South Africa was consistent only in its ambiguity. While the United States rebuked the South African government following the Sharpeville attack and joined in a UN Security Council resolution condemning it, three different facets of the antiapartheid movement still troubled those crafting US policy to South Africa. First were the heavily skewed US economic interests in the country. Americans had long been closely aligned with the profitable mining sector, spilling over eventually into other lucrative sectors such as autos and energy. Dating back to the discovery of gold and diamonds in the late 1800s, Americans joined the rush to the mining fields for quick profits. By the turn of the century, American engineers had established a dominant presence in the largest companies, drawing on their technical skills and experience to support the full exploitation of the mines, including techniques for deep-level mining.

Two, William Honnold and future president Herbert Hoover were instrumental in advocating for the recruitment of Chinese laborers as well as implementing techniques to extend depleted mines deeper. The US bank J. P. Morgan helped raise initial investments to establish the Anglo-American Company in 1917, the conglomerate that came to dominate South African mining through the century. As the government enacted rigid apartheid laws following the Second World War, foreign investors poured into the country, making upwards of 15 percent return on their investments. By 1972, the United States had surpassed Britain as the largest source of foreign investment. Antiapartheid opponents, many of whom came from labor unions, saw these US business interests not only allied with their managerial adversaries but also profiting from a political system based on racial discrimination. South Africans opposed to apartheid came to the conclusion that the United States was on the wrong side of their fight to remove all forms of segregation.

Concerns with the role of the South African Communist Party in the antiapartheid movement exacerbated US suspicions and consternation over the future of foreign investments. These increased with the adoption of the armed struggle by the ANC. The United States officially denounced the recourse to violence, in part because of its concern over the impact on the stability of the economy, but also perhaps because we continued to see the political divide through our prism of the desegregation achievements through the nonviolent tactics of Martin Luther King Jr. When antiapartheid activists reached out to allies inimical to the United States, in the Eastern Bloc and among Middle Eastern groups opposed to Israel, the divide and the suspicions grew.

It may have been the antiapartheid movement's relationship with the South African Communist Party that raised the greatest concerns among US government officials and US business interests. In its earliest days, the Communist Party of South Africa limited membership to whites only, and when it opened its doors to Africans in 1924, many members left the party. Its ranks dwindled during the 1930s, and suspicion among Africans about allowing whites in leadership positions distanced the ANC from the communists. With the rise of the National Party and its apartheid policies after World War II came new legislation, the Suppression of Communism Act. This act effectively banned the party and pushed the membership underground. The ban led to its secret reorganization as the South African Communist Party (SACP), which maintained a close relationship within the broader alliance associated with the African National Congress. The many members of the ANC's executive who shared party affiliation with the SACP helped to foster the impression that communists were leading the ANC. The two organizations shared the goal of Black liberation in South Africa, but for the communists, it was the necessary first step on the path toward a socialist state. When the ANC adopted the armed struggle in 1963, it fell to Joe Slovo, an SACP leader, to organize it from outside the country.

The ANC was open to alliances with organizations, foreign and domestic, that would support its efforts to end apartheid. In his well-known statement during his trial, Nelson Mandela discussed the relationship of the ANC and the antiapartheid movement with communism: "For many decades communists were the only political group in South Africa prepared to treat Africans as human beings and their equals. They were the only political group which was prepared to work with Africans for the attainment of political rights." He went on to conclude: "Because of this there are many Africans who today tend to equate freedom with communism."[25] In 1964 and later, Mandela remained steadfast in seeking alliances where he could find them. Long after his release from prison, he maintained loyalty to whoever had provided support, including the PLO and Cuba, causing no small discomfort in the United States.

It was not just Mandela and the ANC that highlighted the links between communism and antiapartheid efforts. The National Party government repeatedly used the specter of communists in the ranks. This argument fed into the dominant Cold War views in the United States, when we defined our national priorities as the defeat or containment of communism. As the United States sought to remove institutionalized racism within its borders with the passage of the Civil Rights and the Voting Rights Acts in 1964 and 1965, it did little officially to support similar efforts in South Africa, where the government claimed it had to crack down on antiapartheid activists since they were bent on replacing apartheid with communism. This alignment of Cold War aims between the United States and South Africa continued through to the 1980s, as the two countries fought on the same side to support an anticommunist insurgency in Angola.

Not only did we see South Africa's struggle to remove apartheid through our civil rights history, but, as with many places around the world, the United States confused the nationalist aims of antiapartheid activists with support for a broader global communist agenda. The South Africans, on the other hand, were turning to whoever would support their cause, while in the United States we were advocating for a peaceful, nonviolent transition to democracy.

The link with communism became more apparent as the political space for crafting new policies toward South Africa opened up with the demise of the Soviet Union and the Eastern Bloc countries in the late 1980s. These events coincided in the United States with pressure on business through the divestment campaigns and on politicians in Congress. In South Africa with the removal from power of the intransigent P. W. Botha after a stroke, a new National Party leadership felt it could manage a transition away from apartheid without all-out civil war.

In the midst of this, the foreign minister, Pik Botha, came to

Durban for his party's national convention, and in a speech he made explicit the connection between events in the rest of the world and the conscious decision to release Mandela from prison, unban political parties, and begin discussions toward a political transition. Surprisingly honest, Botha said that he (and others in the party) were seeking to avoid the example of Romania, where Nicolae Ceau escu and other leaders were lined up against the wall and shot.

These changes opened up opportunities for the United States to support the political transition that South Africa was undergoing. Within the country, the US Embassy had always been one of a few venues where people across the racial divide could meet and engage each other. Through both aid programs and people-to-people exchanges, the US Embassy was able to reach out to those still able to confront apartheid such as church leaders, university activists, and community-based organizations ostensibly unaligned with any banned group.

The US library in Soweto could not pretend to meet the needs of the African majority in the country, but it did serve as an important symbol in the middle of the country's most well-known township. When the political transition started, these efforts multiplied to support the negotiations and then the transition. We made possible countless interactions between interested parties on both sides of the Atlantic, from constitutional lawyers to economists, artists, educators, and city planners.

There is no doubt that the leadership, talent, and goodwill within South Africa, among South Africans, rode this process through to a conclusion that was far from perfect but could have turned out to be truly horrendous as some repeatedly tried to derail it. The political transition away from apartheid should rank as one of the major international success stories of the twentieth century. In the end, the United States looked beyond our civil rights history and our aversion to communism. Instead, we opted to listen to South Africans, and listen hard; to see through our experiences into the realities that they faced; and to support the transition they chose to pursue, on its own terms. As a result, we were able to contribute to the heroic efforts undertaken by South Africans at all levels to remove institutionalized racism and embrace a democratic future.

The US version of civil rights history that we promoted in Nigeria, South Africa, and elsewhere initially centered around Dr. King, one man who embodied the efforts, in the face of setbacks and resistance, to build a more just society. As the transition in South Africa unfolded, the pursuit of justice once again took the shape of an individual, Nelson Mandela, even as he sought to push the broader movement to the foreground. In some ways, we in the United States have adopted, even appropriated, Mandela and his struggle into our own continuing, halting history of race. But we are not alone. We may best capture the historical legacy of this remarkable once-in-a-generation leader by the cliché that seems to surface in any global turmoil: "Where is our Mandela?"

Suggested Further Reading

Julie Frederikse recounts the history of the emergence of non-racialism in *The Unbreakable Thread: Non-Racialism in South Africa* (Bloomington: Indiana University Press, 1990). Nelson Mandela's autobiography, *Long Walk to Freedom* (New York: Back Bay Books, 1995), provides his firsthand account of joining the African National Congress, the Freedom Charter, his years in prison, and his emergence to negotiate a path to building a new society. Joseph Lelyveld's *Move Your Shadow* (New York: Times Books, 1985) came out a couple of years before my tour and offers insights into the disparities of apartheid. James Campbell explored the history of the African diaspora in the United States in his *Middle Passages: African American Journeys to Africa* (New York: Penguin Press, 2006). John Higgenson described the early years of American involvement in South Africa in his essay "Privileging the Machines: American Engineers, Indentured Chinese and White Workers in South Africa's Deep-Level Gold Mines, 1902–1907," which appeared in the *International Review of Social History* 52, no. 1 (2007): 1–34.

5

Summit of the Americas: Trapped in Our Past

As president, Barack Obama had his eye on history. It was hard not to, and not just because he made history as the first African American president of the United States. He was acutely aware of America's history of race. He noted as much in his first inaugural, appealing to "our better history." He knew, undoubtedly firsthand, that we had a shameful history: the vestiges of our slave past spilling over to destructive Jim Crow discrimination, leading to the ugliness of the backlash to the civil rights struggles, and today's enduring inequalities and prejudices.

We as Americans look back to this sorrier history and its recurrences and shudder when we look too closely. However, Obama knew we also had a better history, one we prefer to remember and to highlight. His political side told him to lean toward the optimism of our better history. It is a version that Obama, in his most stirring oratory, evoked. After the shooting at a church in Charleston, South Carolina, Obama contrasted the two sides of history:

> The fact that this took place in a black church obviously also raises questions about a dark part of our history. This is not the first time that black churches have been attacked. And we know that hatred across races and faiths pose a particular threat to our democracy and our ideals.
>
> The good news is I am confident that the outpouring of unity and strength and fellowship and love across Charleston today, from all races, from all faiths, from all places of worship indicates the degree to which those old vestiges of hatred can be overcome.[1]

This same duality exists in the way many outside the United States remember their history of interaction with us. They also know a *harsher history*, and they devote more time and energy to remembering it than we do. No single moment captured this duality better than when Hugo Chávez, the thorn-in-our-side president of Venezuela, gave Obama a "history" book. It was March 2009, at the Summit of the Americas, just a couple of months after Obama's inauguration. While not his first trip outside the United States as president, it was his first summit, meaning he was on a grander stage, joining thirty other foreign leaders in Trinidad.

The Office of Western Hemisphere Affairs at the State Department has a permanent staff attending full-time to the business of the Summit of the Americas, a process of meetings of heads of state every three years. That's right: permanent staff is in place for meetings held once every three years. This small group follows up on commitments made at the summit, measuring progress and corralling the resources needed to implement programs and agreements. Every third year, six months or so out from the meeting, other offices start getting pulled into the preparations, and one month out from the start of the summit, hundreds of staff focus on organizing and supporting the event. They float plans, redraw them, finalize them, and then after the summit, they drop them. Then a few days before the next summit, they start all over from scratch. That's too cynical a view, but maybe not far from what actually happens on any meeting the president attends.

These summits represent only the latest in a long history of competition between Latin America and the United States over multilateral diplomacy in the region. As far back as 1826 with the Congress of Panama, the issue of control over regional organizations and conferences and the related issue of which countries to invite and who would do the inviting have swirled around these regional meetings. The Summit of the Americas, first convened by President Clinton at the inaugural summit in Miami in 1994, recognized the emergence of democratic governments in the region and pressed the case for a free-trade pact across the region. With the Organization of American

States (OAS) taking over the planning and control of the summit process, the exclusion of the only nondemocratic nation in the region, Cuba, led to boycotts and the creation of the Bolivarian Alliance, led by Hugo Chávez of Venezuela, as an alternative forum. Spain has its regional conference, the Ibero-American Summit, and the Community of Latin American and Caribbean States emerged in 2010 without the participation of the United States or Canada.

This particular Summit of the Americas in April 2009 was unusual because it was President Obama's first, less than two months after his inauguration, and no one knew what his focus would be. It was also unusual since the predictable unpredictability of Hugo Chávez had started in the weeks before the summit. Would he and his three like-minded leader/friends attend? (Evo Morales of Bolivia, Daniel Ortega of Nicaragua, and Rafael Correa of Ecuador.) Would they insist on Cuban participation? And how would they react to the presence of Obama, whose very election ran counter to their preconceptions of the United States?

With all contingencies planned out, with word of Chávez's attendance coming only the week prior, the president and hundreds of people descended on Trinidad.[2] Diplomats, security officials, computer and communications technicians, journalists, press officers, and doctors and nurses joined the entourage, all in support of President Obama. While many anticipated Chávez's ability to capture the limelight, especially given that his coy delays in deciding already succeeded in giving him more attention, no one saw the incident of the book coming.

I suspect that Chávez decided to attend the summit only once he figured out his game plan to hijack the meeting. Early on, he sought out Obama, handed him a book, and shook his hand. This simple act changed the narrative we had wanted to impose of multilateral cooperation that worked to address scores of challenges facing the hemisphere, albeit framed in the heavy, plodding language of international bureaucracy. A handshake and a book.

The book was *The Open Veins of Latin America,* by Uruguayan journalist Eduardo Galeano, originally published in 1971. The Monthly Review Press released it translated from the Spanish in 1973. Shortly after its publication, the Uruguayan government banned the book and imprisoned the writer, both signs of a different Latin America during the Cold War. Hugo Chávez made *Open Veins* a bestseller thirty-five years after its writing and ten years after a new twenty-fifth-anniversary edition was released. His gesture prompted a colleague to run to the State Department library and share the loaned copy with me. Despite more than ten years working in the region, I had never heard of Galeano. A casual glance through the pages was all I needed to appreciate why the book and the author touched a vein throughout Latin America for those firmly on the left side of the political spectrum.

Galeano claims that he writes so people don't forget. "I'm a writer obsessed with remembering, with remembering the past of America above all and above all that of Latin America, intimate land condemned to amnesia."[3] His subtitle reveals his ambition: *Five Centuries of the Pillage of a Continent.* In *Open Veins,* Galeano scours through, yes, hundreds of years of history across the continents, recovering memories and thrusting them in the faces of readers who either never knew or deliberately choose to forget. (This approach also helped lead to the writing of this book and the need to remember and the benefits of hearing competing versions of history.) *Open Veins* was not an easy read, as I caught myself in heightened defensive mode, arguing and angry. He makes no pretense of his partisanship, quoting Marx authoritatively and citing Cuba as a model "new society."[4]

The book's title taps into the dual meaning of "veins," comparing the despoliation of mineral resource veins in the earth to the tapping into the biological veins of the continent's people. Put more directly, as countries like Spain, Britain, and the United States have plundered the resources of the region, the people have bled. Galeano goes so far as to say, "The more the world market desires a product, the greater misery it brings to the Latin America peoples whose sacrifice creates it."[5]

It is a very different history of events from the one the United States remembers, or promotes in its relations with the continent, creating a type of macro history shock of world views. These competing histories help explain why not only leaders such as Chávez or Daniel Ortega of Nicaragua but also many politicians, intellectuals, and activists across the region approach relations with the United States with such mistrust and suspicion. This view of history has spawned and sustained a political left in Latin America that is both further left and more numerous than its counterparts in other regions.

Galeano pulls together a wide variety of unconnected events and trends across centuries. He signals his intention from the start that he will "chronicle our despoliation and at the same time explain how the current mechanisms of plunder operate, [and] will present in close proximity the caravelled conquistadores to the jet-propelled technocrats, Hernán Cortés and the Marines, the agents of the Spanish Crown and the IMF; the dividends from the slave trade and the profits of General Motors."[6] He organizes his thesis around resources: sugar in Cuba, bananas in Guatemala, copper in Chile and Peru, and oil in Venezuela. Complaining of the profits made by foreigners at the expense of Latin America, Galeano contrasts initial investments with the significantly larger earnings leaving the countries. And he goes further. Resources such as coffee, he claims, produce more jobs in the United States than in Latin America and earn more in levies and tariffs for the European community than for the supplier countries.[7]

Galeano decries the alliance of foreign usurpers—diplomats, marines, bankers, and merchants—working in concert to ensure that these types of arrangements continue for the benefit of outsiders. USAID and the Alliance for Progress also come under blistering criticism as tools, on a par with the marines, for securing dominance through tying economic assistance to purchasing US products and through promoting economic policies advantageous to US interests in the region.

Given the book's references to the role of US embassies and ambassadors throughout the region, the only surprise is not that there are heightened levels of mistrust and suspicion, but that there are not more openly hostile leaders like Chávez. Galeano claims the US ambassador in Bolivia began attending cabinet meetings in that country, and his counterpart in Cuba before the Castro Revolution told the US Congress that he was the second-most-important person in the country. Galeano recounts coups and executions aided by US embassies in Mexico in 1910, Nicaragua in 1933, Guatemala in 1954, and Brazil in 1964. The book was published before the downfall of Salvador Allende in Chile.

It's easy to see why this particular book appealed so to Chávez, and generations of Latin Americans, even making its way into US university curricula. Venezuela has not just squandered its oil, its principal resource; it has borne the brunt of "organized looting," using Galeano's language.[8] Foreign oil companies made half of their profits internationally from Venezuela; representatives of the companies drafted the country's law dictating the terms of production, trade, and investment. The Chávez hero Simón Bolívar emerges as the leader promoting a united Latin America, except that, according to Galeano, it is united only in its "serfdom" to "a legion of pirates, merchants, bankers, Marines, technocrats, Green berets, ambassadors, and captains of industry."[9]

The book found receptive audiences throughout the hemisphere whose distrust of US motives ran deep, especially concerning the role of the US military. A year before the 2009 summit, the US command whose area of responsibility covers this hemisphere, SouthCom, announced it was reinstating the Fourth Fleet, as a restructuring of its naval resources in the Western Hemisphere. The announcement caught the rest of the hemisphere by surprise. Much as in the creation of NorthCom described earlier, US officials played down the new Fourth Fleet as a simple organizational reshuffling to place all the naval resources available to SouthCom under a single entity and, unstated, to raise its status to the equal of other fleets in the navy and enable it to call on additional naval resources if needed. After all, the original Fourth Fleet that had operated from 1943 to 1950 helped defend the hemisphere against German U-boat warfare during the Second World War. When it was disbanded in 1950 because its original mission had ended, coverage for naval operations in this region fell to the Second Fleet.

Partners and skeptics through the region drew on a different history as they conjured up a more robust, even aggressive, purpose behind the reinstatement. They feared the United States was placing this region on a par with the fleets operating in the Persian Gulf. Even those who regularly participated in a cooperative joint naval exercise asked for explanations to respond to their voting populations, who were wary of such close ties to the US military. And of course Chávez and his allies saw this as a golden opportunity to stoke the resentment toward the United States and its record of interventions in the hemisphere, raising the prospects that the new fleet was a sign of preparations for another round of gunboat diplomacy. The designation of the fleet prompted Chávez to bolster his efforts to create the Union of South American Nations (UNASUR) as he countered with his proposal to create a South American Defense Council, launched in December 2008. Chávez also drew on the same tactic of distrust of the US military in characterizing the US humanitarian response to the 2010 earthquake in Haiti as an invasion and takeover of the island nation, which will be explored more fully in a later chapter.

It took weeks of reassurances through diplomatic channels and a vigorous public diplomacy media campaign through the hemisphere to set the record straight about the new naval fleet in this hemisphere. The experience demonstrates, just as with the NorthCom announcement, how an action that is conceived in the United States as a bureaucratic reorganization arouses suspicions based on a history that the rest of the hemisphere remembers much differently than we do.

Those suspicions were kept alive by Galeano's book written decades earlier, but still popular enough to cause Chávez to hand a copy to Obama. Never mind that the book grew out of the context of the Cold War and carries anachronistic paeans to Karl Marx and the "model society of Cuba." While some predictions, such as the deterioration of the dollar in the world economy, could be used to cite the book's irrelevance, others anticipating the 1980s debt crisis in Latin America seem prescient indeed, even if couched in terms of responsibility for such a crisis lying in the hands of foreign banks.

More important is that the book has endured beyond that era, even though Galeano disavowed it in 2014, some five years after Chávez presented a copy to Obama at the summit. Speaking at a book fair in Brazil that was intended to honor the forty-third anniversary of its publication, Galeano said he would "keel over" if he had to read it again. His self-criticism seemed to center on his lack of training as he wrestled with complex concepts of the political economy of the region and on the "extremely leaden" prose employed by the left at the time. He did not elaborate on the overall content of his argument, though he did admit to a "much more complex" reality than his book painted.[10]

Even with that disavowal, the book still holds enough sway to remain on the curricula of many universities, if only to reflect attitudes and perceptions of the era. It was well known enough to be the one selected by Chávez to make a highly public point to Obama, which some interpreted at the time as a publicity stunt, designed by a leader who knew how to capture global public attention. But to Chávez, this was more. It was history. More than a narrative to be resurrected or remembered, to Chávez, this was *his* history. It helped shape his attitude and dictate his behavior—as well as those of his supporters throughout the continent—in their encounters with the United States. The Cold War rhetoric of that book had shifted easily to newer paradigms of leftist criticism, such as neoliberalism to explain the bundle of economic reforms linked to privatizing government enterprises and free trade that replaced the rhetoric of the Cold War. Not that Chávez minded that earlier rhetoric either, since his goal was to build a socialist state in Venezuela. He wanted Obama and the rest of us to confront our history, that part of our darker history, which was what he and other like-minded Latin Americans saw when their attention turned to the United States.

In Trinidad, Obama responded with his approach to history, answering a litany of US offenses presented by Nicaraguan president Daniel Ortega earlier in the proceedings:

> I didn't come here to debate the past—I came here to deal with the future. [Applause.] I believe, as some of our previous speakers

have stated that we must learn from history, but we can't be trapped by it. . . . To move forward, we cannot let ourselves be prisoners of past disagreements. I am very grateful that President Ortega— [applause]—I'm grateful that President Ortega did not blame me for things that happened when I was three months old. [Laughter.] Too often, an opportunity to build a fresh partnership of the Americas has been undermined by stale debates.[11]

The official transcript only says laughter, but it probably was nervous. And maybe a little relieved, that a new US president whom they liked and were willing to give the benefit of the doubt to had deflected the tension in the room.

If Chávez intended this presentation as a means to rewrite or resurrect an alternate version of history, he succeeded. Sales of *Open Veins* skyrocketed the day after he promoted the book, jumping from number 54,295 on Amazon's rankings of books to number 6 the next day.[12] The durability of the book as a best seller is questionable, as its ranking five years later had fallen to 26,390, but it was still ranked the fifteenth most popular book of those related to Central America.

Suggested Further Reading

As mentioned, I first read *Open Veins* by Eduardo Galeano (New York: Monthly Review Press, 1973) only after Hugo Chávez presented the book to President Obama. Galeano's book was excoriated as the "idiot's bible," in a mocking and harsh critique of the Latin American left, by Plinio Apuleyo Mendoza, Carlos Alberto Montaner, and Alvaro Vargas Llosa in *Guide to the Perfect Latin American Idiot* (Lanham, MD: Madison Books, 2001), first published the year before I arrived in Peru and immensely popular there during my assignment, since it was cowritten by the son of Peru's famed author and presidential candidate. Over the course of my tours in Peru and Mexico, the essays of Mario Vargas Llosa, his Nobel laureate colleague, Gabriel García Márquez, and Mexican author Carlos Fuentes regularly appeared in newspapers with varying degrees of criticism of the US role in Latin America and beyond. Collections of their essays include Llosa, *Touchstones: Essays on Literature, Art, and Politics* (New York: Farrar, Straus and Giroux, 2011); García Márquez, *Scandal of the Century* (New York: Knopf, 2019); and Fuentes, *Contra Bush* (Buenos Aires: Aguilar, 2004).

6

Haiti: Recovering Heritage

Tragedy and heroism. And history.

The 2010 earthquake in Haiti lasted barely three minutes, but the devastation ranks as one of the most destructive natural disasters in recorded history. Each passing hour, reports out of Port-au-Prince painted a worst-case scenario, only to be surpassed with later news of even greater catastrophe: hundreds of thousands of people dead, the collapse of nearly every government building as well as homes across the capital city and beyond, and the breakdown of already limited services.

When the quake struck, on January 12, 2010, I was back in Washington at the Bureau of Western Hemisphere Affairs, in an office supporting cultural and press programs at embassies throughout the hemisphere. My wife and I had just stepped out into the cold, dark early winter evening following a swearing-in ceremony for a colleague who was off to South Africa when my Blackberry rang. It was the bureau's executive assistant; he never calls, I thought. Calmly, he told me about the quake from three hours earlier and asked if I would fill the second shift overseeing a twenty-four-hour task force to monitor the crisis. I had never been to Haiti but knew enough about its tenuous economic situation to expect the worst. I agreed, and by the time I arrived the next morning around five o'clock, three different task forces were running out of the operations center, including one run by the consular bureau, fulfilling its responsibility for the protection of US citizens abroad. In just the first four days following the earthquake, the consular task force logged four hundred thousand phone calls, responding to queries about relatives and friends in Haiti.

While I would end up doing only two shifts on the task force, the crisis occupied the full attention of the bureau and offices across the Department of State and other federal and state agencies for months to come. The extent of the destruction quickly became apparent, surpassing the worst fears. The storm destroyed more than 105,000 homes and damaged another 208,000, leaving an estimated 1.3 million people homeless. It reduced all but two of Haiti's government ministry buildings to rubble. At least fifty hospitals and clinics that would have treated victims were not usable. Well over 200,000 people died, and 300,000 were injured. Total cost in damage came to $7.8 billion, according to the Government of Haiti. Among the casualties were hundreds of UN peacekeepers who had been stationed in Haiti to provide security since the 2004 departure of ousted president Jean-Bertrand Aristide.[1]

Such large and abstract numbers tend to lose meaning. But in stark personal terms, the tragedy hit closer to home. The cultural attaché and a Foreign Service colleague whom I had met several months earlier, Victoria DeLong, was missing and a day later was found lifeless in the rubble of her home, a victim of a "pancaked roof," a new term I learned to describe collapsed buildings that took so many lives during the earthquake.

The rescue and relief efforts, first from individual Haitians on the ground before outside help could arrive, and then the efforts of nations across the globe descending on Haiti to provide support, made heroes of neighbors, of government bureaucrats, of soldiers. The day after the earthquake, a depleted Haitian government turned control of its damaged airport over to the US military to coordinate arrivals of aid and aid workers. The first US disaster relief teams arrived, followed shortly after that by a growing number of international disaster assistance staff, along with increasing amounts of supplies. Two aircraft carriers, the USS *Vinson* and USS *Bataan*, and a US Navy hospital ship were mobilized to the area, along with thousands of soldiers to support relief efforts, to distribute food, and, if necessary, to protect against looting.

That Saturday, as Secretary of State Hillary Clinton visited Port-au-Prince, I was at my desk in a largely empty State Department building trying to find ways to get press officers into the country. Not only had relief teams arrived from around the world, but so had hundreds of journalists and their crews, trying to file their stories of the earthquake and the relief efforts. I received a call from the switchboard. On the line was a journalist in Nicaragua, who asked for a comment on a claim that his president, Daniel Ortega, had made the day before. A longtime antagonist of the United States, Ortega claimed (and I paraphrase) that the United States was invading Haiti, with intentions to take over the country.

Stunned into momentary silence by the idea that there would be any reason why the United States would want to take over the poorest country in the hemisphere, which had just suffered an unimaginable disaster, I asked him to repeat his question to make sure I heard it right. I then politely responded by denying the claim, and noted that only the military had the organizational structure and resources to deploy quickly and provide the relief needed in such devastation. The call ended, and I thought I had put the story to rest.

It did not take long for this claim, though, to become a counter-narrative to US assistance to a neighbor in desperate need. The story spread quickly across Latin America and on to other parts of the world, especially those places predisposed to distrust and criticism. Hugo Chávez of Venezuela became the loudest voice, but others soon joined the refrain. The ground on which such claims fell, while not fertile, was tilled with recollections of the history of US intervention in Latin America, a history taught in universities, retold in books like Galeano's *Open Veins of Latin America*, and regularly reinforced in the pages of newspapers across the continent. While I was unaware of a single voice in Haiti making such a connection, surely people inside and outside of Haiti remembered an earlier era—going back to 1915—when the United States had intervened in Haiti and then governed for the next nineteen years.

And in Haiti and beyond, the inhabitants remember the US presence as an extended, unwanted occupation. How many who descended on Haiti that January after the earthquake, with troops and aid workers, were aware that the United States had occupied Haiti for almost twenty years? I was not.

Haiti could have been the model historical case study for Galeano's *Open Veins*, except that the country's largely mineral resources of gold, silver, and copper were still largely unexploited and might have sent Galeano off in search of a metaphor different from veins. Foreign powers over centuries, not just the United States, had leveraged their military, diplomacy, business, and even aid presence in Haiti to exacerbate political and economic problems that have plagued the country since its founding. The rebellion of slaves against the brutality of French colonial sugar plantation owners in the 1790s should, by all counts, take its place, perhaps even ahead of the French Revolution, as a historically transforming event, placing the campaign to end slavery and racial oppression on the global conscience for centuries.

Haiti's independence leaders—Dutty Boukman, Toussaint Louverture, Jean-Jacques Dessalines, and Henri Christophe—are revered inside and outside Haiti for abolishing slavery on the island and for turning it into the first country in the Americas after the United States to declare independence from a European colonial power, in 1804. When the French finally admitted defeat, they demanded compensation for the loss of property, in this case, slaves, and for the next one hundred years, the nation was burdened by debt payments to France.

Even with these links to France, Haiti's history is played out in the shadow of its large, imposing neighbor to the north. In the years immediately following independence in 1804, political infighting in Haiti continued to plague the country in its aspirations for a unified state. At the same time, it struggled externally for political recognition. In the United States, we delayed the recognition of Haitian independence, because we viewed it through the lens of our contentious divide over slavery. Fear of slave revolts on US soil dispelled any move toward recognizing Haitian independence. It wasn't just Southerners who stood in the way. Even John Quincy Adams, known later in his life as an ardent foe of slavery, used his position as secretary of state under James Monroe to warn against recognition: it would not be "advisable either to recognize them for the present or at any time in that manner."[2]

Adams in his capacity in 1823 as top diplomat drafted the document warning against European interference with newly independent nations, later known as the "Monroe Doctrine." That doctrine was positively received initially by Simón Bolívar and these new Latin American nations. The seminal document did not extend to Haiti, since the United States still withheld formal recognition of its independent status. Ironically, Bolívar, the hero of South American independence, had fled to Haiti for refuge and regrouping after one of his early attempts to defeat Spanish rule failed.

Even without formal relations, though, trade between the United States and Haiti continued. Trade with Haiti in the 1820s was valued at more than $2 million, placing the island nation on the list of top ten trading partners with the United States. Despite the internal disputes over its plantation system upon Haiti's independence, agricultural production remained strong enough to account for one-third of the coffee consumed in the United States.

Still, recognition was not forthcoming, for decades following the French acceptance of its former colony's independence. Only the United States and the Vatican continued their denial of accepting the political reality of a Black-run sovereign nation. Not until December 1861, in the first year of the US Civil War, did Abraham Lincoln formally recognize Haiti. He used his first message to Congress to argue, "If any good reason exists, why we should persevere longer in withholding our recognition of the independence and sovereignty of Hayti and Liberia, I am unable to discern it."[3] Freed from Southern legislators in Congress, Lincoln used recognition, more as a point of symbolic propaganda, to acknowledge the successful revolt by black slaves and pronounce the futility of the South's clinging to that "peculiar institution."

The issue of delayed political recognition looms over the US perspective in the history of our relations with Haiti, principally because of its connection to the debate over slavery and the Civil War. But even then, it remains a sideshow in the context of those tumultuous years. So peripheral was this issue to our remembrance of that conflict that there was no reference in Ken Burns's *The Civil War*, his twelve-part documentary television series, Doris Kearns Goodwin's *Team of Rivals*, nor David Herbert Donald's biography, *Lincoln*.

The memory of the United States withholding recognition may cloud the relationship between the two countries, but it was not the issue that kept alive the mischievous statements from Daniel Ortega and Hugo Chávez accusing the United States of taking over Haiti during the rapid emergency response to the earthquake. They hearkened back to the US occupation from 1915 to 1934, nearly twenty years of military and political control over this island nation, relegated in the United States to a "footnote of history," in the words of historian Mary Renda.

Several aspects related to the occupation may account for the amnesia in the United States. First was the blatant economic and strategic grab behind the decision to intervene in Haiti; second was the unexpected resistance and the brutality of the US response to quell it; and third, the manipulation of Haiti's political and legal foundations to advance US interests did little to ensure long-term stability.

The case for intervention was a result not of one cause, but of a confluence of interests. First were those related to business, where Americans who controlled railways, large tracts of land for banana plantations, and eventually a dominating interest in the National Bank of Haiti, argued at the highest levels of the US government for intervention to assure the stability of their investments. The US Navy's removal of $500,000 in gold bullion from the National Bank of Haiti the year before the intervention was a clear sign of US concern over Haiti's instability and a fierce determination to protect US financial interests. Also, the United States had been eyeing for decades the deepwater port of Môle Saint Nicholas that could give the United States an additional base from which to patrol the Caribbean and could preempt any prospects of the port falling into European hands.

Finally, the case for intervention was based on the fact the United States *could* invade, that it had the uncontested power to intervene, as demonstrated in the still freshly remembered experiences in Mexico, Nicaragua, and the Dominican Republic.

Political violence inside Haiti precipitated the intervention, prompting US business interests to advocate for military action to protect their investments. With a US steamship en route to Haiti and rebel forces marching to the capital, President Vilbrun Guillaume Sam ordered the execution of 167 prisoners, including a former president of Haiti. Street protests erupted immediately, forcing Sam to flee to the French Embassy, but mobs stormed the premises, seized the president, and executed him on the spot. The brutal violence was the pretext needed for the US Marines to land. The initial intervention of just 330 Marines in July 1915 turned into a full-blown occupation. The occupation included a declaration of martial law, the removal of Haitian officers in the army, the establishment of a gendarmerie under US authority, the seizure of customs houses, and the selection of a new president who would accept the terms of the occupation and eventually a new constitution, drafted by a young assistant secretary of the navy, Franklin Delano Roosevelt. Almost twenty years later, it was the same man, in his new role as president, who brought an end to the occupation.

From its start, Haitians resisted the US presence, and they called ending it their "second independence." New Haitian heroes who fought against another foreign intrusion emerged and took their place besides Toussaint Louverture in monuments on their streets and portraits on their stamps and coins. Historians debate the toll of the occupation, with estimates of the violence claiming as many as 11,500 lives. Haiti does not share the relegation of this event to a footnote, nor is it forgotten in other parts of Latin America, lending credence—far-fetched though it seemed to me at the time—to Daniel Ortega's accusation that the United States had long-term plans to take over Haiti.

Much of the violence came from two distinct but related rebellions against the occupation. Both emerged from the remnants of the Haitian army but also took advantage of guerrilla-style warfare waged by the Cacos, rebels who had actively fought in rural areas for decades since independence from France in 1804. By September, just two months after the arrival of the US Marines, fighting broke out from the Haitian military remnants who refused to submit to the new authority. One of the first acts of resistance came from the town of Léogâne (by coincidence, also the epicenter of the earthquake in 2010). A Haitian officer, Charlemagne Péralte, refused to hand over the town to the newly established US authority.

When removed by the handpicked new president of Haiti, Péralte left, but his departure sowed the seeds of the second, more ruthless, rebellion. Meanwhile, other soldiers, likewise, refused to submit to the US forces, including General Benoit Rameau, who drew on Haiti's own independence struggle for inspiration: "For almost 112 years, we have been a free and independent people. Our sweat and courage gave us our independence. In that time, we have never been governed by a head of state chosen by a foreign power."[4] Haitian military remnants combined with the rural Cacos to establish a fighting force, but one that proved ineffective against the superior arms and overpowering tactics of the US Marines. The fighting that quelled this initial rebellion proved so one-sided and inflicted such a tragic loss of life to Haitians that it prompted Josephus Daniels, the secretary of the navy in Washington, to order a suspension of the offensive. A Southern Democrat who shared Woodrow Wilson's progressive views, Daniels also aligned with Wilson's racial prejudices. Still, the scorched-earth campaign proved too much, as it contradicted his paternalistic view that the marines were on the island to protect the Haitian people.[5]

When it became clear that it was former military officers who were leading the fight, occupation authorities removed them and placed power in a new gendarmerie with former Haitian soldiers filling the rank and file, but reporting to US officers. US Marines took up their positions as regional administrative officers, replacing Haitian governors and controlling a broad-ranging set of affairs, from budgets and taxes to policing and judicial matters, with no outside authority to check their behavior. So all-encompassing was their grip on power that one marine, Faustin Wirkus, entitled the memoir of his tenure there as *The White King of La Gonâve*.

The invading marines initially achieved their goal of quelling the uprising of the Cacos. However, the decision to build roads into the interior that enabled them to move troops quickly into rebel strongholds—and, incidentally, to allow peasants to move their goods to market—required labor. So, in 1916, the occupying forces turned to a little-known law, not used in Haiti for decades, called the *corvée*, which allowed for the conscription of forced labor. By itself, this practice was more than enough to remind Haitians of their own past experiences of slavery and the struggle to free themselves.

The particularly brutal implementation of the corvée in the recruitment, imprisonment, and harsh work conditions made its captive workers little different than slaves. Workers were tied up, bludgeoned, tortured, rounded up into what one Haitian official called "concentration camps," and even executed as examples to others to sustain the large numbers needed to build the roads. Stories of these atrocities and growing protests against it filtered up to the occupation authorities and Washington. They decided to abolish the corvée in 1918, but not before it had driven those under its yoke into the arms of newly reconstituted Caco forces, who launched another rebellion.

Both the guerrilla fighting and its suppression surpassed the violence of the first Caco war. One of those forced into labor was Charlemagne Péralte, the same military officer who had resisted the US takeover of his jurisdiction at the start of the occupation. Péralte at one point claimed he had forty thousand forces under his command, using the hit-and-run tactics of guerrilla warfare and managing to control large swaths of the rural north of the country. He took on the persona of leading not just an army, but an alternative government, and solicited support from British and French diplomatic representatives in Port-au-Prince. His propaganda appealed directly to heroes of Haitian independence and even cited as a tactical role model the Belgian resistance against German occupation a few years prior on the other side of the Atlantic.[6]

The US military countered the armed resistance by relying again on superior and overwhelming force. They executed those captured, and destroyed villages presumed loyal to the resistance. They brought in reinforcements from the naval base at Guantanamo and even employed aerial bombardment of villages. Finally, two marines infiltrated a camp where Péralte was based and shot him. They then dragged his body out of the camp and photographed the corpse to prove his death; without his leadership, the revolt eventually ground down. Still, Péralte attained the enduring status of a Haitian martyr for independence, for freedom.

At the same time as the rebellion, US occupation authorities were able to maneuver through Haiti's nominal governmental structure a plan to remove a constitutional ban against foreigners owning property in Haiti. Achieving this goal, long sought by US businesses, the occupation had to convince the figurehead president, Philippe Sudré Dartiguenave, to dissolve parliament and hold a referendum approving a new constitution with the provision allowing foreign ownership. With only 5 percent of the population voting, the new constitution was approved by a vote of 98,294 in favor and 769 opposed. The constitution provided for a new legislative body, but the government never held elections during the remaining years of the occupation.

Revelations of these abuses, both political and violent, surfaced early on during the occupation years and became a matter of public record. The US Senate launched an investigation and conducted hearings that included testimony from US military officials, observers on the ground, and Haitian citizens. An American missionary told the Senate hearing that he believed more Haitians died as a result of the corvée than in "open conflict."[7] Soldiers involved would acknowledge their discomfort with the occupation. Lewis Puller, a marine hero of World War II, wrote a friend that he feared he would be court-martialed for killing Cacos, but instead he received a military decoration. Smedley Butler, another honored marine who commanded the suppression of the Caco war, oversaw the gendarmerie and dissolved the Parliament at gunpoint during the drafting of the constitution. He later recalled his actions as nothing more than making "Haiti and Cuba a decent place for the National City Bank boys to collect revenues in."[8]

James Weldon Johnson, who left a career as a US diplomat to head up the NAACP, went to occupied Haiti in 1920 and wrote a series of articles for the *Nation* and the NAACP magazine *Crisis*. His criticism was most damaging, reflecting on the goals of an occupation that was originally justified to usher in stability in a nation that presumably couldn't govern itself. While acknowledging benefits of the occupation in the building of the main national road, a new hospital, and improved sanitation, he concluded:

> The United States has absolutely failed in Haiti. It has failed to accomplish any results that justify its military occupation of that country, and it has made it impossible for those results ever to be accomplished because of the distrust, bitterness, and hatred which it has engendered in the Haitian people. Brutalities and atrocities on the part of American Marines have occurred with sufficient frequency to bring about deep resentment and terror on the part of the Haitian people.[9]

The occupation had ended up exacerbating the violence and instability that it had sought to eliminate.

With the death of Péralte and the completion of the Senate inquiry, the occupation settled down into an extended period of steady calm, with no elections, but also no further violent rebellion until 1929. A new model agricultural school inaugurated in July of that year became the site, just a few months later, of student protests over the failure to provide promised scholarships. Unrest spread, and the US Marines fired on a crowd of 1,500 protesters, killing twelve, ushering in the end of the occupation.

Within two months of the shooting, a commission appointed by President Herbert Hoover arrived to make recommendations on a plan to restore Haiti's government. The commission held hearings in Haiti and wrote a report citing benefits from the occupation (the road, a hospital, and a school building) but faulted the US authorities for failing to initiate any process of "Haitianization," turning over administrative responsibilities to Haitians. Hoover did not act on all of the recommendations but did begin a process of training Haitians to assume control of their government. It took a new president, Roosevelt, amid an economic crisis, to complete the pullout of the marines and the handover back to Haitian officials.

The question remains, though, if all this was a matter of public record then, why were so many of us involved in the earthquake-relief efforts unaware of this history? It was this narrative that lent credibility to those, such as Daniel Ortega and Hugo Chávez, who wanted to claim that the United States was not just taking over Haiti, but taking it over *again*. I do assume that my colleagues at the embassy in Haiti and those in Washington more closely responsible for Haiti and Caribbean affairs were aware. I also accept responsibility for not knowing; yet, in the entire effort, never once did I hear anyone refer to this history, or perhaps its relevance to the presence of US soldiers providing relief.

The historian Mary Renda offers one easy, but fallacious, explanation: "The real stuff of U.S. history during those years was taking shape within U.S. borders and in Europe, not in a small Caribbean nation."[10] The invasion occurred while war had broken out in Europe with the debate over US participation. Later, displacement occurred through Woodrow Wilson's involvement in the Versailles treaty negotiations and proclamations of self-determination, ironically at the same time the United States was drafting and forcing acceptance of a new constitution in Haiti.

Such an explanation may account for relegating the occupation to the status of forgotten history in the short term. In the long term, though, it may be that the negative fallout from the extended occupation did not coincide with our view of ourselves. We would rather forget.

It took weeks for the Ortega claims of a US takeover to fade, largely as a result of actions on the ground to dispel the notion that the United States intended to "occupy Haiti." US soldiers made sure that international relief flights, including from Cuba and Venezuela, were allowed entry; journalists from the United States and all over the world visited the island to see for themselves what was happening; the departure of the US ships, the drawdown of forces, and the resumption of Haitian control over their airports were highly publicized. The State Department officials addressed the accusation from the pressroom podium and in dozens of broadcast interviews in countries across Latin America and Europe. The story did not endure, but it did represent an arena where history and competing versions of history influenced the conduct of our foreign relations, even casting our most generous spirit in a cloud of controversy.

Amid this controversy, and not long after the relief efforts took hold, I received a call from a Foreign Service colleague detailed to the international division of the Smithsonian Institution. He passed along news that Smithsonian officials had learned from their cultural counterparts in Haiti of tremendous damage to their archives, museums, art, and national patrimony. Haiti had been one of the countries featured at the annual summer Folklife Festival on the Washington Mall, organized by the Smithsonian, so they had close contacts reaching out for help. I was heading to Haiti for a brief TDY (temporary duty) and said I would explore what the prospects were of Smithsonian assistance.

If it wasn't the last thing on anyone's mind in Haiti, I am not sure what could have followed it. A makeshift tent encampment was set up for all Haiti's government operations, and their officials were overwhelmed with the magnitude of the disaster and the effort to provide relief, while at the same time they were grieving and suffering their own losses. These officials strove in vain to stay ahead of the numbers of aid agencies that arrived to support different slices of the relief—shelter, food, medical help, orphans, potential mass migration, water, crime, security, radio, telephone, and electricity.

Any embassy building has a normal quiet dignity. Our new embassy in Port-au-Prince was designed to push offices out of sight of the main atrium. After the disaster, it was transformed into a blurred whirlwind of energy and confusion, hosting thousands of people from multiple US government agencies detailed to Haiti, and attending to requirements unique to their responsibilities. The staff determined which victims could receive medical treatment in Haiti and which ones required evacuation to US hospitals. They planned for distributions of water and food, set up temporary housing for the displaced, handled the repatriations of affected citizens, coordinated with other countries and international relief efforts, dealt with the arrests of US citizens accused of trying to abduct Haitian orphans out of the country, organized transportation to affected areas, managed visits by US officials, and patrolled the streets. Tents for US soldiers crowded the compound; thin mattresses were flown in so people could sleep on the floors of their temporary offices; long lines formed for embassy cafeteria egg sandwiches and hamburgers as the only food available; showers in two small change rooms around the compound's swimming pool ran continually for the several thousand people occupying the compound. And, amid this disorganized order, aftershocks continued to rock the building and all inside.

Of the many tasks that fell on my desk during my short time in Haiti following the earthquake, one was to arrange a public event to hand control of the airport back to the Haitian authorities. Ports were devastated, and the global response was immediate. Flights and ships were backed up trying to land with needed supplies, with Haitian port officials either themselves lost in the earthquake or tending to their own families and neighbors. Lack of electrical power and telecommunications compounded the difficulties in the landings. The US military stepped in to play an indispensable coordinating role, repairing the airstrips and queuing up hundreds of flights from around the world. After several weeks, with the first electrical grids repaired, phone service reinstated, and Haitians back at work, the first commercial flights were ready to resume operations, and the US military was eager to turn control back to the proper authorities. The US command wanted some formal public ceremony to mark the event, to show some semblance of a return to normalcy, but also to counter the Chávez and Ortega notion that the United States was "taking over" the country.

I tracked down the Haitian government official responsible for communications; she was at the huge tent complex that served as headquarters for the hundreds of relief organizations. Harried, she emerged from one tent, holding a radio in one hand and talking with several people around her. With the eyes of someone who hadn't slept in days, she purposefully made her way through a lineup of relief officials, each with their request. I managed to get her attention, introduced myself, and explained my purpose of arranging a handover ceremony with the US commander when the first commercial flight landed.

She stopped, looked at me, looked through me, and then away, and walked on, without a word. That was about as firm a "no" as I received in my career. The demands placed on this woman were simply too great for a "nicety," however well-intentioned. Or was it perhaps too public a reminder that Haitians, who took pride in their independence, had not been in control for however brief a time? When the first flight arrived a couple of days later, with Haitian authorities back in the air traffic control tower, no publicity was needed to send those messages through the broader community.

The earthquake exacerbated Haiti's already troubled experience with the army of international organizations operating in the country, from the UN peacekeeping forces to the humanitarian relief and development agencies and NGOs, mixed in with a host of know-nothing do-gooders who ended up doing not much good, such as the organization that came to "rescue" orphans from the country without permissions from government or families. Worse yet, the introduction of cholera into the country, which has taken the lives of an estimated ten thousand Haitians, was traced to a contingent of UN peacekeepers from Nepal who arrived after the earthquake. The government had a hard time just tracking the agencies present, let alone trying to control and coordinate their efforts. According to the historian Laurent Dubois, some in the country went so far as to compare the "foreign presence in Haiti with the era of the U.S. occupation."[11]

In this environment, replete with all the stark life-safety demands, the Smithsonian representatives made a case that Haiti's cultural heritage was at risk, already seriously damaged but even more so, vulnerably exposed to the elements and potential looting. Attending to the national identity of Haiti held out the possibility of restoring an intangible sense of pride and confidence in a people, to support them psychologically through the long physical process of rebuilding. I went to Haiti knowing little about it except its revolution in the early 1800s, but I was aware of its art and even owned a small painting, a gift from a friend who had lived there.

Haitian art is known for its bold, primary colors, depicting a romantic, idyllic life and cultural/religious motifs as well as recounting recurring themes of Haitian struggles for independence, justice, and dignity. Both elite and folk, democratic and capitalist, art provides a living, attested to by any trip through a Haitian market. Haiti's art rests close to its people, part of its everyday life. Through all the years of turmoil and struggle, it has been, according to prominent figures in the Haitian art world, this cultural connection that helped hold the country together, a unifying source of national pride. A Haitian architect who signed on to the Smithsonian's effort affirmed that "it is our culture that gives the Haitian people the courage to survive and dream of a better life."[12]

The earthquake devastated that heritage. The Galerie Nader, which held the largest private collection of Haitian art, estimated that three thousand paintings and sculptures were damaged or destroyed. The Centre d'Art, opened by Haitian artists with the help of two Americans in the 1940s as a training and exhibition space, collapsed, and many of its artworks lay strewn through the rubble, openly exposed, as torn and twisted as the steel rods holding the concrete buildings. The Holy Trinity Episcopal Church was completely destroyed—incuding its fourteen wall-length murals, painted in the early 1950s, depicting Christian themes, but in a Haitian context. Even those buildings spared from the worst, such as the National Library and the National Archives, still suffered unseen structural damage, as well as havoc to collections, pushed off shelves and strewn across dusty, lopsided floors. The quake destroyed private art collections, universities' and schools' art collections, and reduced to rubble the archives of prominent historians and writers.

Few in the relief effort focused on this damage. Initial recovery of the art proceeded like much of the early response in Haiti, through the efforts of staff, friends, and neighbors, sorting through the rubble, pulling out paintings and twisted sculptures, trying to rope off sites to prevent looting, and obtaining containers in which to store and secure the salvaged art. Quickly, international organizations dedicated to supporting museums and cultural protection mobilized and began to bring their resources to bear. UNESCO provided crates and fencing. Haiti's Caribbean neighbors, in the form of the regional organization CARICOM, sent supplies to Haiti's conservation experts. Additional funding appeals came through other organizations but arrived only slowly, given the extent of the damage. It became clear that no such international fund existed for emergency cultural recovery, despite the high-profile cases of both human-made and natural disasters to patrimony in the years before the quake, in Iraq, Afghanistan, Italy, Mexico, Pakistan, and India.

Frustrated by the glacial pace of international recovery efforts, the Smithsonian and its persevering, energetic, and creative under secretary for history, art and culture, Richard Kurin, stepped up to take a leadership role. In close contact with his Haitian counterparts, Kurin reached out to many US private and public agencies for support. State Department cultural patrimony funding was inappropriate since it operated on a fiscal-year basis and was too small for the enormity of work. After receiving offers of assistance from concerned artists, he tapped into the goodwill of a New York–based actors association, the Broadway League, for an indispensable initial donation to allow the Smithsonian to begin the preparatory work while seeking larger US government funding.

The first step consisted of a fact-finding visit to Haiti to assess the damage, but Smithsonian officials were advised not to travel. The embassy refused to give a fact-finding team country clearance, a step required any time a US government employee travels officially. A small group headed by Kurin went anyway, claiming correctly that the Smithsonian was an independent organization, publicly funded, but not technically a government agency. Despite the initial recalcitrance of the embassy, the acting cultural affairs officer helped the team with transport and other logistical support. By March, they had completed their damage assessment and began work on a restoration plan, in conjunction with Haitian authorities.

Back in Washington, Kurin continued to lobby hard to have a small amount of funding from the massive USAID package for Haiti relief set aside. The Smithsonian proposed a project to restore the art, the murals, the archives, and the museums, but were turned down repeatedly in internal discussions. They were running into the same concerns about the relevance of such a request, in light of the humanitarian needs. More specifically, in a time of budgetary fighting with Congress, the perceptions of funding diverted to cultural patrimony protection was not a high priority.

However, through a visit to Washington by the Haitian first lady, the Smithsonian caught the ear of Michelle Obama, and funding was restored. By June 2010, just five months after the earthquake and at the start of another rainy season, the Smithsonian had people on the ground who set up the Haiti Cultural Recovery Center to store and then restore works of art. One of their goals was to work side-by-side with Haitian experts and train on-site a group of volunteers to handle, secure, stabilize, and repair damage to the art.

All can appreciate the life-saving priorities in the wake of a disaster. But what is the value of rescuing a nation's heritage? Kurin, later, put it in ways we could better understand:

> If we had a terrible disaster in Washington in which the White House, the Capitol, the National Archives, the Library of Congress, the Smithsonian and all the museums had collapsed, we'd surely rescue people first, and then we'd deal with the deceased. At some point, after that, we'd think about going into the rubble and pulling out the Declaration of Independence, the "Star Spangled Banner," the treasures in the National Gallery of Art, the rare books, and so on. Similarly, Haitians have their treasures, their icons, the objects that express and represent the Haitian experience.[13]

Throughout the next eighteen months, the Smithsonian, in conjunction with the Haiti Cultural Recovery Center, trained more than 130 Haitians in restoration techniques and cultural management. Together, more than 80 specialists who traveled to Haiti worked with their counterparts on the ground to treat well over fifty thousand paintings, sculptures, manuscripts, and books, to help recover three of the surviving murals at the Holy Trinity Episcopal Church, and to restore more than one hundred paintings and art pieces from other sites.

In the face of a reluctant, even skeptical, interagency apparatus, the Smithsonian pushed through its project, not only recovering the objects so crucial to Haiti's heritage and identity but leaving in place a larger group of Haitians technically capable of continuing this work. Understandably, life, safety, and other basic survival issues rose to the top of the priority list following the devastation, but attending to the Haitian sense of pride and self-worth, in their storied past and glory of their art, occupied a prominent place on that list as well.

Over and over during those first few months following the earthquake, we heard of the resilience of the Haitian people, their self-reliance in attending to their needs and those of the families and neighbors. I saw it firsthand in the faces of the Haitian staff at the US Embassy, who started coming to work in the first days after June 12, even as they were living out of cars and were caring for their families. I saw it at Quisqueya University, a private university in Port-au-Prince. There, I met the rector, Jacky Lumarque, who had made his way to a local radio station to appeal for help, before he secured the assistance of about twenty young men from the neighborhood. In the first hours following the disaster, these young men responded by sorting through the debris and saving the lives of people trapped. With deteriorating health in the surrounding neighborhood, Lumarque used the only space left to him after so many of the university's buildings collapsed, the parking lot, to turn it into a community health clinic, continuing the practical studies of his medical students in meeting the needs of the community. This self-reliance makes up the fabric of Haiti so that even at times of government breakdown, Haitians were helping themselves. There were cases of looting, but not anywhere near the level the United States and the rest of the international community had prepared for; there was no mass exodus, no flotilla of people seeking to hop into makeshift rafts and boats to flee the island, heading for the United States. As much as people look at the breakdown of Haiti's governments over its history, this national self-reliance is also a part of its history, a trait its people had proven since the 1790s, when they fought for their independence, which is the heritage and history that were so important to protect.

Ultimately, it's in our national interests to understand, appreciate, and even support our partners in defense of their national identity. In this specific case, Haitian self-reliance in the earthquake, as attested to in its cultural heritage, saved lives. It translated into people staying on the island to help each other, rather than flee and seek safety elsewhere. More broadly, understanding this heritage of self-reliance as seen and promoted through Haitian culture would help reduce the shock for foreign observers and actors living and working in Haiti. We outsiders might have a better, fuller grasp of why, for example, Haitians rebelled against occupation in 1915, or why they might, almost one hundred years later, in one simple, isolated interaction, be reluctant to engage in a public ceremony to return control of the airport. Both offend their sense of independence and self-reliance.

Suggested Further Reading

In *Haiti: The Aftershocks of History* (New York: Metropolitan Books, 2010), Laurent Dubois provides a comprehensive account of the legacies of Haitian history from its independence through the earthquake. Michel-Rolph Trouillot looks at the impact of erasing memory in Haitian history in his *Silencing the Past: Power and Production of History* (Boston: Beacon Press, 1995). Mary Renda looks closely at the US occupation in *Taking Haiti: Military Occupation and the Culture of U.S. Imperialism, 1915–1940* (Boston: Beacon Press, 1995). Richard Kurin describes the efforts of the Smithsonian in Haiti, politely avoiding mention of the bureaucratic squabbles, in his *Saving Haiti's Heritage: Cultural Recovery after the Earthquake* (Washington, DC: Smithsonian Institution, 2011).

7

Peru: Getting It Right

At a distance, the brown hills looked like piles of dirt, as if they were massive heaps of tailings extracted from mines. But in this equatorial desert all along the coast of Peru, the ground was hardened rock with a tan/brown pebble surface. These are the smooth foothills of the Andes that descend to the sea. Apart from the interspersed rivers that carry water from the mountains and sustain the cities and towns, most of the Peruvian coast is stark, arid, and empty "moon rock."

We were climbing around one such hill that looked no different from its surroundings in the Chillón River valley just north of Lima. Our guide was Peruvian archaeologist Jorge Silva. My wife and children had joined me during the long Southern Hemisphere summer vacation. My son leaned over and picked up something he saw on the ground. It was a skull. We were walking on top of an eroded pyramid from more than a thousand years ago that Jorge had established as a work site. Looters had discarded the skull in their hunt for more valuable items: textiles, clay pots, or metals, such as bronze tools and gold decorative art. Not far from the skull were plastic bags and wrappers that had blown on to the site.

Jorge invited us to the site that he had started excavating and that would consume his life for the next decade. He told us that in Peru, even with UNESCO World Heritage sites extending from Sipán in the north to the Nazca Lines and Machu Picchu in the south, only about 10 percent of the pre-Columbian civilization had been uncovered. Indeed, it was after we left Peru in 1999 that archaeologists concluded that one long-ignored site, Caral, was the oldest city in the Americas at an estimated age of 4,700 years. Located about two hundred miles north of Lima, Caral became the focus of intensive excavation and research to open up this site to the country's scientific community and the economically important tourist business. Months later, archeologists discovered another site of Incan funeral bodies beneath the streets of a squatter settlement on the outskirts of Lima. People fleeing violence in the interior of Peru had moved down to Lima in the 1980s and staked claims on the foothills surrounding the capital, not knowing that the brown hill they claimed was a funeral site called Puruchuco-Huaquerones.

While we climbed the hardened hills of packed gravel and dirt, it was easy to see how a massive structure or even an entire city could be lost under nature's destructive processes. The skull that my son found and replaced on the mound prompted Jorge to note how his first unfinished item of business was completing the security fence around the perimeter of the site. The reality haunting Peruvian archaeology is looting. These sites that are so important to Peru's identity are at the same time so tempting an opportunity to make a living.

Peru is a case where the United States got the history right, through simple, inexpensive use of soft power. By supporting a small but important and growing group of Peruvians determined to protect their nation's archaeological patrimony, we acknowledged the importance of Peru's ancient history to its national identity. For Peru, this was more, though, than just ephemeral "feelings" of identity; the economic benefits from tourism to these archaeological sites is a source of foreign revenue. Furthermore, our cooperation generated goodwill, that, in turn, allowed us to address the hard issues of diplomacy, such as balancing antiterrorism efforts with respect for human rights.

Shortly after I arrived in Peru, with the ink barely dry on a memorandum of understanding between the two governments, the United States committed to returning historic artifacts that were coming into the country or illicitly sold on the open market. The official title of the bilateral agreement signed in 1997 underscored its heavy legalistic and bureaucratic nature: Memorandum of Understanding between the Government of the United States of America and the Government of the Republic of Peru Concerning the Imposition of Import Restrictions on Archaeological Material from the Prehispanic Cultures and Certain Ethnological Material from the Colonial Period of Peru. We referred to it simply as the "MOU."

The bilateral agreement gave practical force to a 1970 international agreement negotiated at UNESCO to prohibit illicit trafficking in antiquities. It only took two more years for the United States to ratify this cultural property convention. That ratification alone is a jarring reminder that the United States once understood that it was in our national interests to ratify international agreements and cooperate with other countries to address problems and challenges that cross borders. Still, the UNESCO cultural property convention remained nothing more than a nice piece of paper until the US Congress enacted the laws to implement its provisions. That legislation took twelve years to work its way through Congress. The Convention on Cultural Property Implementation Act in 1982 set up an office in the State Department that would oversee the type of bilateral agreements envisioned in the original convention to protect cultural property.

The same Jorge Silva who showed my family around the archaeological mound helped negotiate the bilateral agreement with Peru. A professor at Catholic University in Lima and a former Fulbright scholar in the United States, he played an instrumental role in bringing a divided Peruvian side to the table and in preparing the extensive supplemental information. Two colleagues in the Cultural Section of the Embassy, Helmut Fisher and Elba de Cuba, also aided in this effort. They helped compile an appendix consisting of page after page of historical items paired with exemplary photographs that supplemented the agreement so that US border agents would be able to identify objects under scrutiny. The pre-Columbian materials covered a broad period, "ranging in date from approximately 12,000 B.C. to A.D. 1532." The listing included "objects comprised of textiles, metals, ceramics, lithics, perishable remains, and human remains," and came from a wide array of cultures from across the breadth of Peru: "Chavin, Paracas, Vincus, Moche (including objects derived from the

archaeological zone of Sipán), Viru, Lima, Nazca, Recuay, Tiahua-
naco, Huari, Chimu, Chancay, Cuzco, and Inca." This bilateral agreement was only the second that the United States had undertaken,
after El Salvador's agreement in 1995. Peru broke new ground in that
it also encompassed objects from the Spanish colonial period, specifically religious artifacts and paintings, "used for religious evangelism
among indigenous peoples." Such inclusion underscored the loss to
the looting of abandoned and unprotected church buildings, some as
old as three hundred years, serving peoples in the most remote areas
of the Andes.[1]

Responsibility for the protection against looting did not fall only
to the realm of the US Customs Service. Language in the agreement
and the subsequent extensions stipulated that the government of Peru
would commit to improving enforcement of its laws. These laws related to trafficking in archaeological artifacts, coordination with other
countries that would either buy or facilitate the transit of these materials, development of training programs for staff involved in the
management and enforcement of cultural patrimony, and educational
programs for the public at large.

This cultural property protection agreement culminated a long,
troubled history of US involvement in Peru's cultural past that rises
to the level of history shock in our bilateral relations as each country
views that aspect of our relationship quite differently. In this case,
though, the agreement allowed us to improve our bilateral relations
and advance the broad array of other US interests, most of them
clearly higher on our list of priorities. By demonstrating US respect
for Peru's ethnic and cultural past—in essence, a source of its identity
and pride—the agreement blunted mistrust and suspicions that lingered in Peruvian attitudes toward the United States.

One precise point where history clashed in Peru and the United
States centered on the figure of Hiram Bingham, the Yale University
historian whose travels to Peru led him to discover, or perhaps more
aptly, uncover Machu Picchu, as its neglected ruins lay hidden in forest growth. It was Bingham who, in successive expeditions to South
America starting in 1906, became intrigued by the lost city in the

Peruvian Andes where the Inca ruler Manco Capac II led his loyal subjects away from the capital, Cusco, in 1536 to escape the onslaught anticipated from the conquering Spaniards. In a preliminary visit to Lima and then Cusco in 1908–1909, Bingham first engaged Peruvians on the whereabouts of the last capital of the Inca empire.

Two years later, in June 1911, with the aid of recently unearthed colonial documents, Bingham once again set out for Peru, focusing on the Urubamba Valley just outside of Cusco. Residents told Bingham to seek out an innkeeper named Melchior Arteaga, who had spoken about ancient Incan ruins on the top of a mountain. With Arteaga as a guide, and in the company of a Peruvian military escort, Bingham ascended the mountain and came upon buildings so overgrown with vegetation that he was unable to identify the extent of the complex, lodged on a ridge between two mountains, Machu Picchu and Huayna Picchu. In subsequent trips, he brought with him other members of his expedition as well as Peruvian workers to start clearing away the site.

Bingham referred to his finding as more of a rediscovery of Machu Picchu. Not only was Arteaga aware of these ruins, but so were the three families who lived on the mountains and who were still using the terraces up and down the sides of the mountains for their gardens. In his journal, Bingham jotted down the graffiti he found on the main temple, painted "Lizarraga 1902," a name he tracked down to a local farmer named Agustín Lizárraga. He also gave credit to a French explorer, Charles Wiener, who referred to ruins near Machu Picchu and Huayna Picchu, although he was never able to visit them. When Bingham later mentioned discovering Machu Picchu, he qualified the use of that word "in the same sense of the word as it is used in the expression, 'Columbus discovered America.'"[2]

Even his most critical detractors acknowledge that Bingham brought the site to the world's attention. Yale University and the National Geographic Society financed a return trip the following year, 1912. *National Geographic* dedicated one entire issue of its increasingly popular magazine to Machu Picchu. With more than 250 photographs, Bingham wrote a text that wove together the elements that make Machu Picchu so breathtakingly inspiring. These include the sheer audacity of siting the city on top of a mountain. The natural beauty is enhanced by snow-capped mountains in every direction. The frightening precipices lead down to a roaring Urubamba River that curves around the mountains into a lush green tropical forest. The walls have jigsaw-puzzle pieces that weigh thousands of pounds, stones as large as twelve feet in length carved to fit together so tightly that mortar was not needed. Scholars near and far assembled hypotheses for the various purposes and placements of the buildings, crowded together and separated by hundreds of stairways and alleys. Alignment with the sun, moon, and another nearby mountaintop Incan site adds to the sense of wonder for the scientific and spiritual capabilities of the engineers and builders. It is hard not to sit down at any spot on the premises and drift off, imagining a thousand people walking up and down the steep stone staircases, moving to markets and worship sites through the maze of alleyways, greeting and chatting with neighbors, and carrying on, perhaps even inured to the glory of their surroundings.

Suffice it to say that Machu Picchu ranks highest on my list of recommended places to see. Further, the mountain city is just the final destination of a trip starting in the Incan capital of Cusco, with its grand sixteenth-century plaza, and the nearby walled ruins of Sacsayhuamán. Then, you can travel through the Sacred Valley with its terraced hillsides and Incan walls scattered randomly along this fifty-mile fertile stretch of land. The narrow streets of Ollantaytambo seem to have not changed at all since the 1400s. Stone walls that lead to an old Incan palace border their cobblestone paths.

Bingham erred, though, in his conclusions over the importance of the site. Not only did he feel that this was the secret Incan capital where Manco Capac II had led his followers, but he also overemphasized three large windows in a temple to conclude that they represented the three caves out of which a people emerged "on that migration which led them to conquer Cusco and to establish the Inca empire."[3] Subsequent scholarship has led archaeologists and scholars to conclude that this site was one of several royal summer palaces for the Incan rulers based in Cusco, with construction set much later than Bingham had guessed, probably around 1450.

The publication of the April 1913 *National Geographic* edition made Bingham a household name in the United States, catapulting him to fame that saw him leave academia and enter the world of politics, first as lieutenant governor, then governor, and then US senator from Connecticut. In 1948, in his retirement, he wrote *Lost City of the Incas*, a book that retraced his steps in finding Machu Picchu and helped re-create interest in the ancient site. He died in 1956, just two years after Hollywood's release of *The Secret of the Incas*, filmed at Machu Picchu and very loosely based on Bingham's Peru expeditions. That movie, in turn, inspired the Indiana Jones franchise, featuring an archaeology professor whose four filmed adventures to find lost treasure around the world made a treasure for Harrison Ford, George Lucas, and Paramount Pictures. Hiram Bingham's expeditions roughly correspond to *Indiana Jones and the Temple of Doom*.

In Peru, different perceptions of Bingham's expeditions arose as early as his first encounter with Machu Picchu in 1911, escalating to outright hostility during his second trip to Peru in 1912. At first, Bingham received support, advice, and encouragement from both Peruvians and American residents in Lima and Cusco, who provided information, guides, and workers to lead him to the region, and eventually to the actual site. Then, in the wake of Bingham's rediscovery, interest in Latin America's indigenous past grew into an *indigenista* movement among scholars and intellectuals on the continent, in Peru, and specifically in Cusco. Bingham's findings in 1911 prompted Cusco officials to prohibit any excavations on the site. Despite a national decree prohibiting the removal and export of any artifacts from the site, Bingham brought back to Yale for further study bones and other artifacts from the site.

As he was assembling his return expedition under the auspices of Yale and the National Geographic Society, Bingham ran into a new set of obstacles set up by government officials in Peru, which complicated any understanding of what he could and could not remove from the site. The parties reached a preliminary understanding after

President William Howard Taft intervened directly with his Peruvian counterpart, Augusto Leguía. With an agreement to divide evenly all artifacts found on the site, the 1912 expedition began. Once in Peru, Bingham learned that this understanding failed to receive approval in Peru's legislature, leaving open the disposition of the hundreds of items Bingham was uncovering.

What exactly he did find made its way into the article Bingham wrote for *National Geographic*, which appeared after his return to the United States. Offering Peruvian workers a reward of one sol (about fifty cents) to find burial sites in caves scattered throughout the site led to "more than 100" burial caves and "a large quantity of skeletal material secured."[4] Also, he noted that the team had found "200 little bronzes, a lesser number of pots, and 50 cases of shards." Besides the lack of agreement with the authorities, Bingham's biggest issue was a practical one: how to carry ninety-three boxes, each weighing upward of ninety pounds, of materials down the mountain, across the Urubamba River, and through terrain that he described as "the most inaccessible part of the Andes."[5]

With the work proceeding, Bingham still had no permission to remove anything from the site. The unpopular president Augusto Leguía lost the 1912 election and a new, leftist populist president, Guillermo Billinghurst, came to power. The first meeting between Bingham and the new president did not go well, with the Peruvian president calling the first agreement "a disgrace" since no Peruvian experts participated in the excavations of "their own" ruins.[6] Finally, Billinghurst hit upon an arrangement allowing Bingham to export all that he found, with three conditions: all work on this expedition had to be completed by December 1, 1912 (earlier than Bingham had planned); Peru had the right to inspect everything removed; and Yale would be required to return the objects when the country asked for them.

While newspapers hailed Bingham in the United States, the Peruvian press grew sharply more critical. In December 1911, upon Bingham's return from his initial expedition, the *New York Times* headline read "Yale Expedition Back from Peru," noting that Bingham was the first white man in four hundred years to enter Machu Picchu and that the team had placed a Yale flag on the mountain. *National Geographic* elevated Bingham's accomplishments when they published a photo of him seated with Robert Peary and Roald Amundsen, the explorers of the North and South Poles. The press in Peru that had embraced his first expedition turned against Bingham before his return. They printed quotes attributed to Bingham in which he complained about the dirt and smells in Cusco.[7] Local papers in Cusco portrayed the members of the Yale team as pillagers, and the papers in Lima referred to Bingham as a "Yankee imperialist."[8] Peruvian objections centered on Bingham's exclusive hold over a Peruvian historical site, shutting out local scholars and removing artifacts.

In public, the expedition leader only obliquely referred to the problems he was encountering in Peru, with the government, in the newspapers, and among the scholarly community. To him, these were bureaucratic hurdles to be surmounted, but his letters back to his wife revealed his growing anxiety and discouragement. He would return to Peru in 1915 for further explorations and excavations, but with increasing public and official harassment. This time, failure to secure the proper permits led to charges of illegal excavations and export of archaeological artifacts, halting his work. Newspapers printed rumors of him bringing in a steam shovel to excavate ancient ruins and smuggling gold through Bolivia. Bingham was able to clear his name legally, but with the understanding that any artifacts removed belonged to Peru.

Bingham took thousands of items back to Yale from Machu Picchu over his three trips, enhanced by his purchase of hundreds of items from local collectors. There is much evidence, though, that the site had seen many of its most treasured items lost well before Bingham's arrival, mostly to looters from neighboring villages. One theory points to a German mining prospector, Augusto Berns, who chanced upon the site in the 1880s and took many of the valuable items. Another looted site centers around the tomb under the highest structure, the Torreon, or the Temple of the Sun. The tomb under the temple likely held the mummies of Inca royalty and quite possibly gold statues. The loss of those statues might have occurred in the earliest days of the Spanish conquest of Peru.

Looting archaeological sites for precious metals and materials predates the time when these sites were even considered archaeological. In 1529, Queen Isabel of Spain signed off on Francisco Pizarro's appeal to explore Peru after he described the abundance of gold and silver objects he saw in his initial forays along the northern coast. Three years later, Pizarro promised to release the Inca emperor Atahualpa, whom he captured in the town of Cajamarca, when the ruler offered rooms full of gold and silver in exchange for his freedom. An estimated six tons of gold arrived in the town from the far corners of the empire, much of it melted down from art and artifacts made for royal and religious leaders and buildings. Speculation is that gold from Machu Picchu, including gold from the tomb under the Temple of the Sun, was sent for Atahualpa's ransom. None of the gold sent to Cajamarca saved Atahualpa. With riches in hand, Pizarro then reneged on the agreement and executed Atahualpa. Subsequent conquests throughout the empire all the way to the Incan capital of Cusco led to more looting by the first conquistadors.

Today, Cajamarca is a city of more than 225,000 people and the capital of the province. Its ignominious history led the Organization of American States to designate it as a Landmark in the History of Culture and the Art of the Americas in 1986.

Within fifty years, though, a backlash emerged against what must have seemed a wholesale unfettered extraction of indigenous treasures, art, and materials from archaeological sites in Peru. In 1574, the fifth Spanish viceroy of Peru, Francisco de Toledo, laid out a set of conditions to protect against looting of indigenous "treasures." In recognition of the importance of these relics, monuments, and remains, less than a year following its declaration of independence in 1821, Peru promulgated a decree to create a national museum and prohibit "extraction or excavation" of archaeological sites without receiving permission of the government. The original decree was expanded by two more decrees, the first in 1893 to set up a permitting process for archeological explorations. A second, in 1911, spurred on by Hiram Bingham's findings, stipulated that all objects uncovered in explorations belonged to the state. Subsequent laws clouded the issue of ownership but generally acknowledged that private ownership of historical artifacts is allowed in Peru, but the owners have to register those items with the state.

In addition, it is illegal to sell any such object outside the country. The agency responsible for Peru's cultural heritage is the Instituto Nacional de Cultura (National Institute of Culture.) Established in 1972, the government agency combined the responsibilities of various offices dating back to 1929, to oversee the national museum, to set up an inventory of past sites and artifacts, and to encourage the development of local talent in archaeology.

These laws and decrees underscore not only Peru's commitment to protecting its past but also the depth of emotional attachment that these materials and sites have for the national identity and character. Despite this source of national pride and the long history of legal protections, enforcement against looting remains a problem.

The potential wealth from illicit trade in artifacts and materials from the multiple archaeological sites in Peru still tempts. Those involved in the trade are not just the impoverished rural inhabitants living close to *huacas*, sites whose name is a derivative of the Quechuan word for a burial mound. Looters are often the first to find a site, happening upon a mound near their own homes. Word spreads quickly of a new find, and more professional *huaqueros* with experience to mount quick exploratory digs move in. They seize whatever treasures they can find, leaving the sites littered with unwanted artifacts and multiple, random holes, compromising whatever archaeological value the site may have had. At one site, Batán Grande, northeast of the coastal city of Lambayeque, one archaeologist arrived after the looting to count more than one hundred thousand pits.

The *huaqueros* are just the first in a long line of collectors, exporters, museums, art galleries, and auction houses that stand to profit from such looting. While the traffic in stolen artifacts is difficult to quantify because it operates underground, UNESCO estimates the value of this industry worldwide at $5 billion a year. Collectors and dealers pay looters hundreds or even thousands of dollars for items, then turn around and make a profit of easily one hundred times the amount they paid for it. One report cited that a "top-quality Paracas weaving (from Peru's south coast) can sell for half a million dollars."[9] Looters have been able to sell rare gold pieces for double that amount.

Established private collectors in Peru rely on the *huaqueros* to identify materials they have uncovered. Enrique Poli, who owns one of the largest and best collections in the country, told one journalist, "My looters are my angels. They bring me anything I want."[10] While Peruvian law makes it illegal to buy materials looted from archaeological sites, the buyer needs to register the artifacts with the Instituto Nacional de Cultura in order to retain legal ownership. Poli's house in Lima is a museum, open to visitors. Knowing his brazen acknowledgment of buying from looters, I hesitated to go to his museum for a long time, and when I finally did go, I was amazed at how he had filled every corner of his home and inch of wall space with his collection. It is not just the large collectors who displayed such objects, either, but offices and homes of Peru's professional and business class often showcase archaeological treasures.

One key provision of the Memorandum of Understanding on Cultural Property with Peru was its effective date. For a variety of legal reasons, the MOU could not be made retroactive; only looted items trafficked after 1997 were subject to the restriction on conditions of return. Anything that left Peru before the agreement was not covered by it. The one exception was items from Sipán.

Shortly after arriving in Peru, my family and I joined a small group of embassy families at the National Museum for a tour of artifacts retrieved from a mud-brick pyramid near the village of Sipán, on the north coast of Peru. Our host was Walter Alva, the curator of the exhibition and the archaeologist who led the find and excavation of a burial tomb that held the remains of a high warrior-priest and several attendants as well as thousands of artifacts made from gold, silver, clay, turquoise, copper, and cotton. Animated, and limited only by his imperfect English and our worse Spanish, the short, bearded scholar took us around the cavernous museum halls. He paused at the display cases, which lit up to reveal large polished gold shields and flaps that covered the body, along with gold necklaces and earrings adorned with turquoise. The cases also contained painted pottery depicting the history, the rituals, and the wars of the Moche people who inhabited the northern coast of Peru roughly fifteen hundred years ago, well before the Incan empire. The centerpiece of the exhibit was a tomb, recreated to show what the warrior-priest, whom Alva named the Lord of Sipán, would have looked like on the day of his burial. Two men and two women were buried on each side, and the surrounding niches were filled with human remains and hundreds of ceramic pots.

The exhibit had recently opened in Lima, but Alva was quick to point out that this home was temporary. He interspersed his description of the artifacts with his plan to complete the fundraising needed. His goal was for new space near the Brüning Museum in Lambayeque that he directed to permanently hold this Sipán collection. At the time, such a museum seemed like a fanciful dream, but Alva and his archaeologist wife, Susana Meneses, had unbridled pull in the cultural world in Peru and the field of archaeology beyond Peru. Through the force of personality and the importance of this find, the couple persevered, and the museum opened in 2002. Unfortunately, less than a year after, Susana succumbed to cancer.

Just as Hiram Bingham achieved his fame through the pages of *National Geographic*, Alva revealed his archaeological find in the October 1988 edition, just over seventy-five years after Bingham's article on Machu Picchu took over the entire edition of the magazine. Also, like Bingham, Alva gave a suspenseful, blow-by-blow narration of his discovery of the burial tomb. That find, Alva pointed out, was not his, but unfortunately had been the work of looters in a nearby village. In early 1987, Peruvian police began to notice new gold specimens making their way to the illicit market of trafficked archaeological artifacts. They traced the items from the dealers who registered them with Peruvian authorities (to claim ownership) back to a family near the mounds. A raid on their property revealed ancient gold pieces hidden around their yard. In his article, Alva told how the police had called him, as they had on previous occasions, to verify the origin of the items.

Upon inspection, Alva knew that these "treasures unearthed by the looters could only have come from a tomb of unprecedented magnificence."[11] With a sense of urgency, he moved to secure the archaeological site as quickly as possible, setting up camp with his wife and a few colleagues at the mound, with police posted as security guards. Alva recalled waking up regularly to the sound of shots fired as looters were anxious to return and uncover more gold treasure. What he initially found were holes dug randomly over the structure, penetrating and wrecking one tomb. He wrote of his suspicions that more tombs were nearby but lay further and deeper, based on the structure of wooden platforms.

Alva described the archaeological brushes, squeeze bulbs, and other tools and techniques he used to excavate this find, narrating layer by layer what he uncovered. He documented, for research purposes, what the looters had destroyed in the companion tomb just a short distance away. At twelve feet below the surface, he found what looked to be a "guardian." Sure enough, twenty inches below that lay another platform, under which lay the Lord of Sipán.

This tomb mirrored the looted one and convinced Alva and the Peruvian authorities of the scope of illicit artifacts from the Moche era on the market. Dealers and collectors in Lima owned some, while others were making their way out of the country, in part with the help of a retired US Embassy employee, Frederick Drew. Drew allegedly used his connections among foreign diplomats and their immunity to spirit items out of the country. As pieces from Sipán began to show up in US and European museums, the Peruvian authorities approached the United States to obtain its assistance in retrieving the looted items and preventing their future import. Further excavations by Alva and his team unearthed even older tombs below the Lord of Sipán, which Alva described in a follow-on piece in *National Geographic* in June 1990. The publicity in *National Geographic* and elsewhere surrounding the discovery of a tomb, comparable to Tutankhamen's in Egypt, helped convince the State Department in 1990 to impose emergency "import restrictions on culturally significant archaeological artifacts from the Sipán Region of Peru."[12]

This agreement effectively brought a halt to the import of Sipán treasures into the United States. While the agreement was ground-breaking, that emergency restriction only limited the import restrictions to Sipán, one region of Peru. With proof that the restriction was working, Peru and the United States discussed a broader binational agreement, which resulted in the 1997 MOU covering pre-Columbian artifacts from sites across the country and from the colonial era. The MOU incorporated the 1990 emergency restriction on Sipán.

Because the MOU was not retroactive, absent from the coverage under the agreement were those items in possession of the Yale Peabody Museum that Hiram Bingham had removed from Peru almost ninety years earlier. These artifacts were not part of the official discussions leading up to the signing of the MOU, but informally Peruvian officials and leaders in the archaeology and museum world discussed the need for their return. Well aware that this collection was in the hands of a private organization, our counterparts in Peru did not press the US Embassy to arrange for their return. Rather, Peruvian officials acknowledged the active enforcement of the US Customs Service in seizing items at the border and in auction houses, resulting in their highly publicized returns. In addition, they followed closely two high-profile FBI cases involving the attempted sale of a rare, gold decorative backflap worn around the neck by Sipán elites and the donation of other valuable Sipán items to a museum in New Mexico.

Still, now and then, an article appeared in the Peruvian press criticizing Yale's refusal to return the collection Bingham had amassed from Machu Picchu and other sites. The university did not display the collection but held on to it for research purposes. It was unclear how much research was taking place until the 1980s. At that time, two Andean scholars at Yale, Richard Burger and Lucy Salazar, sifted through the boxes and concluded that the site was a summer palace, thus dispelling Bingham's theories on the origins of the Inca empire.

Twenty years later, these same two scholars decided to mount an exhibition of the Bingham collection, ultimately leading to its repatriation. In January 2003, Salazar and Burger, now the director of the Peabody Museum of Natural History at Yale, opened an exhibit at the university that laid out their theories of Machu Picchu through the display of more than 120 collected artifacts. The show then traveled on to Los Angeles, Pittsburgh, Denver, Houston, and Chicago.

In planning the exhibition, the Yale scholars approached officials in Peru, presumably hoping to work out a level of cooperation that might include placing Peru on the exhibit's itinerary. Given the years devoted to studying Incan history and culture, Burger and Salazar had to be aware of the controversy of Yale's retention of the Bingham collection. While they may have hoped to preempt controversy for their upcoming exhibit, the decision to display the artifacts and photographs that Bingham took reopened the wound of the loss of the material for Peru and a blow to its national dignity.

The Yale couple reached out to Peruvian officials, including the nation's first lady, Eliane Karp-Toledo, a Stanford-educated anthropologist who had studied indigenous groups in the Andes since the 1970s. She had met her husband, Alejandro Toledo, while he was earning his doctorate in economics at Stanford. With a lengthy résumé as a government official, international consultant, and university professor and administrator, Toledo had become the first elected president with a rural indigenous background in South America. His French-born wife had championed her husband's roots in the campaign, drawing on her contacts and understanding of the rural mountain cultures of Peru.

Armed with both political instincts to advance her husband's popularity and a long-standing commitment to Peru's indigenous communities, Eliane Karp-Toledo agreed to meet with the two Yale scholars planning the Machu Picchu exhibit, but only on the conditions that Yale allow Peruvian experts to inventory the collection and that Yale would return all items to Peru. Such a meeting never took place as Burger and Salazar could not meet those conditions. Armed with grants from the National Endowment for the Humanities, the National Science Foundation, and even Peru's diplomatic missions in the United States, they went ahead with their traveling exhibit in the United States without Peru's support. The US press made little mention surrounding the ownership title to the pieces in the exhibit, and Burger and Salazar acknowledged the "historic collaboration" and "mutually beneficial" relationship they enjoyed with Peru in the catalog accompanying the exhibit.

Still, the exhibit reawakened the public clamor in Peru for the return of the Bingham collection. Eliane Karp-Toledo continued to press Yale. She met with the board of the National Geographic Society, Bingham's collaborator in 1912, in Washington, and convinced them to acknowledge that the material belonged to Peru. It was only in 2007, after Toledo had left the presidency, that Yale eventually reached an agreement with the government of Peru. However, its stipulation of only a partial return incensed Peruvians, with Karp-Toledo leading the charge as a private but still influential citizen. The government turned to the US courts, and it got ugly. Peru leveled seventeen charges against Yale, including fraud, conspiracy, and "unjust enrichment." The evidence against Yale included Peru's somewhat confusing history of laws and decrees forbidding the export of archaeological items as well as a letter from Bingham to Gilbert Grosvenor, publisher of the *National Geographic* magazine in 1916. He stated, "The objects do not belong to us, but to the Peruvian government, which allowed us to take them from the country under the condition that they be returned."[13] Finally, in 2010, following the intervention of the outgoing US senator from Connecticut, Christopher Dodd, Yale signed a memorandum of agreement with Peru. This agreement included the return of all objects, the commitment to support the establishment of a joint International Center for the Study of Machu Picchu and Inca Culture in Cusco, where the artifacts would be housed and remain accessible to scholars from Yale, Peru, and the international community.

What is the relevance of cultural patrimony protection as a foreign affairs tool when considering the full range of priorities in advancing and protecting US interests abroad? Issues such as security, investment and trade, and promotion of democracy and human rights seem to relegate protections against looting to a rung near the bottom of any agenda. The foreign policy justification for pursuing these agreements on the cultural property was best spelled out in the 1990 emergency restrictions covering imports from Sipán: "The appearance in the United States of stolen or illegally exported artifacts from other countries where there has been pillage has, on occasion, strained our foreign and cultural relations."[14]

In Peru, the cultural property agreement went further in practice than just removing an irritant from the front pages of the newspapers. The protection of Peruvian archaeological treasure became linked to broader US goals to promote the rule of law, to disrupt drug trafficking, and to protect human rights. Even more, though, the agreement helped create public tolerance for US advocacy on these harder issues, as Peruvians came to see the return of items seized under the agreement as gestures of respect for their nation's history that ultimately defined their national identity.

The first years of this agreement coincided with the unraveling of democratic institutions in Peru. Wracked by years of domestic terrorism at the hands of two different groups, the country made key arrests and was returning to normalcy. Still, at the same time that we negotiated the agreement, seventy-two hostages remained in the Japanese ambassador's residence. Three months before I arrived, members of the MRTA (Túpac Amaru Revolutionary Movement) had stormed the ambassador's National Day reception and took hundreds of guests hostage, capturing global attention. While all seven of the US diplomats initially held were released, the anxiety in my own family mounted. They confronted a different reality that they had not signed up for when they agreed to leave the comfort of suburban Maryland to face this type of danger in Peru. As a public affairs officer handling both press and cultural affairs, I joined the embassy staff three months later when they were dealing with both the global media interest in the hostages, still running high, and the national interest in emerging human-rights abuses.

On my first day at work, the Peruvian media swarmed our ambassador, Dennis Jett, at a book donation organized by the cultural affairs office of the embassy at the University of Lima. Despite the backdrop of the books, the ambassador was well aware that the journalists did not come to ask him about political science books. The night before on television, with hostages still held in the Japanese ambassador's residence, a story broke in the Peruvian media about the torture of Leonor La Rosa.

Shocking images of this former Peruvian Army intelligence officer showed a gaunt, crippled woman, lying in bed with a neck brace, unable to hold up her head. Privy to the secret activities of Peru's antiterrorist activities, La Rosa was accused of leaking intelligence reports to the press that uncovered plans of targeting not just terrorists but journalists and opponents of the regime. La Rosa told her story of torture and rape and showed the evidence of burns on her feet and hands. At a time when seventy-two high-ranking Peruvians and international diplomats were still held hostage, this was national news. Ambassador Jett's forthright response noting US concern about these torture allegations and call for an investigation set the stage for the next two years.

When Alberto Fujimori became president in 1990, he promised to deal with the terrorists with a *mano dura*, which translates directly as "hard hand" but reads more like "iron fist." More than fifteen years of violence spread from the highlands of the Andes to the cities, putting Peru alongside Lebanon and Angola as the most violent countries of the 1980s. Fujimori's tough measures included emergency rule, the installation of police and the army on university campuses, secret army units, night raids, and (as La Rosa made known) torture and secret prisons. He produced the security Peruvians desperately sought to enable them to resume normal lives, but at a cost to its democratic principles and practices.[15]

In speaking out on the case of Leonor La Rosa, the US ambassador used his prominent public platform to call for respect for human rights and the rule of law. Even for a nation that was in the grip of terrorism for more than a decade, these were universal democratic principles that extended beyond borders.

At the time, especially with international attention focused on the hostages in the Japanese ambassador's residence, many Peruvians were open to Fujimori's no-nonsense, autocratic measures to deal with this scourge. In a dramatic raid to rescue the hostages less than three weeks after the La Rosa story broke, Peruvians hailed Fujimori, as he stood in the doorway of a bus taking the freed hostages to the hospital following their release. Newspapers the next day showed pictures of him stepping over dead bodies of the MRTA hostage-takers in the residence, helping his popularity soar among Peruvians. Statements from Washington and Ambassador Jett praised the rescue attempt without qualifications.

In the ensuing weeks, with his rising popularity, Fujimori moved to position himself to run for another term, one prohibited by the constitution. He fired judges so he could change the constitution and run for president again, packed the courts with his loyalists, and threatened the press with measures to curtail newsprint, which led the media to the US Embassy's doors and phones seeking reaction. Ambassador Jett did not hesitate to speak out against the erosion of democracy, drawing quick criticism from Fujimori supporters in the Congress and the press. Later, graffiti appeared around the city, in English: "Jett go home." Eventually, Fujimori himself reacted to Jett's comments: "The last time I looked we do not have a viceroy," referring to Spanish colonial rule. The political opposition and a national media under duress appreciated Ambassador Jett's remarks. Still, they felt torn, as the misgivings they had about the state of democracy in Peru equaled those about a US ambassador intervening in their domestic politics.

Every four to six months the government of Peru had the opportunity to announce a return of looted archeological artifacts. This ritual never lost its importance, as government officials arranged a ceremony with Ambassador Jett making a presentation. The rolling cameras ensured prominent news coverage. These returned items reminded Peruvians of the problem of looting, but more importantly, they offered an alternative view of the United States, one in which the United States respected the deep and rich cultural history of their country. These treasures, even seemingly insignificant vases, tools, or pottery shards, formed Peru's enduring identity, beyond the current strife of violence and erosion of democratic institutions. These artifacts had endured thousands of years, and returning them also implied they would survive in their proper context, well beyond the politics of the day, the human rights abuses, and one president.

The protection of Peru's archaeological treasures from looting and resale across borders paralleled and reinforced other US foreign policy interests in Peru, especially stopping the illicit drug trafficking. Fertile soil in the Andean valleys and a conducive climate made for bumper crops of coca leaf. Farmers had grown it in the region for centuries, and indigenous inhabitants used it for medicinal purposes, as a stimulant and a corrective to adjust to high altitudes. Just as with archaeological looting, the illicit drug trade depended on poverty, similar transit routes out of the country, and corruption in law enforcement and the judiciary to fuel profits in the drug trade, but to an exponentially higher degree.

The US Embassy oversaw a series of programs in cooperation with Peruvian authorities to prevent smuggling, to develop alternative crops for farmers, to provide training for police and judges, and to reform the loopholes in the judicial system. Returning looted pre-Columbian artifacts underscored US commitment to the rule of law.

The July 4 Independence Day reception in 1999 came a few days before the departure of Ambassador Jett. Security was tight, with the taking of hostages at the Japanese ambassador's National Day reception still fresh in everyone's minds. President Fujimori did not attend, but a number of his cabinet members did. Ambassadorial remarks are customary on these occasions. Typically, they are forgettable fluff. However, Jett used the opportunity as a valedictory for his three-year tenure in Peru. His message was pointed, but without finger-pointing. Jett did not mention the increasingly autocratic Fujimori by name. Instead, he spoke of the choices that Peru had ahead, laying out the alternatives for the type of country Peru could shape for itself. The choice lay between becoming a pariah nation turning its back on democratic principles or a model for the hemisphere, respecting the rule of law and reaping the benefits from a stable, reliable, and predictable climate conducive for economic growth—a choice, Jett concluded, for Peruvians to make.

Perhaps the applause the ambassador received was louder in my mind than in reality. What remains fresh, though, was the sight of the man leaping forward to be the first to shake Jett's hand. It was Francisco Toledo, the Stanford-trained economist. He would run for president against Fujimori the following year. Fujimori had stacked the courts and Peruvian Congress to change the Constitution and allow him to run for a third term. Toledo lost the election, but it was so full of irregularities that it was eventually thrown out, with Fujimori escaping into self-exile. Toledo won the runoff election. His anthropologist wife, Karp-Toledo, became the first lady and used her platform, as we have seen, to promote the protection of Peru's indigenous heritage.

By coincidence, I left Peru the same day as Ambassador Jett. Ten years later, I returned on a short visit in connection with my regional position in public diplomacy. I found myself walking over another archaeological mound, this time at Caral. During my assignment, this ancient site was not on anyone's radar, but subsequent research showed Caral was the oldest city in the hemisphere, 4,700 years old and home to three thousand people, earning it global recognition as a World Heritage Site. With the wind whipping the dust into my face, members of the archaeological team who were preserving the plazas, the circular arena, almost twenty different temples, canals, and a multitude of artifacts guided colleagues from the embassy and me around the site.

The US Embassy in collaboration with the archaeologists applied for funding from the Ambassador's Fund for Cultural Preservation. They received one of the largest grants under this program, $800,000, to demonstrate US support for Peru's conservation effort. Even though the amount paled in comparison with other government funding, the grant offered another demonstration of how a simple nod in the direction of history supported our foreign relations. By making what was vital to Peru (its history and heritage) also important to the United States, we continued to strengthen our capacity to work together on a host of other fronts, including the hard diplomacy of counternarcotics and combat against global terrorism. When we signed a trade agreement with Peru or called on their government to support us in regional forums against the maneuvers of opponents such as Hugo Chávez or Fidel Castro, this strengthened cooperation advanced the broader US national interests.

Suggested Further Reading

Roger Atwood outlines the impact of looting in Peru and other world sites in his *Stealing History: Tomb Raiders, Smugglers, and the Looting of the Ancient World* (New York: St. Marten's Press, 2004). Mark Adams uncovers Hiram Bingham's trips to Peru and subsequent controversies in *Turn Right at Machu Picchu: Rediscovering the Lost City One Step at a Time* (New York: Dutton, 2011). Hiram Bingham recreates his own expeditions in *Lost City of the Incas* (New York: Phoenix Paperbacks, 2003). The pages of *National Geographic Magazine* also contrast Bingham with Walter Alva, seventy-five years apart, in the April 1913 story written by Bingham, "In the Wonderland of Peru," and the October 1988 account by Alva, "Discovering the Tomb of a Moche Lord."

8

Mexico: Coming Home

"That doesn't look so bad. That looks like where I come from. That's my life." The young man in blue jeans, boots, and short sleeves made the comment during a focus group session on a series of public service ads sponsored by the press section at the US Embassy in Mexico in collaboration with the Mexican National Immigration office. Six different ads recounted the hazards of trying to make an illegal crossing into the United States. Pictures and stories of the desert and mountain crossings, heat and cold, rescues in fast-flowing rivers, overcrowded hidden compartments in trucks, and polleros and coyotes (the hated, feared, but unavoidable people smugglers) had little impact.

Only one of the ads produced an effect on the focus group. It was of a mother holding a baby, talking about the risks she had taken, not thinking of the harm that could have come to her child. In Mexico, where Mother's Day is part national holiday, part colossal traffic jam with everyone taking their mothers out, only the mother's tale had an impact of dissuading treacherous border crossings.

After the election of Mexico's president Vicente Fox in 2000, the issue of immigration moved to the forefront of the relationship between the two countries, outpacing the contentious exchanges we had over counternarcotics cooperation. With staggering numbers, history was occurring right in front of our eyes, amid what could be the third great wave of US immigration, or fourth depending on how one counts. And counting is hardly a science, especially in seeking any accuracy of those who are in the country without documents. Still, the numbers available impress. In the year 2000, an estimated four hundred thousand Mexicans came to the United States to stay each year and added to a population of almost ten million who had been born in Mexico and were here without documents. Half of the new entries and nearly half of those Mexicans already in the United States were undocumented, constituting roughly half of those from all countries making their way to the United States without legal documents.

More than three hundred Mexicans died each year along the border trying to cross illegally. The number of deaths was too high and propelled us to pursue collaborating with the government of Mexico to create public service ads. At the same time, perhaps, those of us in the embassy naively imagined that the ads, describing the harsh conditions of illegal crossings, would reduce deaths by reducing the numbers of illicit crossings. It was naïve only because the economic and cultural pull from the United States was so much greater than a small ad campaign, but the situation moved us into "we-have-to-do-something/anything" mode.

I came face to face with the historic proportions of those numbers when I traveled to our consulate in Nogales, whose district had within the last two years surpassed Tijuana/San Diego as the site of the largest number of illegal border crossings. I wanted to see firsthand the routes people took trying to cross into the United States illegally. Those routes had shifted as border enforcement and construction of barriers along the California coast sharply reduced the numbers of illegal crossers there. A few years before, the problem had become so severe that highway road signs in California warned motorists to be aware of crossers, using pictorial images akin to wildlife crossings, but in this case with silhouettes of two parents holding a child's hand in running position.

In Nogales, a small group of us, including the consul general and members of the Border Patrol, hopped into very conspicuous Chevrolet Suburbans (that we were thankful were running the air conditioning on high). We first drove southwest from Nogales to a small town, Altar, about forty-five minutes from the border. There we passed lines of small stores and market stalls selling their wares from the sides of the streets. Hanging from their porches were brightly colored back-packs, water bottles, sneakers, and other items intended for the market of migrants. Catering to these crossings was good business.

We next turned the car onto the dirt road to Sasabe, the town at the border. Along another forty-five-minute drive, this time heading northwest, we counted seventeen vans returning to Altar, each of them empty. Those vans could probably carry fifteen people each. In that short ride, we saw what two hundred thousand undocumented immigrants a year looked like at ground level. Not only do migrants send money back to their families and villages, but, as the satellite dishes on top of the recently constructed cement block houses in Sasabe attested, they also leave a fair amount at the border, in the attempts to get across.

It's not exactly an entitlement that many Mexicans feel about coming to the United States to work, but it comes close. It is more like a cultural expectation, a coming-of-age requirement in many villages. Family members and neighbors have made the trek and returned with cash to build a house. One anthropologist likened the time Mexicans spend in the United States to university, preparing young workers to return home with new skills and habits.[1] Others study the adverse impact on villages in the sending areas that comes from wholesale loss of residents at their most productive years. However, what's most revealing about this historical movement is the widespread impression in the United States that Mexican migration is not historical at all—or that it is historical only to the extent it compares with earlier waves of Irish, German, Italian, and Polish immigrants in previous centuries. There's a tendency to view Mexican migration in its current volume and forms as new and different.

History shock tells us otherwise. And the history of immigration from Mexico has its own unique set of waves, contradictions, and conflicting policies and regulations. That history reveals a recurring pattern since the nineteenth century of encouraging Mexicans to come to the United States to fill the shortfall of labor in the gold mines, on the railroads, in agriculture, and in manufacturing. At the same time, other forces have discouraged this immigration and worked to expel and deport those already in the country. It's a historic whiplash of "we need you," followed by "go home."

Mexicans in the United States may be able to lay claim that they are not the immigrants. Through their ancestors who became absorbed into the country following the redrawing of the border in 1848, they can legitimately call themselves "original settlers." They were one of the earliest groups to arrive in the territorial homes of Indigenous groups as varied as the Apache and the Yurok. Certainly, some of the buildings in Santa Fe predate any structures built by the Pilgrims by decades.

Ironically, both Spain, as the colonizer, and then Mexico, newly independent, exhibited their ambivalence and contradictory policies toward immigration into their territory. In the early 1800s, both welcomed and then reversed course to prohibit immigrants—in this case, settlers from the United States expanding into the territory west of Louisiana. Initially, Spain recruited agents, with a promise of payment, to identify and lure hundreds of settlers to colonize the territory north of the Rio Grande, Texas, for fear that the "integrity of the national territory continues to be weak, [and] risks being lost," in the words of one observer.[2] One of the earliest agents, Moses Austin, was recruiting the first settlers under this arrangement, but within a year, Mexico gained its independence and canceled all grants Spain had offered. After Moses died, his son Stephen made the long trek to Mexico City to seek to reverse the decision and preserve his grant. He ran into the factional politics of the new nation but eventually won back his original grant. A new law passed responsibility for the issues of settlement and migration to the individual Mexican states, and the Coahuila and Texas government approved the original dispensation for the agents as an effort to populate its northeastern regions. Also, these new dispensations for colonizing Texas had their schemes of preferences. First, those colonists who married Mexicans received priority citizenship credit, as a way to integrate the colonists into their new nation. Second, the laws gave preference to those "wandering tribes," offering land to those who settled and pledged loyalty to both church and state, with the explicit statement attached, "always preferring native Indians to 'strangers.'"[3]

Led by Stephen Austin's colony between the Colorado and Brazos Rivers, the new colonists, who were intended to fortify Mexico's claim to the region and to serve as a buffer zone between the United States and Mexico, ended up with greater links, politically and economically, to the United States. The numbers swelled to the point that Alexis de Tocqueville in his visit in 1831 noted: "Daily, little by little, the inhabitants of the United States are filtering into Texas, acquiring land there, and though submitting to the nation's laws, establishing there the empire of their language and mores. The province of Texas is still under Mexican rule, but soon there will, so to say, be no more Mexicans there."[4] Where de Tocqueville erred was in the claim that the settlers were submitting to Mexico's laws. Discontent among the new arrivals grew as the central government in Mexico alternately ignored these faraway colonies or sought to impose controls, specifically over slavery. Settlers entered Texas with their slaves to work the fields, but Mexico had long since abandoned the practice of slavery. From its earliest days as a new nation, Mexico abhorred slavery, declaring that no individual could be enslaved for life. A law passed in 1824 went further and prohibited slavery, including a clause that freed any slave who entered Mexican territory. The settlers ignored the law, calling their slaves "indentured servants" and choosing to interpret the new law as pertaining only to the commerce of slaves.

Faced with another restriction passed in 1830 prohibiting further immigration into Texas, the settlers not only ignored the new law, but turned their increasing resentment toward it into an unshakeable desire for independence. A Mexican-organized boundary commission sent to investigate the territory in 1827 had prompted this law. The commission was alarmed at the pull of the region toward the United States in trade and cultural links. By 1835, de Tocqueville's prediction had come true: these settlers and their slaves outnumbered Mexicans in the Texas region by ten to one. The influx of settlers did lead, precisely as the head of the boundary commission, General Manuel de Mier y Terán, had predicted, to the residents' clamor for independence and ultimately to annexation to the United States and war with Mexico.

Following the war, those on the northern side of the border launched their ambivalent policies and entreaties toward the roughly eighty to one hundred thousand Mexicans living in the territory annexed by the United States. The 1848 Treaty of Guadalupe Hidalgo stipulated that those living in territories ceded by Mexico could claim either US or Mexican citizenship, but they had only one year to make a choice. After a year, those who had not elected Mexican citizenship would automatically become citizens of the United States. Scattered unevenly in the vast territory stretching from Texas to California and north into Colorado, these citizens of Mexico faced pressures to stay as Americans or leave.

Despite the protections of property guaranteed by the treaty, expulsions of Mexicans in Texas and California proceeded. In the case of Texas, fears of Mexicans aligning with slaves in the region to incite rebellion contributed to expulsions and deportations ordered by local jurisdictions across the state, with Matagorda County claiming expulsion was preferable to lynching.[5]

In California, the discovery of gold, one month before the signing of the Treaty of Guadalupe Hidalgo ending the war, led to a mass influx of wealth-seekers from all over the world, but also from northern Mexico. This competition from *outsiders*, especially those with significant mining experience in the Mexican state of Sonora, led to a tax imposed on foreigners working the gold region. The tax opened the way to more informal, extralegal, and even violent efforts to discourage, repulse, and expel all foreigners—not just Mexicans but also Chileans, Peruvians, and Chinese. Many of the Mexicans ended up moving to other parts of California and the recently ceded territories to work in other mines from Colorado to Arizona.

Mexican diplomats in the United States argued that the violence against their citizens in California constituted a violation of the terms of the Treaty of Guadalupe Hidalgo, but back in Mexico, government officials hoped for their return. With so many residents of the already underpopulated border states of Sonora and Chihuahua migrating north to the gold mines, a weakened Mexican government worried that areas along the new border were becoming increasingly vulnerable to raiding. They feared those indigenous groups who had not taken up earlier offers of settlement and whose nomadic lifestyles did not respect these recently drawn lines in the sand. Others targeted for populating this area included those of its citizens caught north of the treaty line following the war. By urging them to move south, the Mexican government hoped that these returnees who harbored negative experiences in the United States, from either the gold rush or the aftermath of the war, could oppose any further secession attempts as well as provide protection from periodic raids.

As early as August 1848, just months after the signing of the treaty, Mexico issued a decree outlining the conditions for repatriation of its citizens, including the establishment of a repatriation commission and the offer of enticements in the form of land, payment for transportation, and subsidized agricultural seeds to work the land in the border states. The government underestimated the cost of these benefits to returnees and later had to renege on fulfilling them.

The Mexican states were reconstituted as military colonies along the border to prevent further loss of territory and to provide some authority. Representatives of the new commission traveled into their former territories to recruit individuals appealing to national loyalties and complaints about loss of status in their new nation. However, delays in transferring some of these promised financial enticements prompted some who had returned to change their minds and head back north.

Given the expulsions and mistreatment of Mexicans in Texas and California in the years after 1848, it is surprising to learn that officials in the territory of New Mexico opposed these recruitment efforts from the southern side of the border. One commissioner who had traveled north to encourage returns, a Catholic priest named Ramón Ortiz, was removed from New Mexico. US officials made the technical claim that repatriation of this type was not part of the treaty.

In the end, how many of those who found themselves in the newly absorbed territories opted to maintain their Mexican citizenship and leave their homes? Not surprisingly, there is little consensus on these figures, as they vary from as low as one thousand to thirty-one thousand. The larger estimates usually extend the period of national determination past the one year allowed for in the treaty, even taking into account the fact that some who left the United States ended up returning when financial incentives were not forthcoming.

The remaining years of the nineteenth century reflect migration between the two countries in the context of broader international trends in global movements of people, which included Europeans arriving in the Western Hemisphere in historic numbers, but also Asians and Africans moving not just to the region, but also within their regions, to escape problems of hunger and lack of work due to overpopulation.

Mexicans continued to move north. They were lured by employment, particularly on the railways, after the exclusion of Asians in the late 1800s left a vacuum in filling the available jobs to lay the new track throughout the western United States. While Mexico did serve as a destination country for European immigrants, much as did the United States, in the years before 1910, the country still lost two people to the United States for every one new immigrant.

The year 1910 marks the beginning of the revolution in Mexico and a period of tremendous instability and upheaval, resulting in an increased exodus, so that the loss of Mexicans for every new immigrant reached a ratio of five to one. More than 890,000 legal Mexican immigrants came to the United States for refuge between 1910 and 1920. "Mexico is the only country in all of the Americas where its nationals migrate abroad," lamented Francisco Madero. Madero was the opposition candidate turned leader of the revolution that toppled Porfirio Díaz, who had ruled Mexico for more than thirty years.[6] It wasn't just the violence from the revolution that sent Mexicans north. It was also the continuing lure of work. A congruence of new rail transportation, refrigeration, and publicly subsidized irrigation projects opened up the Southwest to new agricultural possibilities. Produce from the southwestern states filled store shelves, growing from practically none in 1900 to about 40 percent of the total market by 1929.[7] To work the newly irrigated fields, growers looked south and to the temporary nature of Mexican labor. Thus, another cycle of push-pull started. The lure of jobs pulled Mexicans north, and they were pushed out by the threat of violence and instability in the South.

Push-pull is not the only cycle related to immigration. When groups in the United States called for restrictions and expulsions, citing worries about the loss of jobs and cultural change coming from large numbers of immigrants, there was a corresponding push-back reaction. Even though Mexicans and other Latin American countries received an exemption from the national quotas established by the 1924 Johnson-Reed Act restricting immigration, the start of the depression five years later created a backlash against foreigners in the United States. The 1924 law also created the Border Patrol. After the depression began, the Border Patrol embarked on a campaign to deport immigrants. The threat of those deportations resulted in many more departures than actual expulsions, but the result was the same. An estimated 150,000 Mexicans returned to their homeland in the 1930s.[8]

Regardless of actual figures, patterns in the conflicting attitudes toward Mexicans in the United States have deep and persistent roots in our shared history. That dissonance is not exclusive to the US residents. Mexicans also have had conflicting attitudes toward those who leave their country for their northern neighbor. On the one hand, and in very broad and general terms, Mexicans view those who abandon their country with suspicion—especially those heading north. The historian José Hernández unearthed references to "Bad Mexicans" in government documents from the prewar era. This pattern continued after the war, as Hernández cited prominent Mexican writers from the nineteenth century who described those who fled north as "contaminated by contact with the U.S." and, more recently in the twentieth century, as "cockroaches."[9] Another historian, Timothy Henderson, cited Mexicans who referred to those who left as "traitors who peddled their labor abroad rather than stay and work where they were needed."[10]

On the other hand, those who left were making a contribution that few could discount. They sent back increasingly large remittances to their families and communities, providing one of the top three sources of foreign exchange for Mexico over the past thirty years, along with oil and tourism. Migration offers an economic escape valve, holding out promises of employment elsewhere when none exists in many rural areas. However, many acknowledge that the depopulation of those sending areas leaves them without the workforce to develop the region, particularly with the exodus of young, robust men and women.

At his inauguration as president of Mexico in December 2000, Vicente Fox inherited this situation. Fox openly embraced Mexicans residing in the United States during his presidential campaign. He courted them to persuade their family members, friends, and neighbors in Mexico to vote for him. Analysts in both countries credited this group with helping put him over the edge in his election. They sent back money to their relatives, offsetting the showering of financial gifts that his opponents in power were able to spread throughout the country, especially in rural areas. Fox had no ambivalence toward those who had left.

Fox elevated the basket of issues surrounding immigration to the forefront of the diplomatic dialogue. He commonly referred to that basket as "the whole enchilada," his colorful term for seeking a comprehensive immigration reform package in the United States. The specifics included protection and better treatment of Mexicans in the United States. It also included a guest worker program to allow for circular movement of those going to the United States for employment, improvement of border operations, expansion of development in the sending areas within Mexico, and amnesty for those undocumented who resided in the United States. Even Fox knew the political toxicity of the word "amnesty," preferring the euphemism "regularization." Because of the general enthusiasm in the United States for Fox, the candidate who ended seventy-one years of PRI rule in Mexico, his initial entreaties on immigration met not quite an open endorsement, but at a minimum muted resistance. Certainly, with President Bush, who came from Texas and who himself had captured enough of the Hispanic vote in both his gubernatorial races in Texas, but also in the deciding but divisive electoral vote in Florida, the idea of reaching out to Hispanic voters in the United States through the immigration issue had a certain appeal.

So, when President Bush broke with the tradition of going to Canada for his first foreign trip and opted to go to Fox's ranch outside of Guanajuato, Mexico, the excitement was palpable. With an agreement to commence high-level ministerial talks on immigration, expectations of a breakthrough ran high in Mexico. Secretary of State Colin Powell, Attorney General John Ashcroft, and their two counterparts, Jorge Castañeda and Santiago Creel, led the talks.

Three elements, however, combined to make the odds for passage of such a comprehensive reform on immigration insurmountable. The first element was the divided politics of immigration within the United States, with each side—conservative and liberal—showing divisions in their ranks. Simply put, Republican probusiness and Democratic pro–civil rights groups supported an immigration overhaul while Republican border-security advocates and Democrat prolabor groups opposed reform. Secondly, less than a week after Fox's return official visit to Washington, the 9/11 attacks happened and took over the national agenda. We argued in Mexico that even without 9/11, the politics behind the issue made reform very difficult. Finally, and tied to politics, came the inescapable reality that immigration was a domestic issue. Any reforms would be negotiated by the US Congress, not with foreign countries.

That last formulation became the mantra for those of us in the embassy as we advocated with both our official counterparts and the broader Mexican public. Immigration was a domestic issue and was not open for negotiation. However, the history of immigration, specifically concerning Mexico, contradicted that point. We *had*, in fact, negotiated a guest worker program with Mexico, the Mexican Farm Labor Agreement, to recruit workers during World War II.

Taking its more common name from the Mexican term for manual laborer, the Bracero program started in 1942 and lasted well beyond the war until 1964. At its height in the mid-1950s, this program accounted for 450,000 Mexicans per year coming to the United States to work, primarily as agricultural workers. President Fox's decision to focus on migration had its roots in this earlier program. He sought a negotiated agreement with the United States to regularize migration in order to protect Mexicans who were working under cover of secrecy there. The Mexicans drew a direct line from the Braceros. The line for the United States was dotted or broken. We had forgotten.

Several aspects of the Bracero program stand out as relevant to the US-Mexico relationship in recent years. First, the program began with an executive order, not with congressional approval. Second, negotiations with the Mexican government occurred, throughout the program's duration, with the State Department taking the lead in those talks. Finally, this guest worker initiative, originally conceived as a wartime emergency, evolved into a program in the 1950s that served specifically to dampen illegal migration.

Even before Pearl Harbor, growers in the Southwest faced labor shortages in their fields. They had unsuccessfully lobbied Washington to allow for migrant workers. It took less than five months following the attack on Pearl Harbor and the declaration of war to reverse the US government intransigence on the need for temporary workers. In Washington, interagency discussions hammered out details of responsibilities, with the Departments of Agriculture, Justice, Labor, and State coordinating with the War Manpower Commission. Informal negotiations had been taking place between the State Department and the Mexican government so that they could sign an agreement on April 4, 1942, between the two countries.

The process that was hammered out started with a grower's request for employees, which then triggered a US Employment Service certification of a shortage of labor. This certification then transmitted an order for workers to Mexican recruitment centers. Funds from the US government initially covered the cost of transportation from Mexico to the place of employment. Contracts were drawn up between the Farm Security Administration and the migrant workers, with subcontracts eventually extended to the employers. Overall, during the war, upward of 219,500 Mexicans came to work on farms across twenty-four states.

The extent of the bilateral discussion on immigration was best captured years later, in 1951, when a commission was established to review the status of migratory labor. The commission concluded that "the negotiation of the Mexican International Agreement is a collective bargaining situation in which the Mexican Government is the representative of the workers and the Department of State is the representative of our farm employers."[11] The language was remarkable, especially looking forward to 2001, when we told the Mexicans that immigration was a domestic issue.

Even more remarkable in the establishment of the agreement was the absence of Congress. Seven months after the first braceros arrived and a year after the signing of the agreement, legislation passed authorizing the program. That law, Public Law 45, appropriated $26 million, and, in a pattern that recurred for the remainder of the existence of the Bracero program, it reversed conditions established in the original bilateral agreement signed with Mexico.

Specifically, the law prohibited the use of any funding to cover the cost of recruitment and transportation from Mexico to the site of employment. Also, it allowed growers to recruit without having to go through the Mexican government, to find available workers right at the border, and to use INS waiver provisions to permit the entrance of otherwise inadmissible workers. These new procedures made it easier for the employers, who, by not complying with the bilateral agreement, could also pay the migrant laborers less. Preference for the latter provisions shows up in the numbers of braceros arriving in the final year of the wartime program: 31,331 braceros were admitted into the United States to work under the original agreement, but an additional 55,000 came under the unilateral provisions of the law and were recruited right at the border.

This initial phase of the Bracero program lasted beyond the end of the war, for two more years, with congressional representatives from grower states arguing that a shortage still existed. Nevertheless, on April 28, 1947, Congress passed Public Law 40, declaring an official end to the program by the end of January the following year. However, growers lobbied hard for a continuation. The House Agricultural Committee organized hearings before the end of the year, during which the commissioner of the INS testified that "the emergency was not over."[12] The hearings endorsed an extension of the program. With no regard for the provisions closing it down by January 30, 1948, the committee focused on details of the extension, such as forestalling the imminent departure of thousands of bracero workers.

At the same time, without the approval of Congress, the State Department was negotiating a new agreement with Mexico, signed on February 21, 1948, weeks after Congress mandated its termination. Seven months later, though, Congress placed its stamp of approval on the new program and authorized its continuation for another year. When the year lapsed, the program still did not end, but carried on under administrative action, without congressional approval or oversight.

The new conditions for the extended Bracero program attempted to deal with the large numbers of Mexicans who were entering illegally outside the requirements of the agreement. The new arrangements included Mexican citizens who were already in the United States as Bracero participants and who may have overstayed their authorized period of employment. Thus, growers recruited fewer and fewer guest workers from the interior of Mexico. In the first two years of the new program, they contracted more than twice the number of braceros in the United States compared with those recruited from Mexico. By the third year, the ratio had increased to five to one. The new provisions worked to encourage potential recruits to enter the United States illegally and regularize their situation with the INS there.

The new arrangement made life easier for the growers, who could contract directly with employees without the bureaucratic requirements of going through government agencies. Budgets and staff for the Border Patrol and the INS were cut, reducing their ability to control the entry of thousands of Mexicans seeking to work on farms in the United States outside of the Bracero procedures. The flow of workers to the border became so strong that, in another twist of history, it was the Mexican government that appealed for greater enforcement. They stalled negotiations in the early 1950s over the program until the United States took action to stop the illegal entries.

So many braceros were failing to return home that in 1951 government negotiators threatened to pull Mexico out of the agreement.

The US Congress heard the message. The State Department invited members of the House Agricultural Committee that sponsored the bill to the negotiations in Mexico. By June 1951, they had passed Public Law 78, which amended an earlier farm bill and authorized the program, determining once and for all that the US government would contract with the Mexican workers. No one already in the United States illegally could apply. Growers who employed illegal workers could not receive braceros. The agreement set wages at the prevailing rate. Public Law 78 became the impetus for a new bilateral agreement with Mexico that lasted until 1964.

A growing urgency to address illegal immigration coincided with the Mexican government's appeal for greater border enforcement and the new provisions for legal contract labor but remained separate from the legislation approving the Bracero extension. The costs to states, the impact on wages and employment, and the McCarthyite fears of communist infiltration across the Mexican border all merged to prompt the INS to launch a major enforcement action along the southwest border that they named "Operation Wetback." Sweeps through farms by an enhanced Border Patrol resulted in apprehensions exceeding one million in 1954. The impact of the removals could be felt almost immediately in enhancing the success of the Bracero program. Contract laborers grew from two hundred thousand in 1953 to almost four hundred thousand two years later.

It would be wrong to conclude, though, that the growth in the Bracero program resulted only from the removals. The new, streamlined procedures for the contracting of braceros served to sustain the reduced flow of illegal workers. That drop-off, in turn, sustained the program well into the next decade.

One of those new stipulations allowed growers to identify preferred workers through the issuance of a border crossing card, the I-100 document, more commonly known as the *mica*, meaning "plastic" in Spanish. Thus, workers who either had provided satisfactory service or had special skills would receive these cards, allowing them to be rehired as braceros without going through the recruitment process again. These new procedures meant that the program, originally designed to fill an emergency need during the war years, would see the largest numbers of Mexican workers enter the country during the late 1950s, averaging well over four hundred thousand per year.

A variety of factors combined to bring about the demise of the Bracero program. Chief among these were (1) bureaucratic infighting in Washington between the Departments of Labor and Justice and (2) Mexican government concerns over the issuance of the micas that moved the program away from its temporary nature. A growing public awareness of mistreatment and lower wages for these guest workers motivated Congress to phase out the program by 1964. Employers in the United States who still wanted to contract Mexicans would have to use the procedures of the H-2 temporary visas that applied for all other countries.

Many questions arising from the Bracero experience speak to the situation in the early years of the 2000s and remain relevant today. There is little consensus over the impact of the program on illegal immigration. On the one hand, apprehensions along the border decreased during the years of greatest recruitment, the late 1950s. The INS justified the program as a means to "assist the Service in its enforcement problems."[13]

Also, the number of apprehensions of undocumented workers increased after the demise of the program, which led historian Kitty Calavita to refer to the Bracero program as "the solution of one period [that] prepares the way for the conflicts of the next."[14] Did the program foster the culture of leaving Mexico to work in the United States, sometimes referred to even as a rite of passage for young Mexicans?

As noted earlier, there were periods of Mexican outmigration to work on railroads and in mines in the late 1800s and to escape the violence in the years following the 1910 revolution. A generation later, the disparity in wages still lured unemployed Mexicans with an estimated one day of wages in the United States equivalent to three weeks of work in a society whose rural population had doubled since

1910. The Bracero program institutionalized the enticement, to fill farm employment gaps in the United States and to provide income for poor, rural Mexicans with few or no other prospects. The numbers alone seem to make the case that this program offering employment outside Mexico became deeply ingrained within the society. The number of participants reached five million; the program lasted twenty-two years and crossed two generations. Add to this (1) the number of people who applied but were not accepted, (2) the numbers of family members and neighbors who knew someone working in the United States, and (3) the number of people who during this period went north without papers, and the number of direct and indirect participants increases significantly.

Notable for its absence was even the briefest reference to the Bracero program during the discussions on immigration after President Fox was elected. Far from flawless, especially in the persistently low wages and questionable living conditions on the US farms, the program nevertheless did contain lessons for any new agreement. The linkage between the program and the decline in illegal immigration, the precedence of negotiating with the Mexican government over immigration, and the experience of executive branch action all seemed to bear directly on a renewed guest worker program.

One possible reason for the silence may have been the unresolved issue of the outstanding pay owed to the braceros. In the early years of the program, 10 percent of the worker's salary was sent directly to the Mexican government to hold until the worker returned. Among other things, this served as an incentive for them to return home. However, many never received this payment, the suspicion being that officials siphoned off the funding for their own gain. Thus, during the Fox advocacy on immigration, the Bracero program came up more in the context of participants demanding compensation for the loss of this portion of their wages.

What was most striking about many of those bilateral discussions between various official visits to Mexico was the extent of agreement on immigration. Our embassy in Mexico hosted hundreds of US government visitors every year. President Bush visited four different times during my tour. Secretaries Powell and Albright came several times, along with the secretaries of homeland security, transportation, education, and housing and urban development, the attorney general, the chairman of the Joint Chiefs, governors, members of Congress, and a host of under and assistant secretaries from a plethora of cabinet departments. So many visitors arrived that the State Department appointed an officer whose job was solely dedicated to tracking and taking care of the logistics behind the visits. Typically, embassy officials would accompany these high-level visitors to their meetings. The protocol level of the visitor dictated who in the embassy would brief the visitor before the meeting, sit in on the meeting, and act on any follow-up required after the meetings.

With a few notable exceptions, these meetings were always cordial and more than just civil or productive. On most topics, we saw eye to eye with our Mexican counterparts. When Eduardo Aguirre, the first director of the Citizenship and Immigration Services of the newly formed Department of Homeland Security, came to Mexico City, the interest level ran unusually high. Even without the aggressive advocacy of the Mexican government on behalf of their ten million citizens living in the United States and another twelve million of Mexican descent, our counterparts were eager to hear how the new Department of Homeland Security was organizing itself and to see what the prospects for immigration reform might be. I joined Aguirre for the meeting at the Department of External Relations with Mexico's undersecretary for North American affairs, Enrique Berruga. He was a polished diplomat as well as a writer of fiction in whatever spare time he could have possibly carved out. What was remarkable about the meeting was how quickly it turned into a policy-proposal brainstorming session between Berruga and Aguirre.

Both men threw out ideas for policies the United States could adopt to deal with the five million undocumented Mexicans residing in the United States and the three hundred thousand more each year attempting to make the crossing without papers. New visa programs, identity cards, amnesty thresholds and provisions, and circular guest worker programs were among the ideas all tossed around to break the impasse for reform. The prospects that any of these could succeed never came up during this meeting. The built-in political logjam on this issue was also never raised. Despite George W. Bush's push on two different occasions to break the impasse over immigration reform, those political stumbling blocks proved insurmountable.

One of the proposals that surfaced in that meeting—and many others—was a reference to Canada's guest worker program. The free movement of labor in Europe under the Schengen Agreement was the gold standard that our Mexican diplomatic colleagues hauled out during these discussions. However, they knew that internal politics in the United States dictated smaller, less ambitious steps, such as Canada's guest worker program, that we in the United States ought to emulate. Under its provisions, Canada offered seasonal employment, for up to six months, for seventeen thousand workers. They applied in Mexico, were screened there, and received a plane ticket to Canada, to Ontario mostly. The Mexican government took out some of their wages, which they were supposed to refund to the worker upon his or her return to Mexico. It was much like the Braccro program, but with fewer numbers, and was likely less cumbersome to administer.

This Canadian program certainly merited thoughtful study, particularly as it offered legal, regular, and predictable employment that benefited both nations, the workers, and employers. One glaringly obvious discrepancy limited its replicability, though. The Canadian program dealt with a universe of seventeen thousand people. The numbers of Mexicans seeking work in the United States, on an annual basis, run into the hundreds of thousands.[15]

Still, an assortment of work programs in the United States was then (and still is) legally available to employers seeking foreign labor and Mexicans seeking employment. With so many different legal ways to seek work, some of which have no ceiling limitation, the question remains why so many Mexicans seek entry outside of these visa categories. One answer is that the process to obtain such a work visa is cumbersome and time-intensive, for both the prospective employer and employee.

The numbers and types of visas, not counting the other roughly seventy-five different types of visas, further underscore the confusing morass of policy and law that is our immigration system. It is complicated at best, offering job security to immigration attorneys. At worst, it is a broken system that has escaped reform efforts and ideas from presidents and legislators and so many others like Enrique Berruga and Eduardo Aguirre on both sides of the border.

Most of all, the numbers point out the historic nature of Mexican immigration. Seen from the embassy level, our newest officers were interviewing more than 1.7 million applicants a year. With 2,000 aspiring visitors coming to the embassy in Mexico City each day, that translated to an officer required to interview more than one hundred a day, roughly fifteen an hour, or one every four or five minutes. That's five minutes or less to go through a series of questions, examine and inspect documents, assess their credibility, determine the individuals' capacity to pay their way while in the United States as well as the ties back in Mexico to ensure a return. In Ciudad Juarez, the requirements for the new consulate where we process all immigrant visa applications for the whole country included more than eighty windows for interviewing. We used to say that one out of every five new Foreign Service officers would end up working in Mexico, primarily to adjudicate visas.

At the visa window or along the dirt roads to the border, we see immigration and history collide in the way we conduct our relationship with Mexico, but also with many other countries around the world. There at the window, we see the numbers that by themselves underscore the historical significance of immigration in our era. And the selling of backpacks and water bottles in remote villages along the border reinforces the latest immigration wave that we might expect history books in fifty years to emphasize.

To tell the story of immigration solely through the numbers is to lose sight of the fact that immigration is ultimately a personal, individual story, retold hundreds of thousands of times. It's the story of the mother we met at a desolate ranch house east of the Sonora border town of Sasabe, where migrants were congregating for the final leg of their journey. They would walk across the desert terrain through the unmarked border, perhaps guided by a pollero (a smuggler of Mexican workers), to take them to a road on the other side where there might be a truck to pick them up and carry them further into the United States. The mother was cradling her seriously dehydrated baby, sponging her down to lower her temperature. She said she was determined to make the crossing that night, even after we advised her to wait for the sake of her child.

Later, after driving through the border entry at Sasabe, we came upon a makeshift detention area along a highway where Border Patrol guards were holding a group of apprehended crossers behind chain-link fencing. They had mist machines directed at the migrants, handcuffed under tents, who had probably spent hours, if not days, in the desert. They were awaiting transfer to a facility for processing the migrants and then dropping them off across the border in Mexican territory. One Border Patrol agent sounded more than a little resigned to the fact that after regaining their strength in a week or two, these migrants would likely make another attempt at the dangerous desert crossing.

Years later, I met another young mother from Mexico, attending a US community college, determined to earn an engineering degree and contribute to society, here and back home. Her story of crossing the border illegally sent me back to the desolate ranch house near Sasabe. She moved north, took English classes, worked in restaurants, joined cultural groups, ran computer fairs, and continues to give back to others. It couldn't have been the same mother; it didn't have to be. It was clear that hundreds, if not thousands, had similar stories.

These stories fit in with one version of history, of our identity, as a nation of immigrants, which still receives more foreigners on our soil than any other country. This constructed identity is closely defined by the Statue of Liberty and the lines in Emma Lazarus's poem on that monument that still speaks to the tired, the poor, and the huddled masses. Nevertheless, this is a narrative not necessarily shared by those who approach the visa window, or those being misted down by the side of the road in Arizona. They see a different, parallel storyline, especially in the wake of September 11, with ramped-up border security. Surely, too, there are other stories, of gang members and drug runners in those illegal crossings. After all, ours is a history not only of immigration, but also of reaction against immigration, of nativism, and barriers, of complicated, even broken, laws and policies that cry out for reform but resist fixing. In this case, history shock isn't even historical; it's history in the making that relies on competing and contradictory versions of the past.

Suggested Further Reading

Beyond Borders: A History of Mexican Migration to the United States (New York: Hill and Wang, 2007) by Timothy Henderson recounts the different periods and conflicting perspectives toward Mexican migration. José Angel Hernández looks specifically at the movements of people between the two countries on either side of the US-Mexican War in *Mexican-American Colonization during the Nineteenth Century* (New York: Cambridge University Press, 2012). Two books explore the impact of Mexican immigration in the United States: Andrew Selee's *Vanishing Frontiers: The Forces Driving Mexico and the United States Together* (New York: Hachette Book Group, 2018) and Edward Telles and Vilma Ortiz's *Generations of Exclusion: Mexican-Americans, Assimilation, and Race* (New York: Russell Sage Foundation, 2008). A third, Samuel Huntington's *Who Are We? Challenges to America's National Identity* (New York: Simon and Schuster, 2004), came out while I was in Mexico and evoked controversy as it raised fears over the changing nature of immigration, specifically from Mexico.

9

Cuba: Our Neighbor Doesn't Know Us

At noon on December 17, 2014, President Barack Obama strode to a podium in the Cabinet Room, where he stood with busts of George Washington and Benjamin Franklin behind him. Unaffected by the "drubbing" he took in the midterm elections six weeks earlier, Obama laid down a marker to show he was prepared to use his executive authorities to advance his agenda and remain relevant in his final two years in office despite Republican control of both houses in Congress. Obama announced he would seek to normalize relations with Cuba. "We will end," he said, drawing on his appreciation for the history in the moment, "an outdated approach that, for decades, has failed to advance our interests." Evidence of that failure? The Castros and communists remained in power despite fifty years of policies to isolate the country and, at times, to overthrow the Castro regime.

Obama noted in his remarks that "when I came into office—I promised to re-examine our Cuba policy."[1] In the days before his inauguration, the latest round of rumors spread that Castro was on his deathbed. This time, though, Venezuelan president Hugo Chávez set off the speculations on January 10, 2009, when he released a statement that "Fidel in his uniform who walked the streets late at night, hugging the people, will not return."[2] That set off street celebrations in Miami, raising expectations, ranging from the reunification of families to the overthrow of the communist regime and recovery of financial and property losses confiscated in the early 1960s after Castro took power. Perhaps the celebrations were delayed revenge for the decades that Castro had used anti-Americanism as a foil to help him stay in power and build an international reputation as one who stood up to and survived the power of the colossus just ninety miles to the north.

It is not just newspapers that prepare in advance for obituaries. The State Department had anticipated writing a death notice for Castro countless times because so many rumors of his demise echoed in the halls through the years. Our small public diplomacy office in the Bureau of Western Hemispheric Affairs unearthed a plan developed in the Bush administration that laid out ideas for the US posture in the event of Castro's death. It was quickly apparent that the language adopted in the early 2000s would be unacceptable to an incoming president who had promised in his campaign to meet with Raúl Castro, who had succeeded his older brother as president of the National Assembly in 2006 and then as head of the Communist Party in 2008. The Bush language emphasized the regime-change nature of the US approach to Cuba for fifty years, implying that the Cuban people, freed from Fidel, would rise up to embrace democracy and open markets that he had denied them for fifty years.

Not only did such language run counter to the Obama campaign messages, but events on the island had conspired to make them obsolete. As Fidel had repeatedly managed over the previous five decades, he had already outmaneuvered those in the United States seeking regime change by overseeing a transfer of power to his younger brother. In this way, he managed his own regime change to ensure stability and continuity past his illness and death.

Public opinion had also changed much in the ensuing years. Since the rupture in diplomatic relations in 1961, polling on attitudes toward Cuba in the United States had varied widely. Some years showed broad antipathy toward reestablishing diplomatic relations, such as the late 1970s in the face of Cuban military involvement in Africa. The Reagan years saw a shift toward approving a thaw in diplomatic relations, but then during the Clinton presidency, opinion shifted against such moves. However, by the early 2000s, a general trend had set in with a majority of Americans in favor of establishing diplomatic relations, even among the most vociferous anti-Castro groups in Florida, who had for so long used their political clout in Florida to dictate US policy toward Cuba.[3]

This notable shift in public opinion, especially among Cubans in Florida, minimized the political risk that Obama took during his campaign. Speaking in Miami in May 2008 before an audience of the traditionally hardline anti-Castro group, the Cuban American National Foundation, Obama boldly asserted, "It is time to pursue direct diplomacy, with friend and foe alike, without preconditions." Even though his opponent, John McCain, hewed close to the anti-Castro rhetoric that had allowed Bush to win Florida in 2000 and 2004, Obama's embrace of a new path toward US-Cuban relations did not get in the way of his winning the state by almost 3 percent, including Miami-Dade County with a comfortable 57.8 percent of the vote.

My office had little concrete guidance on how the new president might want to couch reaction to the death of Fidel Castro, imminent or otherwise. Based on those campaign pronouncements and Obama's executive order to close the Guantanamo Bay detention facility within a year, we were fairly certain that the strategy on paper developed a few years earlier would not align with the new president's preferences.

Furthermore, our public diplomacy office was responsible for communicating outside our borders to foreign audiences. The eight-year-old strategy we unearthed was geared toward a US domestic audience, specifically a narrow one located in Florida, as well as a handful of legislators at the other end of Pennsylvania Avenue. Our task was to communicate to the people of Cuba and the rest of the world how the United States viewed that moment of Fidel's passing. How the United States responded would be closely analyzed in Cuba, in Latin America, and beyond as a signal of the change the new president promised. All we had to work with was outdated language, which was a throwback to Cold War rhetoric, and assumptions gleaned from campaign rhetoric about the new president's views.

The United States wasn't alone in anticipating the death of Fidel, and reading the reaction to the rumors in the rest of the world underscored the challenges as we approached our strategy. Castro strode the world stage as a hero in the eyes of many around the world, and not just because he was the lone Cold War survivor standing up to the United States. His claims on expanding social services such as education and health care for Cuban citizens and his record of supporting independence movements in Latin America, Asia, and Africa contributed to his reputation. Often, these romantic views were balanced against his record on human rights for Cubans, with its political prisoners, its suppression of speech, and control of the media.

Facing the prospects of Fidel's death even pushed one leader, Álvaro Colom, the president of Guatemala, to make amends. Amid our discussions on how to craft a new approach in the wake of Fidel's death, Colom issued this statement on February 17, 2009: "Today I want to ask Cuba's forgiveness for having offered our country, our territory, to prepare an invasion of Cuba."[4]

The divergence between Colom asking forgiveness and the people of Miami celebrating has a lot to do with the clash of different histories. Cuba presents one of the clearest cases in US foreign affairs where competing versions of history dominate a relationship. Even the time frame is different. For many in the United States, the history of our relationship with Cuba begins on January 1, 1959, when Castro came to power, confiscated property without compensation, and restricted the rights and freedoms of its citizens. For Cubans, the time frame is longer. US actions as far back as the 1840s make up a continuity of history that culminated in 1959 and carries through to the adulation Fidel enjoys on the island even in his death. The US relationship with Cuba, however, has always been more than just bilateral, as both countries speak to the rest of the world and to issues of concern through our diplomatic, security, commercial, and people-to-people interactions. At the same time, the relationship barely ventures into foreign affairs, dominated by and directed at domestic politics in both countries.

President Colom's apology for the role of his country in the Bay of Pigs caught me by surprise, even though the failed invasion figures prominently in any assessment of the presidency of John Kennedy, or any cursory review of the highlights of US-Cuban relations, especially since 1959 when Castro came to power. What Colom, and undoubtedly many in Guatemala, remember was the use of his nation as a US training ground for Cuban exiles preparing the Bay of Pigs operation. I was unaware of that history.

The Eisenhower administration developed the plan to use Guatemala as a site to train the exiles preparing the invasion of Cuba. The US president approved the arming and training of Cuban exiles as early as March 1960, barely a year into Castro's rule. Vice President Richard Nixon had urged that course of action for almost a year, since the time he had met Castro in Washington in the spring of 1959. Events in Cuba had moved fast. Since that visit, confiscations of property under Fidel's agrarian reforms (including US-owned land and businesses) and jailing of thousands of people surpassed equivalent numbers under his predecessor. Internationally, his search for arms and trading partners led him closer to an embrace of the Soviet Union. By May 1960, the first Cuban exiles arrived for training at a CIA camp at a coffee ranch near the city of Retalhuleu in Guatemala, with a second group headed to a US military base in Panama. At this time, no specific plan was operative, but Richard Bissell, the director of plans at the CIA and a future director of the agency, started laying the groundwork for an invasion.

The selection of Richard Bissell to oversee the elaboration of a plan added one more link to the connection with Guatemala, which may have prompted President Colom's 2009 apology. As an assistant to CIA director Allen Dulles in 1954, Bissell had a front-row seat on the successful effort to overthrow the democratically elected president of Guatemala, Jacobo Árbenz, in 1954. In Bissell's memoir, published posthumously, he noted that the Guatemala experience weighed heavily on the planning for a Cuban invasion. In Guatemala, following an agrarian-reform law that enabled the government to seize more than two hundred thousand acres of land from the United Fruit Company, Dulles prepared an operation to sow chaos and confusion throughout the country by simulating a broad uprising against Árbenz through fake radio broadcasts of civil unrest, distribution of leaflets, and even pastoral letters read from the pulpits of Catholic churches. A few days of well-placed loud bombing attacks ensued. All this ostensibly was directed by an exile force under the command of Colonel Carlos Castillo Armas, whose presence in neighboring El Salvador caused panic among the population and the government, leading to Árbenz's decision to resign. Castillo Armas replaced him after several days of behind-the-scenes maneuvers.

Planning for the overthrow of Castro, Bissell sought to replicate the success in Guatemala, especially since some of the same people were involved in the earlier overthrow. Bissell recruited these individuals to work on Cuba, including Howard Hunt, later connected with Watergate. The plans for removing Castro included preparing an invasion force of exiles, followed by bombing attacks to sow chaos, the distribution of pamphlets, and broadcasts leading to widespread panic and instability on the island, forcing Castro to resign—all from the same playbook as Guatemala six years earlier. In identifying a site to train the Cuban exiles, CIA planners must have found it only natural to select the country where they had overthrown a leader who had started down the path that Castro seemed to be following.

Guatemala, though, also weighed heavily on Castro's mind from his first days in power. In early speeches following their ascent to power, Castro, his brother Raúl, and Che Guevara invoked the 1954 coup in pronouncing, "Cuba is not Guatemala."[5] Cuba, they insisted, would not fall prey to US subterfuge as Guatemala had.

Even though the US public acknowledgement of its role in the 1954 Guatemalan overthrow did not take place until 1997 with the release of declassified CIA documents, it was common knowledge throughout the hemisphere. In the same year as the 1954 coup, Mexican painter and muralist Diego Rivera created a mural, which he called "Glorious Victory," citing the statement from Secretary of State John Foster Dulles when he called the ousting of Jacobo Árbenz, an elected president, "a glorious day for democracy." Rivera's large mural featured Dulles with one hand on a bomb painted with President Eisenhower's face and the other shaking hands with Castillo Armas. Behind them, Rivera portrayed the US ambassador, John E. Peurifoy, handing out money to Guatemalan soldiers.[6]

In exile in Mexico after the coup, Castro met with several eye-witnesses to these events, including a young Argentine doctor, Che Guevara, who had traveled to Guatemala seeking to volunteer, when he was caught up in the events as an active participant in the effort to forestall the coup. He fled to Mexico after taking refuge in the Argentine Embassy, carrying with him a rekindled revulsion toward anything connected with the United States. A year later, Guevara met Castro, who had ventured to Mexico City following an early release from a twenty-year sentence for his role in leading an attack on the Moncada military barracks in 1953. Long conversations punctuated their first meetings, with one of the topics including Guevara's recounting of what transpired to bring an end to the Árbenz presidency. The lessons from 1954 permeated Castro's new political organization, the July 26 movement, in its efforts to overthrow the dictatorship of Fulgencio Batista in Cuba.

The establishment of a training camp for Cuban exiles in Guatemala in 1960 was hardly a secret, as newspaper articles appeared in several media outlets, and even a map of the base appeared in the *New York Times*, days before John Kennedy's inauguration. Castro was also aware, when he referred days before the invasion to the CIA "preparing on the soil of Guatemala and the soil of other countries ruled by puppets of imperialism, military bases and armies of mercenaries to attack our country."[7]

The outcome of the ill-conceived invasion at the Bay of Pigs proved Castro right that Cuba would not be Guatemala, due in large part to the good fortune of geography. Americans could not attack Cuba as easily as Guatemala because it was surrounded by water, in contrast to Guatemala, where Castillo Armas and his military coup associates were stationed just on the other side of the border in Honduras. Two other reasons, according to historian Hugh Thomas, had to do with Castro, though. First was Castro's firmer "hold over people" after a year and a half of promises of land, education, and health to the populace and large, staged rallies featuring Castro's speeches, which, while long-winded, nevertheless stirred his audiences.

Second was Castro's successful endeavor to dissolve the army that had served under Batista and replace it with a loyal following of officers who had joined in his rebellion.[8] Anti-Castro participants in the invasion (both on the island and in Washington) placed less emphasis on Castro's appeal and actions and blamed President Kennedy's decision not to send in US military planes to support the rebels once Cuban troops had surrounded them.[9] Those US bombers had been instrumental in sowing the impression of widespread rebellion during the Guatemala coup in 1954.

Kennedy's inner circle also had Guatemala on its mind. In a memo that Kennedy advisor Arthur Schlesinger prepared a week before the invasion, he stated plainly, "We simply will not be able to afford another Castillo Armas."[10] Such a statement was prescient in all but one aspect: the thrust of the nine-page memo centered on the post-invasion effects on the image of the United States and Kennedy in his first foray in the international arena. He foretold world opinion rising against the United States, with local nationalists "identify[ing] Castro's struggles with their own cause" and countries using the platform of "the United Nations to defend their future freedom of action by defending Castro." The one glaring omission from Schlesinger's memo was any reference to the consequences if the invasion failed, other than finding someone else to blame besides Kennedy "if things go terribly wrong." The predictions of world reaction damaging the reputation of the United States and Kennedy still proved correct, as Kennedy and Adlai Stevenson at the UN, among others, had repeatedly assured the world that the United States was not involved in the invasion. By not anticipating failure, though, Schlesinger was unable to appreciate how Castro would use his success in repelling the invasion to solidify his standing within Cuba as well.

Schlesinger peppered his memo with references to US-Cuban history and analogies from other historical events such as the Boer War and the Lincoln Brigade in the Spanish Civil War. He had come to the Kennedy White House from his post as professor of history at Harvard. He had also experienced the world of intelligence during his World War II service in the Office of Strategic Services, the precursor of the CIA. Citing the lack of a "grave and compelling" threat to the United States, Schlesinger predicted in his pre–Bay of Pigs memo that "for many people the easiest explanation of our action will be a reversion to economic imperialism of the pre–World War I, Platt-Amendment, big-stick, gunboat-diplomacy kind."[11]

Schlesinger's application of these historical analogies may have just as easily come from just one source, Castro himself. In a speech from Santiago, Cuba, shortly after the dictator Batista was ousted, Castro energized the gathered crowd by drawing a line directly to himself from the previous uprisings in Cuban history. "The dead of the three wars of Independence," he cried out, correctly presuming his audience would recognize the three nineteenth-century efforts to overthrow Spanish rule, "will now mingle in their dust with those of 1956–9." In Castro's narrative, the final uprising that started in 1895 culminated when "the Americans intervened at the last minute and prevented Calixto Garcia [one of the Cuban rebel leaders] from being present at the fall of Santiago."[12]

This last war for independence that Castro referred to in his speech is another of the forgotten wars in US history. Most Americans have only a shorthand paragraph version of the war we call the Spanish-American War. Cubans know it as "the War for Independence." Often, the version taught in US schools is not one that generates national pride beyond the sinking of the USS *Maine* and Teddy Roosevelt's Rough Riders. Emphasis falls on the role of the Hearst and Pulitzer newspapers in drumming up support for intervention in Cuba. It was William Randolph Hearst who famously responded to his illustrator, Frederic Remington, who was seeking permission to return from Cuba since there was no conflict: "Please remain. You furnish the pictures, and I'll furnish the war."[13] The US focus of this war was on ending Spanish rule in Cuba, Puerto Rico, Guam, and the Philippines. US actions toward the newly independent peoples following the end of hostilities with Spain lie outside the conventional narrative, omitting in the case of the Philippines reports of atrocities or the fact that the signatories to the Treaty of Paris excluded representatives from the former colonies.

In the case of Cuba, there is scant reference to the Cuban independence fighters that Castro referred to, or to the imposition of the Platt Amendment in 1903 that restricted Cuban independence. Drafted at the State Department after the peace treaty, but named after Orville Platt, the sponsor in the Senate, the amendment abrogated the spirit of the initial war authorization, which included a provision intended to prevent the US annexation of Cuba. Senator Henry Teller had drafted an amendment to the initial 1898 authorization of military force against Spain that stated the United States "disclaims its intention to exercise sovereignty, jurisdiction, or control over said island except for pacification thereof, and asserts its determination, when that is accomplished, to leave the government and control of the island to its people." Once the Spanish left Cuba, the responsibility to rule the island fell to the US military forces, until, as President McKinley noted "there is complete tranquility in the island and a stable government inaugurated."[14] Five years later, the Platt Amendment landed in Cuba amid their constitutional convention. While quoting the Teller language that promised to leave "the government and control of the island to its people," the new amendment stipulated that the new Cuban constitution should "define the future relations of the United States" by agreeing to the seven Platt clauses, which shocked Cubans eager to assert their newly independent status.

Not only did Platt's language demand the right of the United States to intervene to protect life, liberty, and property, but it also carved out territory for an indefinite lease of coaling stations and a naval base at Guantanamo Bay. After initially rejecting these clauses and proposing a compromise solution, the Cuban constitutional convention approved the Platt clauses by one vote. A threat that the US military would not leave until their acceptance helped reverse the initial rejection.

The provisions of the Platt Amendment stood until 1934, when President Franklin Roosevelt signed a new Treaty of Relations with Cuba that removed the abhorred clauses of the right of intervention but left in place the arrangement to continue the lease of Guantanamo Bay as a US naval base. In Cuba and throughout the hemisphere, particularly in leftist circles, the name "Platt," though, became a one-word synonym for US intervention and influence at the expense of sovereign nations. It was this connotation that Arthur Schlesinger invoked when he used the term in his memo to President Kennedy before the Bay of Pigs invasion.

Fidel Castro also used "Platt" as shorthand to rally his popular base in the early days of 1959. In a speech before electrical workers two weeks after overthrowing Batista, Castro knew his audience remembered: "This is no longer 1901 or 1933, when they interfered here and imposed upon us an amendment which was a shame and a humiliation for the country. In 1933 they bought Batista, and he miserably betrayed the people. Now that there is no Platt Amendment nor is there anyone to buy or to bribe."[15] In this way, Castro even linked the abrogation of the Platt Amendment in the 1930s with a renewed interventionism through the corruption of Batista, the man Castro had just overthrown.

The fallout from the Bay of Pigs, both domestically and internationally, endured, leading directly to 2009 and the dilemma of how the United States should react to the prospects of Fidel's death. Many competing and contradictory elements drove our deliberations on a strategy. We could not overlook the hostile relationship with Fidel throughout fifty years, highlighted by the Cuban Missile Crisis, the use of Cuban troops in the Cold War proxy wars in Africa, his blatant efforts to export revolution across Latin America, or his human rights violations at home. At the same time, our public reaction to Fidel's death would reach world audiences that admired Fidel precisely because he stood up to the United States at the Bay of Pigs and elsewhere. This meant that using the occasion to blast him would be easily dismissed as standard American obsession over Castro.

Since Fidel had engineered his transition, the chances that his death would lead automatically to an uprising and installation of democracy were, by any realistic appraisal, remote. The occasion could, though, bring about an opportunity to speak directly to the Cuban people with sympathy and a pledge for a new relationship with the United States. Such a strategy would surprise the rest of the world, mostly by releasing pressure on diplomatic engagements with countries around the world. Other countries were simply tired of hearing from the United States about Cuba. Whether it was through the annual flurry of demarches to foreign capitals for votes against Cuba at the UN and other multilateral bodies or precious time that the United States used in insisting on raising Cuban issues in high-level meetings, for the rest of the world, the Cuba-US relationship was a distraction from the issues that mattered to them.

Our proposed strategy included, therefore, a statement addressed to the Cuban people expressing concern for their lot and a desire to reengage as two peoples. We came up with a list of actions that could start the process, from lifting travel bans to launching exchange activities on a people-to-people basis. Possibilities of lifting the embargo and normalizing relations were cast only in the long term. The response we received from leadership in the bureau to this paper ranged from an encouraging "no" to a flip dismissal. We came away with the understanding that the timing was wrong. These were early days in a new administration—too early—for such an abrupt, major turnabout in our relationship with Cuba. Such a focus on Cuba might derail other priorities for the administration.

One of the many longstanding irritants in the relationship at the time was the broadcasts run by the US government and directed at audiences in Cuba. As the executive order signed by President Reagan in 1981 stipulated, the broadcasts were intended to "promote open communication of information and ideas to Cuba and in particular broadcasting to the Cuban people of accurate information about Cuba."[16] The actual numbers of listeners and viewers who tuned into these broadcasts and the frequency with which they did so remain a patchwork of estimates by both the station's advocates and its opponents, defeating the purpose of providing accurate information to the people of Cuba. Instead, they forced Castro to divert resources to jamming the signals; anti-Castro exiles saw the broadcasts as political payback, and this secured the stations' survival.

What may have irked Castro most was the choice of the name for the station: Radio and TV Martí, invoking the name of José Martí, the Cuban revolutionary hero and writer of the late 1800s. How

Martí is memorialized embodies much in the US-Cuba relationship, one more example of *history shock*. Martí's complex ideology, as seen through the body of essays, commentary, journalism, and poetry, provides ample testament to competing perspectives. At the same time, Martí unites Castro and his support in Cuba with the hardline Cuban exile opposition in the United States, who both claim Martí as the heroic leader of national independence, against Spanish rule, against American domination, against corrupt dictators. Finally, the lack of awareness of Martí in the United States reinforces the overall lack of awareness of history in the conduct of our relations with other countries.

Killed in battle as a leader of the Cuban independence forces in 1895, José Martí served as an inspiration for Castro from his youth through his almost-fifty-year rule. From the first days of the revolution, Castro repeatedly cited Martí as the ideological inspiration of his movement. From 1953 to 1955, while in prison following his failed attack on military barracks, Castro read deeply of Martí, who came to be "a guiding spirit of his life," according to friends.[17] Attuned to symbols and perhaps strategy, Castro launched his rebellion from the same point, Oriente, where Martí had returned to Cuba in 1895. In Castro's initial speech following Batista's departure from Cuba, he appealed to Cubans using the name they had come to associate with Martí, the Apostle. "As our Apostle [Martí] said, all the glories of the world vanish like a grain of maize; there is no satisfaction and no prize greater than that of fulfilling our duty."[18] And, after putting down the Bay of Pigs invasion, Castro once again threw the cloak of Martí over his leadership. He rallied Cubans to their nation, "where we have won the right to direct our destiny, where we have learned to decide our destiny, a motherland which will be now and forever—as Martí wanted it—for the well-being of everyone and not a motherland for few!"[19]

Ironically, it was Batista, the dictator whom Castro deposed, who helped cement the hero cult of Martí throughout Cuba and eventually beyond its shores into the rest of Latin America. By the time Castro was a young boy, Martí had achieved reverence on the island as the author of its founding document of independence, the *Montecristi Manifesto*, issued two months before his death. Martí's birthday was a holiday on parts of the island as early as 1909, and the first full biography of the nationalist hero was published to coincide with the new fervor demanding the end of US dominance under the Platt Amendment in 1932. The de facto ruler in the ensuing decades, Batista, wrapped himself in the mantle of Martí, overseeing the proliferation of monuments across the island, dissemination of books and articles on Martí's life and writings, and prominent inclusion in Cuban school curricula. In 1953, a year after regaining power through a coup, on the one-hundredth anniversary of Martí's birth, Batista built a monument, with a 60-foot statue of the Cuban revolutionary hero in front of a tower that climbs 360 feet. Castro used this as the backdrop for his many speeches and rallies in the Plaza de la Revolución.

Castro continued the glorification of Martí, establishing the Centro de Estudios Martianos (Center for José Martí Studies) at the University of Havana in 1979. To ensure that the Cuban hero's name would not be sullied or usurped by the broadcasting efforts of the United States, Castro then proceeded to set up more than thirty satellite affiliates around the world, mostly in Latin America. These served as Castro's cultural centers, his public diplomacy effort to disseminate information about Cuba under his rule, as well as to promote the study of Martí and his writing.

Later, in 1999, Castro once again claimed the name of the Cuban independence leader as an anti-American hero when he built the José Martí Anti-Imperialist Platform across the street from the US Interests Section in Havana. Prompted by the high-stakes custody battle over Elián González, the young boy rescued at sea after fleeing Cuba, Castro used the venue to whip up anti-American sentiment and demand the boy's return to his father, who had remained in Cuba.

Two main aspects of Martí's ideology appealed to Castro as a leader of the revolution. First was Martí's commitment to Cuban independence. Martí was a nationalist who was imprisoned, exiled, and died fighting to establish a sovereign Cuban state. Through his speeches and writing, Martí drew on a poet's command of language (both Spanish and English) to stir up sentiment toward nationhood for Cuba, one of Spain's last remaining colonies in the hemisphere. He is Cuba's Thomas Jefferson, the author of the founding documents for the nation, a five-point plan written to unite the opposition; he wrote his "political testament" in the weeks before his death. His quotes have found their way into the national anthem and the national psyche: "My sling is the sling of David's," a cry to arms repeated by Castro in his speeches. The patriotic fervor Martí stoked on the island and in a sizable exile community in the United States in the late 1800s appealed to Castro many years later both personally and tactically, as a way to build his following.

Martí's commentary about the United States, where he lived for fifteen years in exile, also attracted Castro. Here again, Martí employed the indirect language of the poet, referring to his New York years spent "living in the entrails of the beast," but he also adopted the blunt polemics of politics in denouncing "the republic of privilege and the unjust monopoly."[20] Martí was not just fighting for independence from Spain, but he also anticipated the need for independence from the United States. His fear was not unjustified.

Since Thomas Jefferson first contemplated purchasing Cuba in 1805, annexation had been a recurring theme, intriguing Presidents Polk and Pierce, as well as candidates such as Henry Clay and Stephen Douglas, largely because Cuba could be an additional slave state in the contested domestic environment over that issue. In the run-up to the outbreak of rebellion in the 1890s, the cry for annexation once again was raised, prompting Martí to denounce Cubans who advocated for annexation to the United States as ignorant of "giants with seven-league boots."[21]

Annexation was still under consideration in the United States after Martí's death and at the outbreak of the Spanish American War. As we have seen, Senator Henry Teller proposed an amendment to the war resolution that relinquished any claims to exercise control over the island. Martí's prescience in appreciating the influence that the United States would wield over Cuba for the next sixty years became a rallying point for Castro's revolution. The lack of historical awareness of this side of Martí 's views undoubtedly led to the adoption of the Martí name for the radio and television broadcasts. After all, it was Martí who railed against US influence in Cuba, precisely the intention of those broadcasts.

Martí's nationalism and concern over American intentions extended beyond the borders of Cuba, though, further appealing to Castro. Martí drew on his own life experiences and travel in the hemisphere to compose perhaps his most famous essay, "Our America." Its very title suggests an identity distinct from the United States. He tapped into the pride "in our long-suffering American republics" and laid bare the "masquerader" in foreign garb with foreign ideas and forms of government, ignoring the Indian and the Negro (Martí's terms) in their midst. Published in a New York Spanish-language magazine in 1891, the essay carried a Bolivarian call to action in a "time of mobilization, of marching together, and we must go forward in close ranks, like silver in the veins of the Andes."

To redeem the hemisphere, Martí advocated for a form of government that grew out of the history and context unique to Spanish-speaking America, not imported from Europe or the United States. Again, these were themes Castro sought to exploit beyond the borders of Cuba, throughout the hemisphere, as he waged a battle to withstand the power of the United States, surpassing Martí as a hero across the region.

So what did Ronald Reagan see in the same figure that caused him to praise Martí as "a genuine Cuban patriot?" The same man whom Castro revered has his name and face attached to schools, parks, and monuments all over the anti-Castro neighborhoods in Miami. These modern-day exiles and their descendants see in Martí a familiar narrative. They relate to the nineteenth-century exile who lived in the United States while awaiting the moment to return to Cuba and fight for its independence.

These exiles can find plenty in Martí's twenty-six volumes of collected writings to reinforce their rage at the dictatorial turn Castro took with their country. Martí denounced military rule and despots, in Guatemala, Mexico, and Venezuela, where he had lived and visited. He was apprehensive about the intentions of military leaders in the independence movement, concerned that they would sideline their civilian counterparts in any future Cuban government. His letter to Máximo Gómez, who later commanded the military rebellion in the war for independence, spelled out his misgivings: "It is my determination to not contribute one iota, out of blind love for an idea into which I am expending my life, to bring to my land a regime of personal despotism."[22]

Later, in his *Montecristi Manifesto*, written on the eve of his return to Cuba and his death, Martí laid out the cause for "political independence [that] would have no right to ask Cubans for their help if it did not bring with it the hope of creating one patria more for freedom of thought, equality of treatment, and peaceful labor."[23] These were the ideals that Castro overlooked in establishing his fiery nationalistic and personal rule. They were also the same ideals that have driven those who left the island to seek to overthrow his regime that has endured even beyond his death.

The decision to name the radio and later the television broadcasts to Cuba after José Martí shows the legacy of the Cuban patriot. Martí cried out in exile against despotism and tyranny in his island home. Decisions to continue these broadcasts flew in the face of the evidence that few, if any people, received the transmissions. While surveys in a tightly controlled Cuba are inherently unreliable, it appears that for the first six years of the radio broadcasts, research (from the station itself) showed a sizable proportion of people on the island had heard Radio Martí broadcasts. Castro refrained from jamming the broadcasts until the introduction of televised transmissions in 1990. From that point, results from informal surveys conducted on arrivals from Cuba to the United States and among visitors to the US Interests Section in Havana showed minimal, almost nonexistent, audiences. With internet technology allowing for more platforms for dissemination of its materials, Radio and TV Martí should have been able to increase their audiences. A 2015 survey conducted following the normalization of relations did show that 20 percent of Cubans had listened to Radio Martí in the previous seven days.[24] Still, the results did not show for how long, or how often.

Audience size and impact—or lack of either—have not mattered in the continued programming of the two broadcasts. Forcing the Castros to jam the signals shifts funding away from other activities they pursue, putting a little pressure on their budgets and their ability to underwrite like-minded activists and movements beyond their borders. Additionally, the Martís have become less a source of information than a bargaining chip in the negotiations with Cuba for changes on the island. Even though then-president Raúl Castro and previously his brother, placed the elimination of the broadcasts on their lists for improved relations, the United States has held off from such a move. Even Obama would go only as far as proposing to transform the station into a private contractor that would still receive US funding.

The main reason why funding for the Martí transmissions continues emphasizes one overarching feature of the relationship between the two countries. So much of our relationship with Cuba has for so long had little to do with Cuba. The broadcasts have, since their inception, served as a political litmus test for the exile community in the United States, heavily concentrated in Florida. Allowing the Cuban American National Foundation, a hardline group of exiles in Miami, to control the station, its programming, and staffing for so many years set the Martís apart from other broadcasts into other restricted-information countries in Europe, Asia, or Africa. The stations even moved out of Washington, DC, to Miami in 1996, to be closer to the exile community.

Keeping the Martís running, out of Miami, has been good for the hotly contested politics of Florida. Cubans have funded political campaigns in Florida, but also in other states, successfully targeting congressional opponents of the Martí broadcasts and supporting other anti-Castro initiatives. This emphasis on the domestic repercussions of US-Cuban relations dates back to the initial interest in annexing or purchasing Cuba, a slave colony. Such an annexation would have balanced out the free and slave states in the United States. The thread leads through the Spanish-American War when the newspaper publishers William Randolph Hearst and Joseph Pulitzer advocated for military intervention to raise their circulations.

Not just the United States has used the bilateral relationship, but Castro, too, has repeatedly used it to strengthen his domestic base, from the earliest days of his regime. His initial speeches declaring independence from the United States helped rally Cubans to his cause, and he continued to use anti-American rhetoric throughout his rule. The failed Bay of Pigs intervention by the United States helped him consolidate his power, and ever since, he turned every anti-Castro initiative or statement emanating from the United States or private exile communities into an opportunity for him to rally support. Whenever we engaged in this manner, whether it was the furor over the raft survivor Elián González or tightening the embargo with the passage of the Helms-Burton Act in 1997, Castro strengthened his grip on power.

Both countries have also used the bilateral relationship to address issues that extend far beyond the two countries. The Cuban Missile Crisis, for example, had less to do with Cuba than with the Cold War. The most consequential event in US-Cuba relations under the Castros was resolved between the Soviet Union and the United States, without involving Fidel Castro, much to his annoyance. In his memo to President Kennedy on the eve of the Bay of Pigs invasion, Arthur Schlesinger also recognized how our actions toward Cuba related to people well beyond its borders when he warned about inflaming anti-Americanism in Europe and possible attacks on American embassies and diplomats in Africa, Asia, and Latin America.

In this way, President Obama's overture to Cuba in 2014 to embark on a return path to normalization of relations also spoke to people around the world, particularly in this hemisphere, where US interests are realistically greater than what we have at stake on the island. One State Department colleague said it felt as if the Berlin Wall had fallen, opening up space in each of our bilateral relations across the region to discuss our primary interests, such as immigration or transnational crime, and not Cuba, which was fundamentally about regime change.

Regardless of how other countries felt about Castro and his human rights record, no one agreed with US efforts to remove Castro from power by either force or economic strangulation. Obama's steps conversely did give us credibility to emphasize human rights in Cuba and perhaps actually gain support for a position that used to be seen as part of an overall plot to bring down the Castro government.

On the island, Obama also was able to seize the initiative from the Castros, who previously always seemed to outmaneuver any attack from the United States to consolidate their power. By stepping away from a foreign policy founded on regime change, Obama took the space to engage Cuba on the broad expanse of the relationship; we will continue the cooperation on migration issues, but also address issues of human rights and economic trade. When Obama visited Cuba in March 2016, he spent two hours with Cuban dissidents. This conversation was unthinkable at the beginning of Obama's administration seven years earlier, when we were preparing a communications strategy in the event of Fidel's death. Given the changes in US policy throughout Obama's tenure, I assume the strategy we drafted was as obsolete as the one we inherited. When Fidel died in 2015, one US ambassador told me that in the Latin American country where he served "it was a non-event." By reaching out to Cuba, Obama had blunted the hero worship of Fidel around the hemisphere as the leader who had stood up to the power of the United States.

On the same visit to Havana in 2016, Obama laid a wreath at the memorial for José Martí on Revolutionary Square. That gesture recognized Martí in his fullness, a revolutionary thinker and actor, as well as a commentator warning about US intentions in the hemisphere. Obama was not usurping one aspect of Martí's thinking about military rule and demagogues in power as the naming of the US broadcasts to the island had intended. He showed Cubans that the United States understood their history and the appeal of Martí to their identity.

One other strain in Martí's political thought was his criticism of the lack of knowledge in the United States about Cuba and the rest of the hemisphere. "The scorn of our formidable neighbor," he wrote in his most famous essay, "who does not know us, is our America's greatest danger. . . . Through ignorance, it might even come to covet us." Here too, Martí was prescient. Nowhere, for example, in Theodore Roosevelt's written record of letters, journals, and commentary does he refer to Cuba's revolutionary leader. Roosevelt and many others in the United States at the time did, as Martí predicted, later covet Cuba.

In writing about the ignorance of the United States toward Cuba and the hemisphere, Martí could as well have been writing in 2017. As much as President Donald Trump would have liked to undo the entire overture to Cuba that Obama made, he only drew back a few aspects related to tourism. Trump fell into the same unfortunate pattern that Obama had tried to break away from—the harsh rhetoric driven by US domestic politics, which once again helped Raúl Castro shore up his support. With Cuba occupying the attention of US foreign policy for just one brief Friday afternoon in June 2017 when Trump announced repressive measures at a campaign-style political rally in Florida, the United States reverted to its century-old scorn for a Cuba that it does not know, just as Martí anticipated.

Suggested Further Reading

In *Fidel Castro: A Biography* (Malden, MA: Polity Press, 2004), Volker Skierka covers Fidel's emergence as a revolutionary leader and his extended rule in Cuba. The classic biography of Castro and Cuba by Hugh Thomas still is relevant: *Cuba, or the Pursuit of Freedom* (London: Eyre & Spottiswoode, 1971). Anthony DePalma takes a different tack in outlining Castro's life, through the eyes of a journalist assigned to Cuba in the 1950s and 60s in *The Man Who Invented Fidel: Castro, Cuba and Herbert L. Matthews of the New York Times* (Cambridge, MA: Public Affairs, 2006). Alfred López traces the travels and writings of José Martí in his biography, *José Martí: A Revolutionary Life* (Austin: University of Texas Press, 2014). Stephen Kinzer recounts the history of American interventions, including Cuba and Guatemala, in *Overthrow: America's Century of Regime Change from Hawaii to Iraq* (New York: Times Books, 2006). Daniel Walsh recounts the history of the Martí broadcasting in *An Air War with Cuba: The United States Radio Campaign against Castro* (Jefferson, NC: McFarland & Company, 2012).

10

Choosing to Remember: Laying a Wreath

We will never know if Secretary Clinton would have laid the wreath at the monument to the Argentine hero José de San Martín. The request never made it past the first level of clearance. It was the brainchild of Peter Samson, a colleague in the Public Diplomacy Office of Western Hemisphere Affairs. As a historian, he grasped the symbolic importance of the simple act of laying a wreath. He proposed the occasion of the bicentennial of the May Revolution that launched that country's war for independence, but the year 2010 coincided with the anniversary of independence movements across Latin America, with other countries celebrating their bicentennials that year: Mexico, Chile, Colombia, as well as Argentina.

The statue of San Martín first came to Washington, DC, in 1924 as a gift from the people of Argentina to the United States, a copy of the monument located in the central plaza of Buenos Aires, depicting San Martín astride his rearing horse, pointing his right hand to the sky. It was moved during the building of the first subway, from its original site in the District of Columbia, near Judiciary Square. The statue was rededicated during the US bicentennial year, and now stands within a block of the State Department.

A request for the secretary's time is never simple. Memos are prepared and cleared across the building and sent up into the rarified stratosphere of department leadership. The secretary may have had plans to be out of the country on or about May 25, the day marking Argentina's bicentennial. Even the thirty minutes to walk out of the building, meet and greet the Argentine ambassador, and say a few remarks is a significant block of time for the secretary who attends to crises around the globe. Security arrangements would make a simple walkabout exceedingly complicated. Besides, the regional bureau probably had ten or more other requests on the secretary's time that didn't just fall to the bottom of the list, but never made it to the list. There are multiple reasons why the wreath laying did not occur, including the friction between the two countries at the time. It seemed, though, that the likely explanation was that my colleagues felt this request did not rise to the level of importance to justify the secretary's time.

San Martín, in the collective Argentine imagination, strikes their national core, their psyche, in deeply rooted ways. His reputation runs high across the entire continent, on a par with Simón Bolívar, the other great liberator who led revolutionary forces down from the north while San Martín moved up from the southern cone of the continent after securing Chilean independence. He met up with Bolívar in Peru to defeat the Spanish royalist forces there. The pride in this son of Argentina's liberating neighboring countries helps frame Argentina's identity as a regional leader.

In the annals of US foreign affairs, not laying this wreath to commemorate Argentina's bicentennial doesn't rise even to the level of a footnote. Other gestures recognizing this milestone did take place, emanating from the US Embassy in Buenos Aires. The request to the secretary was a small bureaucratic incident, forgotten a week later. It is, though, a window on one avenue for confronting history in our relations with foreign nations with whom we seek to build cooperative relationships. The US foreign-policy approach in any nation, even when there are disputes, benefits when the United States acknowledges what is important to its partners. Even if those partners happen to be reluctant and unwilling, such recognition can keep the channels open for the changes that history shows will inevitably come. In this case, we simply chose not to remember.

As a reference point, consider the global commemoration of the US bicentennial in 1976, just two years after the resignation of Richard Nixon and three years after the withdrawal of US forces from

Vietnam, events that tainted perceptions of the United States around the world. In that climate, 102 nations still found a way to mark the two-hundredth anniversary of US independence, according to historian Todd Bennett.[1] Dozens of foreign leaders visited the United States during the bicentennial year and offered gifts, including an original copy of the Magna Carta from the country that we defeated to gain our independence; dozens sent exhibits and artists to participate in the annual Smithsonian Folklife Festival, normally host to one or two foreign partners every year. Japan, which we had engaged as bitter combat enemies just thirty years earlier, built a new theater in the Kennedy Center, while the other axis power held more than four hundred events in West Germany to commemorate the year.

These gestures acknowledged what was important to the United States. They also reinforced our self-image as a nation whose founding and subsequent history made important contributions to the world. But countries extending themselves on the occasion of our bicentennial were not acting solely out of altruistic purposes, but in their self-interest. Their gifts also reflected positively back on their nations, either by recognizing their connections to the United States (Magna Carta), by showcasing some positive aspect of their own cultures (Smithsonian Folklife Festival), or by building an enduring monument to friendship (Japanese theater at the Kennedy Center).

Most often associated with the military, wreath laying is an act of remembrance, a solemn symbol of respect. On various occasions throughout my time in the Foreign Service, I participated in wreath-laying ceremonies. When we mark Veterans Day in the United States, the president lays a wreath at the Tomb of the Unknown Soldier. The Canadians mark November 11 as Remembrance Day, noting the eleventh hour on the eleventh day of the eleventh month as the moment when peace was signed, ending the First World War, during which the Canadians endured more combat deaths than the United States. In the weeks leading up to November 11, Canadians from all walks of life pin red poppies to their lapels as a sign of remembrance. At 11 a.m. on November 11, members of foreign embassies lay wreaths at the National War Memorial in the center of Ottawa, a block from the Parliament buildings. Picture this: in the seriousness of the ceremony, dozens of foreign emissaries stand outside in freezing weather for over an hour, waiting to lay their wreaths at the memorial, shuffling their feet and slapping their hands to try to stay warm. No one would miss it, though, on account of the weather.

Too many times to count, other members of our embassies, particularly from the Defense Attaché Service's offices, regularly participated in wreath-laying ceremonies and other services of remembrance. The left-wing mayor of Mexico City and future president of Mexico, Manuel López Obrador, joined embassy officials to mark the restoration of the statue of Franklin Roosevelt and used the occasion to talk of FDR's inspiration in helping the downtrodden during the Depression. The binational centers across Latin America hosted wreath-laying ceremonies and even parades through the cities marking our July 4 holiday. At Deadman's Island in Nova Scotia, the lieutenant governor general unveiled a plaque commemorating the American soldiers who died in that prison off the coast of Halifax during the War of 1812. The American Battle Monuments Commission, which operates twenty-six military cemeteries in sixteen countries, also oversees the Mexico City National Cemetery, where we would lay wreaths on Memorial Day to commemorate the remains of the 750 unknown US soldiers who died during the Mexican-American War from 1846 to 1848. National holidays, military parades, and gravesite ceremonies all call for remembrance, usually by the simple act of laying a wreath.

Presidential visits to foreign countries often raise the prospect of participating in a remembrance ceremony. In Mexico, the visit of Harry Truman in 1947 included a wreath laying that ended up reshaping the nature of the bilateral relationship, at least in the short term. The first sitting US president to show interest in visiting Mexico, Truman heeded the advice of his Mexican hosts to avoid traveling there in 1948, the one-hundredth anniversary of the end of the war, which saw the loss of almost half Mexico's territory to the United States. Determined to go, though, to press for Mexico's support in launching a new multilateral organization in the hemisphere, Truman advanced the timing for his visit to avoid the association with that conflict. After laying a wreath at the Angel of Independence monument along the central avenue, Truman proceeded to Chapultepec Park to see the monument to the Niños Héroes, six tall columns in a plaza, one for each of the soldiers who threw themselves off the walls of Chapultepec Castle rather than be taken prisoner by invading US forces.

The recommendation to lay a wreath for the Niños Héroes came from Walter Thurston, the US ambassador who had heard from his Mexican counterparts that such a "gesture would obliterate any lingering traces of bitterness over the war."[2] Truman's stop produced the intended effect, at least temporarily. A huge, spontaneous outpouring of emotion sprang from witnesses and spread through the country, reaching the Mexican president, who called Truman the "new champion of hemispheric solidarity."[3] A *New York Times* account of the ceremony reported that "tears of emotion streamed down the faces of the honor guard composed of cadets of the Colegio Militar, now housed in Chapultepec Castle, and as the President drove off, old men wiped their eyes."[4] The wreath laying helped usher in a period of unprecedented cooperation between the two nations, which included Mexico signing the Rio Treaty in September of that year, establishing in the hemisphere the principle of reciprocal assistance when attacked by outside forces. A year later, the Organization of American States was launched with Mexico as one of the founding members. Both these instruments were still functioning more than forty years later when the OAS activated the Rio Treaty of mutual defense in the immediate aftermath of the 9/11 attacks.

Fifty years after Truman's visit, in 1997, when President Bill Clinton paid a state visit to Mexico, he reenacted Truman's gesture. At the request of Mexican president Ernesto Zedillo, Clinton overcame objections from his staff, who were concerned that a stop at the Niños Héroes monument would unnecessarily remind Mexicans of the outcome of the US intervention in 1848. The response in the city to his wreath laying was not as effusive as Truman experienced, but more mixed in emotion. One onlooker quoted in the *New York Times* noted:

"It still hurts. But maybe this is a way to make peace."[5] (Such was the need to make peace 150 years after we forced the original peace treaty on Mexico.) Another journalist overlooked the bailout that Clinton pushed to stabilize Mexico's currency and affirmed that Clinton's visit to Chapultepec Park "did more to restore the confidence and trust of the Mexican people than any agreement between heads of state could have."[6]

The staff's reluctance to have President Clinton pay his respects to the Niños Héroes may also have come from concern over how the people in the United States would view such a gesture. Notably, neither Clinton nor Truman made any remarks at the site. Neither wanted the political blowback from what some might perceive as an apology or a confession of guilt, such as the one given by Nicholas Trist, who negotiated the treaty that ended the war and absorbed half of Mexico's territory: "That was a thing for every right-minded American to be ashamed of."[7]

President Truman did refer to the war in his speech the night of his visit to the war memorial: "Mr. President, you refer to 1847. We did have tragic difficulties then. We had difficulties with our northern neighbor Canada in 1814. We also had a terrible quarrel between our States." After mentioning the two world wars, Truman came close to a statement of regret when he offered that "we have found that the victor loses in total war as well as the vanquished."[8] Truman may have also had on his mind his decision to use the atomic bomb, again coming as close as he ever did to acknowledge the horror of that weapon. More common were his sentiments expressed in a letter to a journalist almost twenty years later: "I have no regrets and, under the same circumstances, I would do it again."[9]

Laying the wreath at the Niños Héroes monument was not an apology, nor a confession of guilt, but for the Mexicans, the act of remembering was in many ways interpreted in just this way. Mexicans did not need, as Clinton's staff worried, a visit to Chapultepec Park to remember the war and the Niños Héroes. That memory is part of the Mexican identity—teachers instruct students from an early age about the loss of the war and territory and the heroism of the six cadets;

they see these stories in their museums and murals; they grow up with them seared into their hearts and minds, helping Mexicans salvage honor in an ignominious defeat. What Truman and Clinton did was acknowledge this pain, pain the United States caused. They chose to remember while many Americans decide to overlook that forgotten war. The two presidents did not need words; the gesture spoke to the Mexicans without the printed quotes that might have cost the US presidents politically at home.

In this way, wreath laying seems to lie on the spectrum of apology, a line that moves from "acknowledging, disavowing, repenting, and [to] offering restitution,"[10] according to the sociologist Erving Goffman. Proceeding further down that spectrum is politically difficult in the United States, and not just in the case of Truman or Clinton in Mexico City. When President Obama became the first sitting president to visit Hiroshima and its Peace Memorial Park, he laid a wreath. The wreath laying occurred after a debate raged in the United States about the prospect of his offering an apology for the horror and destruction the bomb inflicted on the city and innocent lives. Opposition in the United States to any such statement ran deep, recalling Japan's attack on Pearl Harbor that prompted US entry into the war and raising the argument that the use of the bomb avoided a costly land invasion, which would have meant the loss of life for many more US soldiers.

Such debates over the use of the atomic bomb had flared in the past over the Smithsonian Air and Space Museum's canceled exhibit on the *Enola Gay*, the plane that carried the bomb, because the interpretation focused heavily on the destruction caused. The Japanese also engaged in a similar hand-wringing debate over Hiroshima and their role in the war. In 1995, they added a new wing on the Peace Memorial Museum—forty years after it first opened. The wing included an exhibit focusing for the first time on Japan's role in the war, noting Hiroshima as a military center and host to factories producing military armaments, recalling the Nanjing Massacre in China, and admitting that they employed Chinese and Koreans as slave labor in their factories and that they were among those killed in the bombing.

In Hiroshima, Obama opted for wreath laying, with both leaders characterizing the visit as an opportunity to "heal the wounds of the past."[11] His remarks focused on the need for healing, but also on the future, as he reiterated his calls early in his presidency to move toward a nuclear-free world. When Japanese prime minister Shinzo Abe returned Obama's gesture seven months later with a visit to Pearl Harbor, he, too, sidestepped the politically wrought issue of apology, and instead offered condolences to the families of those who lost their lives at Pearl Harbor. After referring to Pearl Harbor as a symbol of reconciliation, Abe joined Obama in laying a wreath at the USS *Arizona* Memorial.

While the notion of moving further down the apology scale than simply laying a wreath at Hiroshima arouses sincere and heated arguments on both sides, the broader issue of apologizing in our foreign relations has become anathema in the political sphere. George H. W. Bush repeatedly drew on the "no apology" theme during his run for the presidency, stating in the early primaries that he "would never apologize for the United States of America. I will stand up for her."[12] Later, after winning the nomination, he even included a follow-on talking point: "I don't care what the facts are."[13] The facts Vice President Bush likely had on his mind were those he had played down in his defense a few weeks earlier before the UN following the shooting down of Iran Air Flight 655 over the Persian Gulf, which killed 290 civilians. On the day of the tragedy, President Reagan had issued a statement expressing sadness and regret over the loss of life, with an account of the events causing the USS *Vincennes* to mistake the airliner as the US ship was, at the time, under attack from five Iranian boats. In his defense at the UN, Bush again referred to an ongoing attack and accused the Iranians of allowing "a civilian aircraft loaded with passengers to proceed on a path over a warship engaged in battle."[14] The UN Security Council did pass a resolution that expressed distress over the shooting down of the airline and the need for a resolution to the conflict between Iraq and Iran, but did not condemn the United States for its actions. There was still no formal apology eighteen years later when President Clinton, while he expressed regret, also agreed to compensate Iran and the families of the victims by paying $131.8 million to settle a suit that Iran had brought before the International Court of Justice.

In Durban, my station, five thousand miles away, the news of the downed airliner ran across the front pages of the newspapers the following day, July 4. My colleagues and I were in the last throes of preparations for the midday reception to be held at the consulate. We spent time discussing whether to call off the reception completely, but decided to go ahead with a subdued event, with no formal remarks. The acting consul general, Terry McCulley, offered a toast, using standard language remarking on the freedoms won by our independence, an indirect reminder referring to the lack of freedom for so many South Africans. The day after the United States shot down a civilian airliner was hardly the time to give any lesson to anyone. The event passed quietly, until the next day when I opened up the local newspaper and saw a picture of Terry McCulley and myself raising our champagne glasses. What caught my eye was that the picture ran below a story about the downing of the Iranian plane. Another photo accompanied that story, this one of a civilian airliner, with a missile drawn in, aiming directly toward the plane. Underneath was our picture, two Americans toasting, and making it look like we were raising our glasses to the downed airliner. When I called the newspaper editor, a friend, to protest, he laughed and claimed innocence, stating that the two halves of that page were put together by different layout staff. Nothing he said could shake me from my view that they had acted mischievously at best, but more likely mixed with a gleeful vengeance.

Mitt Romney carried the theme of never apologizing forward in his 2012 run for the presidency. His campaign biography published two years earlier carried the title *No Apology*, in which he laid out the case for never having to say you're sorry for stating "the United States is the greatest nation on earth and the hope of the world."[15] His favorite talking point on foreign affairs during the campaign ran along the lines that he, unlike President Obama, would "never apologize for the greatest nation in the history of the Earth." Indeed, Karl Rove and other Republicans grabbed on to the characterization of Obama's travel to Europe as "an apology tour," a slogan that lingered well past the time when experts debunked the concept as false.[16]

Romney's pledge never to apologize turned the brutal attacks in Benghazi, Libya, that killed Ambassador Chris Stevens and three other Americans into a crass tool for political advantage in the 2012 presidential campaign that carried to the next presidential campaign. As details were beginning to emerge in the hours following the attack, candidate Mitt Romney held a press conference to criticize President Obama for failing to condemn the attacks and accusing him of choosing "to sympathize with those who waged the attacks." The following day, Romney stood by his earlier comments, calling the Obama response "akin to apology."

In their rush to take political advantage, Romney and his staff erred in stating the basic facts and timeline of what transpired. Romney confused the response to protests at the US Embassy in Cairo with the attack in Benghazi. Those protests, against the imprisonment of Sheikh Omar Abdel-Rahman in the United States for his role in the 1993 attack on the World Trade Center in New York, became inflamed by the diffusion of an anti-Islamic YouTube video. The video was produced and directed in Los Angeles by Nakoula Basseley Nakoula, a Coptic Christian, who immigrated to the United States from Egypt. It portrayed the prophet Mohammed in grossly disparaging and offensive terms. About two thousand protesters were planning to converge on the embassy. To defuse a potential volatile situation, Larry Schwartz, a colleague on short-term duty in Cairo, drafted for release the following statement, cleared and distributed by the embassy to all major media in Cairo ahead of the protest:

The Embassy of the United States in Cairo condemns the continuing efforts by misguided individuals to hurt the religious feelings of Muslims—as we condemn efforts to offend believers of all religions. Today, the 11th anniversary of the September 11, 2001, terrorist attacks on the United States, Americans are honoring our patriots and those who serve our nation as the fitting response to the enemies of democracy. Respect for religious beliefs is a cornerstone of American democracy.

We firmly reject the actions by those who abuse the universal right of free speech to hurt the religious beliefs of others.[17]

The protesters managed to breach the walls and tore down the US flag. While authorities in Egypt eventually dispersed the rioters, hours later another attack erupted in Benghazi, which led to the deaths of the US diplomats. Without knowing all the facts, but determined to score some political advantage, candidate Romney conflated the two attacks. In his statement after we learned that US diplomats were killed in Libya, Romney cited the press statement in Cairo as evidence that the Obama administration apologized to those who killed the US diplomats in Libya. Had he paused, he and his staff would have seen that the statement in Cairo was released before the attack in Benghazi, and had nothing to do with Benghazi. Still, Romney stood his ground, shifting the apology insinuation to an accusation that Obama took twelve days before he called the Benghazi attacks an act of terror. That, too, was false, as Obama later stressed in a debate with Romney, citing transcripts from a Rose Garden ceremony where he used that characterization the day after the killings in Benghazi.[18]

The Embassy's Cairo statement did not explicitly issue an apology for the video, but by condemning the movie's offensive message, it did employ one of the four behaviors cited by sociologist Erving Goffman as components of an apology.[19] For my focus in this book on historical incidents, this example dealt with a contemporary event, rather than one in the past, with a notable exception. Undoubtedly, those officers in the US Embassy in Cairo, looking at crowds of rioters breaking into the compound, had in the back of their minds another similar breach of embassy security that had occurred thirty years earlier in Iran. My colleagues in Egypt were willing to pursue a course of action that may have looked from afar like an apology to prevent a recurrence of a similar hostage ordeal.

Aversion to an apology is not a recent predilection. In the early 1900s, relations with Latin America became strained following the machinations of Theodore Roosevelt to support Panamanian independence from Colombia with the intervention of the US military.

Singularly focused on building a canal across Central America, Roosevelt failed to secure Colombian approval for siting the canal in their territory of Panama. He encouraged Panamanian rebels to proclaim independence and sent the US Marines to take over the railways and the US Navy to patrol the waters to prevent Colombia from reasserting its authority over their territory. When Roosevelt's successor, Woodrow Wilson, sought to repair relations in the hemisphere, he opened negotiations with Colombia to redress the loss of Panama. The proposed treaty included language expressing "sincere regret that anything should have occurred to interrupt or to mar the relations of cordial friendship that had so long subsisted between the two nations."[20]

Senate ratification of this treaty in 1914 quickly devolved into a debate over whether the phrase amounted to an apology or a "simple expression of regret."[21] The inclusion of the language in the treaty did not admit wrongdoing, one notable feature of apology, but many who supported Roosevelt labeled the phrase "an apology." One senator, George Perkins from California, a Roosevelt supporter, went so far in his rejection of the language in the treaty that he claimed "Colombia should apologize to the United States."[22] Wilson was unable to convince the Senate to ratify the agreement, and it took another eight years before the Harding administration was able to secure treaty approval, but only without the phrase expressing regret.[23]

Because of the political risks involved, leaders both in the United States and abroad steer clear of issuing an apology for past behavior in foreign relations. In her book *Sorry States*, historian Jennifer Lind examines the German and Japanese experiences in apologizing for their roles leading up to and during World War II. Lind chronicles periods since the war of denials alternating with genuine acts of contrition and makes a case for an apology. She cites examples when "denials of past aggression and atrocities fuel distrust and elevate threat perception" while "a country's acknowledgment of its past atrocities is important to move relations forward with its former adversaries."[24] At the same time, she recognizes the risks since the common domestic responses from such behavior "typically prompt a backlash from conservatives."[25]

Such backlashes, as portrayed in other countries, can negate the intended effect of moving relations beyond the record of hostilities.

In spite of this political liability, the historical record does include examples when the United States did offer apologies for its past behaviors. In some cases, the United States even went so far as offering redress for its transgressions. Perhaps the most prominent is the apology, financial compensation, and establishment of a national park in memory of the internment of more than one hundred thousand Japanese Americans during World War II. While this action lies outside the realm of foreign relations as most of those affected were US citizens at the time, the internment took place against the backdrop of the war against Japan.

In another case that also has domestic overtones, the US Congress in 1993 passed a resolution apologizing "to Native Hawaiians on behalf of the people of the United States for the overthrow of the Hawaiian Kingdom on January 17, 1893" and for the "deprivation of the rights of Native Hawaiians to self-determination."[26] Similarly, the California legislature in 2009 adopted a resolution apologizing for the mistreatment of Chinese immigrants in the extended period from the 1880s to 1930s. Again, though, this was a domestic political act, directed principally at California's large population of Asian descent, but it had international repercussions and was followed closely in China.

Another case involved the role of the United States in the civil war during the 1980s in El Salvador, and centered around an act of omission, rather than commission. The agreement in 1992 to end the civil war in El Salvador included the establishment of a Truth Commission to investigate "serious acts of violence," and its report a year later cited the massacre at El Mozote "as an illustrative case."[27] The report included forensic archaeological results that confirmed a massacre of more than two hundred men, women, and children in 1981.[28]

At the time, at the height of US involvement in the Central American civil wars, both the US Embassy and the State Department repeatedly refused to give credence to stories of a massacre. Following the release of the 1992 report, then secretary of state Warren Christopher convened a panel to "examine the actions and the conduct of the Department" in its claims of no evidence, despite photographs and articles by two US reporters who visited the scene. Christopher's panel acknowledged errors in the initial conclusions reached in both San Salvador and Washington and in the politically motivated failure to follow up in investigating the massacre. These failures "undermined the Department's credibility with its critics—and probably with the Salvadorans—in a serious way that has not healed."[29] Christopher's acknowledgement of errors carried less political liability since he served in a different administration under a competing political party that had used as much of its legislative power as possible in the 1980s to try to reverse the policies of Ronald Reagan and George H. W. Bush in Central America.

As if to confirm Jennifer Lind's thesis, the record of US foreign affairs also offers up well-known cases when refusal to acknowledge our past actions has lingered in the collective consciousness of other nations and led to disastrous results. The depth of resentment against the United States when Iranians seized the US Embassy and held our diplomats hostage came as a surprise to many Americans, who were unaware of the role of the United States in overthrowing Prime Minister Mohammad Mosaddegh and restoring the shah to power in 1953. Likewise, the "Why do they hate us?" period of self-reflection following the World Trade Center attacks was not centered on the irrational, horrific acts of nineteen terrorists, but more on confusion over reactions from around the world that the attack was a logical consequence of US foreign policies over many years. Stationed in Mexico at the time, I recall opening up the left-of-center newspaper *La Jornada* shortly after the New York attacks and seeing an entire page listing, in small type, dozens of American interventions and policies that harmed other countries, with the implicit conclusion that the September 11 attacks grew out of objectionable American behavior around the world.

One of those events listed on that page had also taken place on September 11 but in 1973. That was the coup against Salvador Allende in Chile, and recently declassified documents show US support for this as well as prior covert actions to destabilize the Allende regime after Allende was elected democratically in 1970.

In Mexico, even though he had just returned from a state visit to Washington, President Vicente Fox took weeks to decide whether to offer assistance to the United States following 9/11, as he took the measure of his domestic voters, who wanted the country to stay neutral in the buildup to any conflict that the United States might launch. Mexico's reaction then, as well as its reluctance to use its vote on the UN Security Council to support the invasion of Iraq, had much to do with its long-standing support for the principle of nonintervention in other states. No amount of wreath laying could overcome those sentiments developed as a result of its painful experience of bearing the brunt of interventions by the United States.

One Mexican senior foreign ministry official took me aside at a service to honor the victims of the March 11, 2004, Madrid train bombings to confide that it was "too bad that we couldn't do this after September 11. We just couldn't, and, besides Spain is our mother country." It fell to a small group of Mexican women who had relatives in New York and had visited fire stations in the city to seek to make amends for the official and tepid unofficial response. They placed a traditional Day of the Dead altar outside the embassy six weeks later honoring the victims and police and firefighters who had given their lives in the attacks.

The Canadian reaction to the 9/11 attacks, in contrast, was both tangible and symbolic. Residents took in passengers from planes grounded in Nova Scotia and Newfoundland while the passengers waited for the international air lanes to open up again. They took in strangers from around the world and offered them more than just beds and home-cooked meals; they showed humanity and compassion in the face of an outrageous, stunning act of evil. A few years later, when I was working at the embassy in Canada, I saw enlarged photos in a display in the US Embassy multipurpose room of the dozens of planes lined up on the runways in Halifax and Goose Bay. In stark contrast to the absence of any such reaction in Mexico, I also saw photos of crowds outside the embassy, lighting candles on the sidewalk. They pushed notes and cards through the iron fence, laying bouquets and wreaths against the fence, and then, several days later, gathered in the tens of thousands on Parliament Hill for a service of remembrance at which US ambassador Paul Cellucci spoke. He later called that the most important moment of his career in public service.

No one in Canada who responded in this way had any expectation of receiving gratitude. The Canadians' actions were a generous, genuine outpouring of solidarity. Still, the omission of Canada from a list of partner countries that George Bush cited during his speech to Congress nine days later hurt, and lingered.

It was an omission that needed rectifying, in the most public way. When President Bush visited Canada, shortly after his reelection, Ambassador Cellucci lobbied for him to go to Halifax, Nova Scotia, as well as Ottawa, to make amends. Deeply unpopular in Canada for more than just the 9/11 slight, Bush started his only public speech on the trip stating what no one said four years earlier:

> Three years ago, Halifax and other towns and villages—from Newfoundland to Manitoba to the Northwest Territories to British Columbia—welcomed, *as the Prime Minister mentioned* [my italics], more than 33,000 passengers on diverted flights. For days after September the 11th, Canadians came to the aid of men and women and children who were worried and confused and had nowhere to sleep. You opened your homes and your churches to strangers. You brought food; you set up clinics; you arranged for calls to their loved ones, and you asked for nothing in return.
>
> One American declared, "My heart is overwhelmed at the outpouring of Canadian compassion. How does a person say 'thank you' to a nation?" Well, that's something a President can do. And so let me say directly to the Canadian people, and to all of you here today who welcomed Americans, thank you for your kindness to America in an hour of need.[30]

Shortly after his arrival in country, our next ambassador to Canada, David Wilkins, also heard of the failure to mention Canada in the congressional speech after 9/11. He used the spontaneous assistance from ordinary Canadians following the devastation of Hurricane Katrina as his opening to make sure such gestures do not go unacknowledged. Wilkins sent an "open letter to Canadians" to every news outlet in the country, thanking them for their tangible support to New Orleans. Newspaper readers across the country saw, many placed on the front pages of their paper, a heartfelt message: "Four years after the devastating terror attacks of September 11, 2001, my country finds itself once again hurting deeply. And today—just as it did four years ago—Canada has come to our aid early and eagerly. On behalf of my grateful country: Thank you Canada for once again being there when we need you the most."[31]

Wilkins's letter came at a moment of American vulnerability, even embarrassment, that we could not provide aid to our citizens. When the devastation of Katrina became apparent, and when countries and private citizens began to send and deliver support, the State Department was unprepared to be on the receiving end of emergency aid. After a few days, the department had set up a task force and procedures for the offers.

In the embassy in Canada, we dedicated one officer to track the calls and letters as well as reports promising and delivering assistance. With the 9/11 omission on his mind, Ambassador Wilkins was prompt with his letter of gratitude, and by tying this spontaneous Canadian reaction to the earlier one following the World Trade Center attacks, Wilkins helped to heal the open wound. A few days later on the fourth anniversary of 9/11, Ambassador Wilkins unveiled a bronze plaque on the side of the embassy whose text—in English and French—made permanent US gratitude for the support of Canada.[32] Finally, on the fifth anniversary of the attacks, the embassy persuaded Secretary of State Condoleezza Rice to come to Nova Scotia, where she reiterated the appreciation for all that Canada did on that terrible day.

No one formally apologized for the omission of Canada in the list of countries that President Bush cited in his speech to Congress. The efforts to make amends for the slight through a simple letter and a handful of gestures were acts of remembrance, and bordered on apology, at least implicitly. As public diplomacy, Wilkins's letter was instrumental in ingratiating him with a Canadian public predisposed to oppose him because he served under an unpopular president. That letter set him down a path of popularity in Canada that later allowed him to secure cooperation for an agenda on trade and security issues, notably resolution of the perennial softwood lumber dispute and participation of Canadian troops in Afghanistan.

In the course of my career, I did apologize for my nation. One occasion that stands out took place during the US-led NATO bombing campaign in the former Yugoslavia in 1999. As public affairs officer, I accepted every request for appearances in the media and public gatherings to explain the justification behind the interventions as a means of preventing Slobodan Milošević from committing further acts of genocide in Kosovo. I knew that one event would have me share a podium with the Chinese ambassador to Peru. The night before the conference, the United States had mistakenly bombed the Chinese Embassy in Belgrade, killing three Chinese citizens. That number could have been higher, but the raid took place at night and China had begun a drawdown of its official personnel in Belgrade. I went ahead with the speech, opting to start my remarks with an apology for the tragic error. The uncertainty of a potential encounter with the Chinese ambassador was resolved when he departed before my arrival, refusing to be seen with an American diplomat.

My discomfort on another continent paled against what my colleagues in Beijing and other consulates in China were living with—including violent protests taking place outside the buildings for days. Still, the issue of US behavior—far from Peru both in terms of geography and national interests—affected our foreign relations on another continent, as Peruvians and many others in Latin America looked at the bombing as another intervention in a long series of military actions dating back a century. One front-page headline, in one of Lima's most responsible papers, asked if Peru were the next country on the list for a bombing. Such a reaction in Peru seemed preposterous at the time. From the Peruvian recollection of a history that saw multiple US interventions in this hemisphere, the headline confirms Jennifer Lind's conclusions—as previously noted—that failure to acknowledge "past aggression and atrocities [can] fuel distrust and elevate threat perception."[33]

While they are symbolic acts, apologies nevertheless do carry power, from defusing potentially violent situations to allowing former adversaries to advance to a state of improved relations. What they have in common with a gesture as simple as a wreath laying is in the act of remembering.

Given the political climate in the United States in the early part of this century, I am realistic enough to acknowledge the unlikelihood of incorporating apology into our relations with foreign countries, from Mexico to Egypt, let alone places such as Cuba, Iran, and North Korea. Donald Trump, with his knee-jerk opposition to diplomacy, would subscribe to the viewpoint that apology is a sign of weakness and political correctness. Trump's version of the historical facts falls short not only in his distorted view of "facts," but also in his sense of history, which seems to be all personal: it started when he became president and includes only that which is in his own experience. Still, I suspect that we as a country, as well as my colleagues representing the United States overseas, are already discovering the value of apology and remembrance, starting with Trump's derogatory statements about other religions and nationalities.

Recognizing our accountability for past actions can offer the opportunity to look forward in our relations with other countries. As Weyeneth concludes in assessing the power of remembering, "It is the conversation about history that is important, rather than judgments about crimes and culpability."[34] The question remains, though, why we as a nation, and more specifically, myself as a representative of the United States overseas, know so little of that history.

Suggested Further Reading

Jennifer Lind cites case studies, including Germany and Japan following World War II, in *Sorry States: Apologies in International Politics*

(Ithaca, NY: Cornell University Press, 2011). Edwin Battistella cites research on apology in multiple situations, not just international affairs, in *Sorry about That: The Language of Public Apology* (New York: Oxford University Press, 2014). Robert Weyeneth explores the links between history and apology in his article "The Power of Apology and the Process of Historical Reconciliation," *Public Historian* 23, no. 3 (Summer 2001).

11

Connecting the Dots: Preliminary Conclusions

Whoever dreamed up the Jefferson Science Fellowship that invites scientists from across the STEM disciplines to spend a year at the State Department understood a few features of American diplomacy. First of all, the role of science in diplomacy, in addressing global issues and bilateral disputes as varied as climate change, arms control, intellectual property, or fishing rights, is increasing in both importance and complexity. With the Jefferson Science Fellows, the State Department can tap into the expertise of scientists across the country. Second, the program allows outsiders to peek into the world of policy making and the practice of foreign relations, helping to lower the cloak of secrecy traditionally associated with and sometimes required in our dealings with foreign countries.

Tim DeVoogd, a neuropsychologist from Cornell University, joined our Office of Public Diplomacy in the Bureau of Western Hemisphere Affairs as a Jefferson Science Fellow. We were not interested in his lifelong study of birdsong and bird memory, but rather in launching an effort to forge linkages between Latin American scientists and their American counterparts. This mutually beneficial research exchange between scientists was taking place naturally between US and European scientists, but only limited engagement occurred in this hemisphere, and it could benefit from a little encouragement. With a good working knowledge of Spanish and an enthusiastic curiosity, Tim was able to spur interest in these cross-border connections.

After his year at State, Tim invited me to Cornell University. In the winter of 2013, I traveled to Cornell to give a talk at the Latin

American Studies Center, which he now headed, an unusual position for a scientist, but a positive result from his year in Washington. Tim invited me to talk to students about some aspect of the Foreign Service. I sent him a few ideas, and rather than the yawning bureaucratic ones such as "strategic communications," he thought one on history and memory in US foreign relations would pique interest. He probably selected that one because of his research on memory and learning in birds.

At Cornell, Tim gave my wife and me a tour of his labs, including a room filled with "his" birds and another filled with thirty years of microscope slides. He proceeded to pull out a few slides, placed them under a microscope, and showed us highly magnified images of brain sections, and cells within those sections in birds. He told us how birds learn songs, which part of the brain remembers places (hippocampus), which part remembers and plans the songs (high vocal center—HVC), and which part controls the production of the songs (*robustus archistriatalis*—RA).

Some birds, he said, have more complicated songs than others, which is important for mating. Females select their mates based on songs; they remember the calls of their mates. Crows, for example, have very simple songs, but mockingbirds, which he has studied, have much more complicated, differentiated songs. What he noticed was that the mockingbird HVCs (which plan out the songs) are two to three times the size of their RAs (which produce the songs). In crows, those two parts of the brain are the same size.

Tim explained how such research bears relevance for humans, in the growth and strength of areas of the brain as a result of use. His research shows as well that the brain continues to change throughout life, growing through continued use or atrophying through disuse, which accounts for how it is possible for stroke victims to recover by developing parts of their brains unaffected by their stroke.

It struck me, as I was giving my talk on history and foreign relations, how the same concept of learning that Tim had been studying could serve as a metaphor for our neglect of history, specifically in our approach to foreign relations, but also as a broader aspect of the

American character that Gore Vidal once referred to as "the United States of Amnesia."[1] Those birds that use memory the most have proportionally larger HVCs; they draw on their memory of songs to learn, to make decisions, to develop new, unique songs. Mockingbirds had developed a heightened sense of learning from the songs they were hearing. The United States of Amnesia uses memory and historical awareness less, making us more like the crows, with an underdeveloped HVC. By neglecting history, we are less able or willing to draw on memory to aid in how we learn, make decisions, behave, or develop new strategies.

Funny how the brain travels. HVCs and learning made me recall a student's question in Mexico City, at a talk in the aftermath of 9/11. Following those events, I joined the millions, in New York or Gander, Newfoundland, who just wanted to do their part, to help. My part was to talk, so in Mexico, I went on a speaking tour, addressing close to fifty groups in the months after the attacks. I spoke with university students and professors, with civic organizations, even with Mexican Muslims at the only mosque in Mexico City. At one university, a student stood up and said that maybe it was time for the United States to embark on a little introspection. My retort: "Welcome to the land of introspection. That's what we do." The young student remained skeptical. He seemed to be saying that the United States was unwilling to look at itself, to look back, to learn.

I, too, was unconvinced, recalling a fleeting episode in a small village in the Central African nation of Gabon, where I taught in the Peace Corps right after college. A math teacher I worked with once wondered how, following the ordeals of Watergate and Vietnam, the United States was so willing to put itself through this torturous, weakening process to fix itself. So far removed from that environment of separation of powers and free speech, he saw the United States through the lens of his own country, his continent, and its colonial ties to Europe. "Seulement l'Amerique," he said. "Only the US" would put itself through that trauma of impeachment, in front of the whole world, to correct its course. The country was undoubtedly momentarily weaker from a realist power perspective of global politics, but in a soft-power, longer-term view, it earned respect and soft-power attraction, even in this remote corner of the world.

Perhaps, though, foreigners like the student in Mexico did not perceive that self-correcting introspection extending beyond our shores. Still, at the time of the 9/11 attacks, the country seemed immersed in reflective discussions that did include an examination of US behavior abroad. Newspapers, magazines, and TV talk shows all were asking, "Why do they hate us?" For a brief period, we worked to see ourselves through the eyes of others. It wasn't a pretty picture: arrogance in calling ourselves "exceptional" or "the indispensable nation." Other countries accused us of making our wealth at other nations' expense, of being indifferent to the plight of other nations, and of seeking power, but only to advance our interests. More generously, through the eyes of a foreigner, captured in Mohsin Hamid's novel *The Reluctant Fundamentalist*, the nation had changed: "I had always thought of America as a nation that looked forward; for the first time I was struck by its determination to look back."[2] Some even mocked the reflective mood, as the same leftist Mexican newspaper that listed all the interventions carried on its front page the headline, "Bush: Amazed the World Hates Us," as it likely was perfectly obvious to all that paper's readers.

That period of introspection, of looking backward, proved short-lived. Soon, other questions shifted the focus away from US behaviors to external sources, ranging from "Who can stop the rage?" to "Who hijacked Islam?"[3] This hatred directed at the United States was schadenfreude: the joy people take in seeing someone else's discomfort, pain, or defeat. Hatred came from misinformation, calling out for a better, more vigorous public diplomacy to showcase the good we did around the world. Some of this shift away from introspection may have been motivated to preserve a national identity built around the concept that the country, despite errors and setbacks, had been a force for good in the world. Or the shift happened with the growing realization that no matter the record of US behavior around the world, the attacks of September 11 had no justification other than misled fanaticism.

Soon, interventions in Afghanistan and Iraq disrupted this momentary period of looking back, and we reverted to our pattern of ignoring history in our conduct of foreign relations. It is a pattern that I experienced through a career representing the United States abroad, and it manifests itself in the most ordinary of interactions, but also in transformational events that continue to shape the way the United States organizes its foreign policy. The personal accounts of historical ignorance included in this narrative are not on the grand scale of military conflict in the post-9/11 world. They do, however, represent the daily interactions that, repeated hundreds of time a day across the world, accumulate and affect our ability to forge the partnerships necessary in advancing our interests, in convincing others that our interests coincide.

The case studies in this volume explicitly show history shock at the intersection of history and diplomatic conduct. These are histories, overlooked or contested, that get in the way of international partnerships and cooperation. As mentioned at the outset, the cases presented here generally fall into one or more overlapping categories of (1) conflicting visions of history, (2) total ignorance of history, either our own or the foreign country's, and (3) misunderstandings of different histories. In several cases, foreigners knew more about American history, especially as it related to their countries, than I did. And in one case, South Africa, misapplying a version of American racial history obscured South Africa's distinctive racial history.

How to account for this propensity of the United States to ignore history in its approach to engaging the world? Undoubtedly, a combination of factors comes into play, sometimes individually, but often in clusters, the weight of each one depending on the individual case. What follows is my take on what might lie behind this reluctance to acknowledge or even be open to exploring history as we interact with the world.

Ignorance

Let me start with a conclusion that readers may already have reached after wading through these accounts this far: personal ignorance, which I am perfectly ready to acknowledge. Upon review, how could it be otherwise that I would have known so little about the US experience in Mexico, Canada, Haiti, or any of the other countries cited here? I confess this, even having majored in US history in college and having taught US history in secondary schools before joining the Foreign Service. While I'm certain that both experiences helped me pass the Foreign Service exam, they were insufficient to prepare me for assignments overseas.

To help fill that gap and provide context for outgoing officers, the State Department's Foreign Service Institute offered an intensive two-week area-studies course, but it typically covered the whole continent and all aspects of the region: current policies, economics, politics, culture, and history. It is understandable that the focus of such rapid overviews would be on current conditions. However, it does crowd out any opportunity for historical analysis, which creates a Foreign Service that fits the historian Michael H. Hunt's description of foreign policy specialists who are "preoccupied with current policy problems . . . [and] hobbled by the same lack of historical perspective that characterizes the public they address."[4]

While these area-studies courses used to last just two weeks, the State Department has reduced them to one week. Mexico is one of the few countries that has its country-specific classes, but I was unable to take any of those. Furthermore, while now the Latin America class devotes a full day to US interventions history, such a perspective was not available when I took the area-studies class. At that time, President Clinton had only recently authorized the declassification of documents showing the extent of US involvement in Chile, Guatemala, and elsewhere, so we were only starting to publicly acknowledge the interventions that many in the hemisphere already suspected.

Even with these classes, undertaking to learn about countries of the assignment is largely left to officers' individual initiative. Unlike the military, where there is extensive training, the Foreign Service assumes individuals will pursue their reading into the history of the country and its relations with the United States. Most colleagues did take it upon themselves to read as much as they could on their country of assignment, but certainly not in any systematic way. I would venture to say that my reading list was as extensive as anyone's in each of the countries I served, and yet as it turns out, I kept bumping into the vast gaps in my knowledge of the history of our relations in the host nation. This ignorance left me at a disadvantage in my dealings with counterparts who were keenly aware of the US involvement in their country and their region.

One other characteristic of the US Foreign Service that compounds this ignorance is the diversity of experiences that recruits bring to the profession. Although that diversity is otherwise a strength, the United States does not field a Foreign Service filled exclusively with individuals steeped in international relations. In my class thirty-five years ago, we had several high school teachers, two Peace Corps volunteers, one high school principal, a navy veteran and journalist, a secretary, one university professor (Russian studies), and a few recently minted graduate students in European history, Chinese, and Middle Eastern affairs. By the end of my career, I was welcoming officers into embassies who had been lawyers from the Southern Poverty Law Center, nongovernmental organization (NGO) representatives, small business owners, even a parole officer from New York City and a country club manager, to round out a profession and really make it more representative of the country as a whole. One counterpart in Peru contrasted this with their Foreign Service, whose entry requirements included a master's degree in international law. The downside to such diversity of experience is the lack of background in international relations. Training on entry and during a career could make up for it, but as noted above, such training falls far short.

Admittedly, the importance of historical awareness in foreign affairs is not a new idea. In his diplomatic memoir, the former deputy secretary of state William Burns recalls entering the Foreign Service with an admonition from Hedley Bull, his professor at Oxford. "History was the key to understanding international relations, he [Bull] insisted, and leaders most often erred when they thought they were immune to its lessons."[5]

Unquestionably, it is too much to expect that every Foreign Service

Officer, either newly minted or departing for a new assignment, could master an exhaustive history of every country and its relationship to the United States. Despite a rigorous selection process, which continues to grapple with allegations of bias, candidates come from a pool that represents the country at large. And the country is, as Gore Vidal and others have pointed out, woefully ignorant of history. In 2018, the Woodrow Wilson National Fellowship Foundation published the results of a survey it commissioned on historical awareness across the US population. The conclusions were damning: over a third of Americans could not pass our own citizenship test, failing factual questions on the original thirteen colonies or historical personalities such as Dwight Eisenhower or Benjamin Franklin.[6] Obviously, there is more to history and the need for historical awareness than the kinds of facts asked for in citizenship tests, but if we require such a base for new citizens, it calls into question the base needed across American society for a functioning democracy, let alone diplomacy. Thus, training for the career of a Foreign Service Officer needs bolstering, but quite emphatically so should American education rediscover the importance of the learning of history at all levels.

Change

Set against this backdrop of generalized historical illiteracy are the organizational rules of the Foreign Service that have developed with a seeming intent to produce and reinforce such a scattershot, superficial understanding of our relations with other countries. First of all, assignments last two or three years before officers move on to their next posting. Even in that short tenure, my point of reference for the first few months in the new assignment was what transpired in my last post, while in the final months, I was already gearing up and beginning to learn about my next post, leaving me with a short time of undivided focus on the US relations in the current country. Second, I suspect my career mirrored many of my colleagues' in that I never returned to a post where I was previously assigned. My own experience may have been unusual in that two of my assignments, Mexico and South Africa, extended beyond the three years, and in each one of those I also ended up working in Washington on those posts.

Not only are those few years insufficient to develop in-depth expertise of the country, but the constant turnover means that among the Americans at the post there is little continuity and scant institutional memory. We rely on the locally employed staff for such information, and while I repeatedly worked with talented, informed host-country colleagues who regularly filled in these gaps in my knowledge, they had two limitations. First, they had access only to the unclassified aspect of the relationship, and second, they could not be expected to advocate for American interests.

Such built-in change results in historical ignorance, but it is not confined to the Foreign Service and finds its way into the upper echelons of decision making. A young analyst for the Rand Corporation, with his PhD in economics from Harvard, was brought into the Defense Department as a senior military analyst to prepare a study on the Vietnam War for Secretary of Defense Robert McNamara. Having served previously in the Pentagon, in Vietnam, and at the Rand Corporation, Daniel Ellsberg discovered documents dating back to the French experience after World War II that prefigured what the United States would face ten to fifteen years later. Ellsberg admitted, "In five years as an American official or consultant dealing with Vietnam, I had remained ignorant of this history or at least of its clear import."[7] Those documents, buried in the files at the Pentagon, were never read by those responsible for military decisions in the 1960s. It's not just Ellsberg as a scholar and official who remained blind to historical events significant for policy formulation. He quotes Henry Kissinger, then national security advisor to President Nixon, responding to Ellsberg's question shortly after Nixon won the election. The question was whether Nixon had ever read the McNamara study of Vietnam, later known as the Pentagon Papers.

The president answered: "No, should I? . . . But do we have anything to learn from this study?"[8] That was three years before Ellsberg saw to it that Nixon, Kissinger, and the rest of the nation did read those papers.

Years before the Pentagon Papers, Under Secretary of State George Ball was a lone voice of dissent against the increasing escalation in Vietnam. In his sixty-seven-page memo prepared in October 1964, "How Valid Are the Assumptions Underlying Our Vietnam Policies?" Ball laid out the case he had been making for several years, with two claims on historical misreading in Vietnam. US policymakers undervalued comparisons to the French colonial experience in Vietnam but also drew an inappropriate analogy to the Korean War in pursuing conflict in another Asian country. By ignoring the links to Vietnam's anticolonial insurgency, US policy would, "in the world's eyes, approach that of France in the 1950s—with all the disastrous political connotations of such a posture." And if the United States failed to make that connection, "Asians would not miss the point."[9] Two Harvard political scientists, Richard Neustadt and Ernest May, cite the attitude of one representative of the Joint Chiefs that may have reflected the broader dismissal of the French experience: "The French also tried to build the Panama Canal," a reference to American perseverance in getting a canal built after years of French failure.[10] Competing versions of history propelled and sustained the United States in this conflict.

Newness

Closely related to this notion of change in grasping our lack of historical knowledge is what I would call "newness." Deeply embedded in a collective American psyche, this notion also extends far beyond the realm of foreign relations. From an early age, we learn we are the "new" world. Marketing hails the "new" product, a regenerating improvement over what came before. The idea of the new nation that holds today is not even new. It goes back to our founding generation, when Thomas Paine commented on the break with England and Europe giving us "the power to begin the world over again."[11] The British historian David Lowenthal argues there is a pride in the United States with this "rupture with the past; each generation was a 'distinct nation' that should erase inherited institutions and choose its own."[12]

By representing the United States as a "break with the world," Thomas Paine captured at least a rhetorical trend that seems to carry over to each successive generation of leaders and citizenry. In this way, newly elected presidents can offer themselves as a break with the excesses of the past that are better off forgotten or that have steered the nation away from its predetermined path of standing as a beacon for liberty for the rest of the world.

Teddy Roosevelt broke with the anti-imperial tendencies of Grover Cleveland and with the caution of William McKinley to intervene in Panama, Cuba, Nicaragua, Haiti, and the Dominican Republic; Woodrow Wilson departed from Roosevelt's big-stick diplomacy, at least initially, when he sought a treaty to restore relations with Colombia and wrap up the status of Puerto Rico and the Philippines, still unresolved from the Spanish-American War. The pattern continues through Reagan moving away from Carter's human rights emphasis, Obama's promise as the non-Bush emphasizing the role of diplomacy, and Trump, as the anti-Obama, working to undo any diplomatic opening Obama achieved.

For Trump, who declares at the end of foreign visits that his trip was historic, history began when he took office. He is unmindful of the historical precedents of the one-China policy, the two-state solution as the foundation for Middle East peace, or the post–World War II institutional framework built to secure a lasting peace and advance US global leadership. Daniel Ellsberg was specifically referring to Henry Kissinger and his reluctance to read the Pentagon study on Vietnam, but he was generalizing about each US leader, noting that "they each thought history started with his administration, and they have nothing to learn from earlier ones."[13]

This break with the past allowed Warren Christopher to investigate the El Mozote massacre at no political cost to the Clinton administration since it occurred under prior Republican presidents. It allowed President Clinton to sign Executive Order 12958 ordering the automatic declassification of government documents after twenty-five years (with the notable exceptions that would reveal sources, contain information on weapons of mass destruction, or fall under a generic view that disclosure would damage relations with foreign governments). Likewise, it allowed a new President Obama, at his first international summit, to urge that nations not be "trapped" by the past, when he expressed gratitude that Daniel Ortega of Nicaragua "did not blame me for things that happened when I was three months old."[14]

Future-Oriented

A corollary to newness is a widely recognized American trait to focus on the future. At the same Summit of the Americas described earlier and on other occasions as well, President Obama saw value in understanding the past, but underscored his bottom line: "The United States is focused on the future. . . . The Cold War has been over for a long time. And I'm not interested in having battles that, frankly, started before I was born. What I am interested in is solving problems, working with you."[15]

Obama is drawing on a corollary to the tradition of breaking with the past that goes back to Puritans arriving in this new world, looking forward to a time when, in the words of John Winthrop, "we shall be as a City upon a hill. . . . We shall be made a story and a by-word through the world."[16] While politicians such as John Kennedy and Ronald Reagan drew on the image of the city on a hill as inspiration to the rest of the world, this sentiment was as much about leaving behind the past, shaping the future, and creating a vision to work toward. The words "a more perfect union" in the first sentence of the US Constitution reinforce Winthrop's notion of a work in progress. Westward expansion, the abolition of slavery, Kennedy's moon shot, and Martin Luther King Jr.'s dream all fall into leaving behind the past and optimistically moving toward the future. Obama was drawing on King in describing the arc of history showing progress, moving in the direction of justice for all and prosperity.

Tom Shannon, under secretary of state, looking back on a long, distinguished career in the Foreign Service, wrote disparagingly of foreign policy references to the past as nostalgia. "Quite apart from the possibility that this past is more imagined than real, it seems evident that the American people want a foreign policy vision that captures and defines the future, and not that parses the past."[17] It may be unfair to draw one quote from Shannon out of context, especially when he may be obliquely referring to the nostalgia of the moment, to make America great again. He is also probably obliquely criticizing the Trump administration for its lack of anything remotely looking like a foreign policy vision. Shannon is right in warning about "parsing" the past, as misreadings and false analogies can steer policy down counterproductive paths.[18] More often, though, this focus on the future often means squeezing out deliberate analysis of the events and trends that presage current situations.

As Obama was able to deflate a tense atmosphere in the Summit of the Americas with a little bit of humor, focusing on the future also enables the United States to sidestep uncomfortable realities of its past behavior. Kenneth Adelman, a conservative policy analyst in and out of government for the past three decades, identified this pattern during the election year of 1980 when he claimed that "Americans have a new penchant for self-flagellation."[19] The past can be burdensome, weighing down and slowing down individuals or nations. Or, more bluntly, in the words of Nobel laureate V. S. Naipaul, "We have to learn to trample on the past. . . . Everywhere else men are in movement, the world is in movement, and the past can only cause pain."[20]

When I served in Canada, this reluctance to discuss even the immediate past (of, for example, the Canadian objections to stricter border procedures or decisions not to join either the Iraqi invasion or the US missile defense system) led to a recurring sound bite in public speeches and comments. Ambassador David Wilkins repeatedly urged his audiences to "stop looking in the rear-view mirror" and focus on the road ahead.[21] It was a simple metaphor that brushed away the controversies of the past so that the two nations could focus on the issues, such as trade and border security, that needed attention. However, failing to address such unhealed wounds in the relationship can "fuel distrust," as Jennifer Lind acknowledged in referring to violent conflict.[22]

So, how to explain, in the face of this inherent, optimistic focus on the future, the dark view of the United States and the world as painted by Donald Trump? Even though Trump harkens back to a nostalgic, great America, he too has painted a vision of the immediate past as America gone astray. His presidency would be future-oriented, promising a future that is a break with the "carnage" that preceded him, toward a future of unbridled prosperity and opportunity. His was a message that resonated, even if with fewer voters than those who responded to Hillary Clinton's "America's best days are ahead."

Exceptionalism

John Winthrop's sermon summoning his congregation to serve as an example to the world has also become embedded in the American collective identity and reshaped into the notion of the country as an "exceptional" nation. Herman Melville continued this sentiment in the mid-nineteenth century, in pronouncing that "we Americans are the peculiar, chosen people—the Israel of our times; we bear the ark of the liberties of the world."[23]

To stray too far from that constructed theme of the United States' greatness would lose the electorate, as Jimmy Carter did when he gave a television address in 1979 on the "crisis of confidence . . . in the growing doubt about the meaning of our own lives and in the loss of a unity of purpose for our nation."[24] This constructed narrative of a nation as a "force for good in the world" appears in the rhetoric of both politicians and school textbooks. It is rhetoric deeply rooted in US culture. It became the easy fallback justification for George Bush when no weapons of mass destruction were found following the invasion of Iraq: the invasion reflected "his deep desire to spread liberty around the world."[25]

I do subscribe to this idea of the United States as exceptional, with certain caveats. My view may be nothing more than knee-jerk patriotism, so deeply ingrained in my upbringing, reflective of the Cold War mentality of the era. Or it may be just a rationalization after a career devoted to advocating for the interests of the United States, but that foundation is still unshakable in reflecting on the impact the country has had on the rest of the world.

My hesitations concerning exceptionalism, though, have to do with its various implications. First, the idea of a beacon to the world, as Winthrop described the Puritan experiment, has its pitfalls when the United States fails itself to live up to its ideals, as inevitably occurs, especially on recurring setbacks related to race relations in the United States. The historian David Brion Davis cites examples of British travelers to the United States as early as the 1820s who "took delight in exposing and ridiculing the extraordinary inconsistency of a free-dom-touting democracy based on slave labor."[26] This inconsistency continued through the Cold War, when American race relations became a recurring element of Soviet propaganda. Faced with such counternarratives, the idea of exceptionalism becomes a trope, easy to use as a club against the United States when shortcomings arise. Even the *Oxford Dictionary* uses just such an example in its definition of the word: "trope: a figurative or *metaphorical* use of a word or expression: 'he used the two-Americas trope to explain how a nation free and democratic at home could act wantonly abroad.'"[27]

Furthermore, exceptionalism implies uniqueness, but in this con-notation, every country embraces its own brand of exceptionalism; every country identifies and promotes those features that make it ad-mirably unique. Most troublesome is extending the notion of excep-tionalism to mean that the United States, by its nature as a democratic ideal, is excepted, in other words, exempted, from international laws that seek to govern conduct between nations and even within nations. Finally, and most relevant to history shock, the widespread view of American exceptionalism obscures our historical understanding. The United States is not unique in developing and transmitting to suc-ceeding generations its version of its history, its place in the world, its identity.

These are, as the historian and political scientist Benedict Ander-son famously described, "imagined communities," in his theory of the construct of nations and nationalisms.[28] Michael Van Wagenen, another historian cited earlier who chronicled the ways the United

States and Mexico have constructed their memories of the 1848 war since its conclusion, finds that "every group has a negotiated story that defines its past, gives meaning to its present and shapes its future."[29] These are our socially constructed identities.

By cherry-picking those events that helped construct a nation that is exceptional, the United States has consistently overlooked that slice of its history that does not correspond to its self-image. Actions that run counter to an exceptional nation spreading liberty are either portrayed as an anomaly, erased from memory, or reshaped. Such was the case described earlier of newspaper accounts and congressional hearings that made known the atrocities during the interventions in Mexico or Haiti, but both the interventions and the atrocities have faded from our collective consciousness. Even the idea of "empire" contradicts a nation that promotes itself as a model of liberty. Richard Nixon reiterated what many Americans believe when he stated in his memoir that the United States is "the only great power without a history of imperialistic claims on neighboring countries,"[30] a view Secretary of State Colin Powell shared years later after the September 11 attacks. They relegated the association of the United States with the idea of an empire to an "imperial moment" at the turn of the last century. The president most linked to that moment, Teddy Roosevelt, conspired to encourage a movement in Panama to secede from Colombia to allow the United States to build a canal across the isthmus; yet, he was able to assert that the United States felt no "land hunger."[31] Presidents from Wilson to Bush recast warfare as interventions in which Americans seek to "persuade themselves that they are acting out of humanitarian motives."[32] The conservative historian Robert Kagan wrote a whole book, *Dangerous Nation*, on the "gap between Americans' self-perception and the perceptions of others." He refers to the self-image "as by nature inward-looking and aloof, only sporadically and spasmodically venturing forth into the world," even in the face of a historical record stretching across "four hundred years of steady expansion and an ever-deepening involvement in world affairs . . . [with] innumerable wars, interventions, and prolonged occupations in foreign lands."[33]

Amid these conflicts, unfortunately acts of atrocity occurred with jarring regularity. Furthermore, they were not forgotten solely to ease the collective conscience. As we have seen, in the cases of the occupation of Haiti and the massacre at El Mozote in El Salvador, there were conscious efforts to cover up or to obfuscate the killing of civilians and the rampant destruction and violence. The actions to pacify Filipinos following the defeat of the Spanish at the turn of the last century prompted news reports deploring the brutality: "We have actually come to do the thing we went to war to banish."[34] Senate hearings run by Henry Cabot Lodge to investigate military behavior in the Philippines resembled "less a whitewash than an exercise in sleight-of-hand." The result for these cases and others, in Mexico, Iran, Guatemala, Chile, and elsewhere, fit the pattern that journalist and historian Stephen Kinzer concluded about the Philippines: "Filipinos remember those years as some of the bloodiest in their history. Americans quickly forgot that the war ever happened."[35]

Repeatedly, in the course of my career, I admittedly was too captivated by the exceptional nature of the United States to acknowledge the times when the United States fell short of its image. When confronted with opposing views in the media or in face-to-face encounters, I fell back on attributing these accounts to conspiracy theories, ideological bias, and even disinformation. Only in the era of declassification was I jarred out of my complacency to accept the history that my foreign counterparts were aware of, but that I had denied.

Secrecy

Closely linked to my reluctance to acknowledge this slice of US history was the fact that many of these events were cloaked in secrecy, covert by nature, to hide any direct evidence of US involvement. Foreign Service officers are instructed to respond to queries that involve covert actions or relationships with a bland comment that we do not discuss intelligence matters. Were we to deny even the most far-fetched charges of US plots, others might judge our failure to deny a future charge as an acknowledgement of its veracity; thus, with only the rarest exceptions, we refused to comment on any charge that involved the activities of intelligence and security agencies.

Our position led to situations bordering on absurdity when foreign counterparts were aware of US involvement in covert operations, even when information was publicly available. As we saw earlier, the Mexican artist Diego Rivera had enough information shortly after the 1954 coup in Guatemala to paint his "Glorious Victory" mural that portrayed the maneuvering of Eisenhower, John Foster Dulles, Allen Dulles, and Ambassador John Peurifoy to effect regime change. However, US representatives were unable to acknowledge our role until 1997, when the United States released more than 1,400 pages of declassified documents that outlined US involvement in the coup. Similar declassifications have revealed the extent of US involvement in removing democratically elected leaders in Chile in 1973, Iran in 1953, or the civil wars in Guatemala and El Salvador in the 1980s. The Iran incident may be the most powerful example of a collective failure, especially in its enduring consequences. Unawareness of previous involvement in replacing a democratically elected leader with the shah in 1953 seemed missing in decisions to stand by him in 1979.

False Analogies

Finally, there is no guarantee that the use of history in the deliberations of foreign policy decisions will necessarily draw on the most appropriate historical analogy. Historical analogies can take on a shorthand imperative in building political support for foreign policy directions, or as historian H. W. Brands notes, they "gain their power by simplifying the present to fit templates imported from the past."[36]

For the United States, several analogies have enduring legacies. The 1938 Munich agreement between Neville Chamberlain and Adolf Hitler has repeatedly been employed to justify decisive US military interventions, from Korea to the Balkans to the Iraq War. The mere mention of Munich or appeasement in policy debates, irrespective of the circumstances, argues in favor of decisive, and usually military, responses to perceived threats and aggressions. More discredited now is the moniker "Who Lost China?" which, following the rise of Mao in China, hovered over US policy debates on East Asia in the 1950s and 60s. The US experience in Vietnam continues to exercise a hold on foreign policy debates, so powerful in fact that opponents in foreign policy debates reach different conclusions citing the same historical analogies. The guidelines developed by former defense secretary Caspar Weinberger for the use of military force overseas, ranging from the risk to US vital interests to clarity of both military and political objectives and the availability of sufficient resources, were designed to prevent the mistakes made in Vietnam. Colin Powell, as chairman of the Joint Chiefs, expanded on Weinberger's lessons on Vietnam to justify the use of overwhelming force with a set of clear, achievable goals in expelling Iraq from Kuwait. When military conflicts do not attain quick objectives, the reference to a prolonged "quagmire" evokes the Vietnam analogy. Similarly, opponents of such overwhelming force pointed to the Vietnam analogy as an appropriate precedent for misreading the nature of the divisions within Iraq and the shift to a counterinsurgent strategy.

At the embassy level, misappropriation of historical analogies entered into the bureaucratic competition for scarce resources. In the waning days of the Cold War, and in corners far from any actual threat, it was customary to cite warnings of potential communist inroads to attract the attention of Washington and the need for enhanced budgets, for aid and exchange programs or increased military cooperation and training. In the post 9/11 world, antiterrorism became the surest way to attract attention and resources. Drawing on the immediate experience of nineteen hijackers entering the United States to launch attacks, embassies identified possible terrorist routes to the United States through their host countries, appealed for security upgrades, and developed programs aimed at youth to counter extremist messaging, among other bureaucratic requests.

Other reasons probably can be found that account for both the generalized ignorance of our history and the lack of historical knowledge and analysis as we approach our foreign relations. Scholars add other factors to this complex web of forgetting. For Alan Taylor, the War of 1812 was relegated to the fine print of history because that conflict ended with no clear winner and resolved little, as was the case with another forgotten war in Korea.[37] In the US-Mexican War where there was a clear winner and loser, historians cite the trauma of the subsequent Civil War obscuring the memory of the war just twelve years earlier.[38] The issue of displacement by more prominent events may account for other examples cited; as stated earlier, Mary Renda notes that "the real stuff of U.S. history during those years [of intervention and occupation in Haiti] was taking shape within U.S. borders and in Europe, not in a small Caribbean nation."[39] War had broken out in Europe with a debate over US participation, and later displacement occurred through Woodrow Wilson's involvement in the treaty negotiations and proclamations of self-determination, ironically at the same time the United States was drafting and forcing acceptance of a new constitution in Haiti. The magnitude of the horrors of the war in Europe surpassed the brutalities in Haiti.

The case studies presented in this volume were selected to demonstrate episodes during my career where history intersected with the management of our relations with foreign countries, distinct from foreign policy development. Other scholars, most notably Richard Neustadt and Ernest May, have examined comprehensively the role history has played in the development of policy in varied situations from the Peloponnesian War to Vietnam, the Cuban Missile Crisis, and arms control.[40] Here, though, at the practitioner level, in trying to manage bilateral relationships, our diplomats are at times unaware of our history in a country or region, or when they do draw on history, they operate from a competing narrative from our counterparts'. In my case, I found myself repeatedly in both situations and felt at a distinct disadvantage in my efforts to advocate for and advance US interests.

There is a danger in reading too much into such episodes. They could be the "off-the-shelf anecdotes or allusions exploited for their emotive appeal rather than consulted for their insight" that Peter

Feaver and William Imboden, two former national security advisors to George W. Bush, cautioned against when building political support for foreign policy decisions.[41] Rather than off-the-shelf anecdotes, though, these are illustrations that I believe Foreign Service officers encounter in assignment after assignment. As I have described this book to colleagues, they readily call up their own encounters in postings as varied as China, Poland, Indonesia, or Colombia with references to immigration history, or territorial infringement, or even wreath layings. Such experiences underscore the need for a broader "historical sensibility," that, in the words of Hal Brand and Jeremi Suri, can help explore alternative solutions and "escape from the imprisonment of the past."[42]

It is not just diplomats who live through the shock of contested memories, but business men and women, tourists, and exchange students. They come to see how other nations have chosen to remember and write their pasts, different from the United States. In *Notes on a Foreign Country: An American Abroad in a Post-America World*, the journalist Suzy Hansen eloquently narrates her encounter as a private citizen in Turkey confronting historical narratives, both new and in direct competition with the ones that she grew up learning. The US-Pakistani writer Mohsin Hamid bases his best-selling novel *The Reluctant Fundamentalist* on an encounter between an American businessman (CIA agent?) and a young Pakistani back from undergraduate study and work in the United States.

A common thread runs through much of the behavior of the United States as it faces outward, beyond its borders. The failure to acknowledge the past or to accept the historical evidence represents an obstacle in US relations with the rest of the world, as the nation seeks to define, protect, and advance its current and future interests. Consequences of this shortcoming can endure, as the seizure of US diplomats in Iran in November 1979 demonstrates. The depth of resentment in Iran toward the United States then came as a surprise to many Americans, who were unaware of the role of the US government in overthrowing Prime Minister Mohammad Mossadegh and restoring the shah to power in 1953. After five years on the job, President Obama cited the Iranian case in a shift away from his warning in the first months of his tenure not to be "trapped by history." In a *New Yorker* profile of the president's foreign policy approach, David Remnick identified this shift: "He is convinced that an essential component of diplomacy is the public recognition of historical facts—not only the taking of American hostages in Iran, in 1979, but also the American role in the overthrow of Mohammad Mossadegh, the democratically elected Prime Minister of Iran, in 1953."[43] Short of the politically sensitive issue of apology, such public recognition of historical facts would at the very least enhance our ability to start the conversations in our relations with other countries from the same baseline of knowledge. Enhancing historical awareness may require additional time for training in anticipation of foreign assignments. One underutilized resource lies in the Office of the Historian at the State Department, which could help officers on their way to foreign assignments explore the personalities, events, and policies that shaped the present. Is it too much to ask outgoing officers to check in with the Office of the Historian before getting their plane tickets? Even a simple recognition of the obstacles to historical awareness alone would be a step in the right direction of instilling a culture of "historical sensibility."

More than fifty years ago, the historian Barrington Moore had a more positive take on contested histories: "Different perspectives of the same events should lead to complementary and congruent interpretations, not to contradictory ones." Moore's take is optimistic. So is mine, based on our ability to adapt. I have seen in my life that change can be abrupt, as in the fall of the Berlin Wall, leading to the fall of superpower confrontation that had defined the previous thirty-five years. It can also be gradual, as we unearth new histories and use them to construct new identities that require a shift in how we interact with the rest of the world.

Public recognition of historical facts, rather than being a sign of weakness, holds out the prospect for strengthening our relations not just with specific, individual nations. Other nations observe the willingness of the United States to reassess our relationships and seek the congruent and complementary ground needed to address the challenges that inevitably arise. That sounds like a platitude—easy to make and harder to instill in practice. The alternative—not taking into account our history in managing our relations with other countries—is the path we're already on, full of costs, restraints, and disadvantages as we seek to advance and advocate for US interests overseas.

Suggested Further Reading

I wish I had read two books before starting my career or starting this project. Richard Neustadt and Ernest May shed light on the role of historical awareness in policy decisions in their study, *Thinking in Time: The Uses of History for Decision Makers* (New York: Free Press, 1988). Hal Brands and Jeremi Suri pulled together a series of articles by academics and practitioners on the role of history in diplomacy in *The Power of the Past: History and Statecraft of the Past* (Washington, DC: Brookings Institution Press, 2016). In *How to Hide an Empire: A History of the Greater United States* (New York: Farrar, Straus and Giroux, 2019), Daniel Immerwahr traces the history of American empire building. Seymour Martin Lipset wrote the classic text on how the United States came to view itself as unique in *American Exceptionalism: A Double-Edged Sword* (New York: Norton, 1996). Paul Pillar explores the long history of American forgetfulness in his book *Why America Misunderstands the World: National Experience and Roots of Misperception* (New York: Columbia University Press, 2016). David Rieff, in his book *In Praise of Forgetting: Historical Memory and Its Ironies* (New Haven, CT: Yale University Press, 2016), takes a contrary perspective on the abuses of history.

Notes

Preface and Acknowledgments
1. William J. Burns, *The Back Channel: A Memoir of American Diplomacy and the Case for Its Renewal* (New York: Random House, New York, 2019, Kindle edition), 102.

Chapter 1. The Past Is a Foreign Country
1. Dana Priest, interview by Steve Inskeep, April 29, 2013, https://www.npr.org/2013/04/29/179762907/u-s-mexico-alliance-against-dug-cartels-in-jeopardy.

2. North American Free Trade Agreement, launched in 1994, lowering tariffs and trade barriers between Mexico, Canada and the United States.

3. Carlos Fuentes, *The Old Gringo* (New York: Farrar, Straus and Giroux, 2013), 9.

4. "2014 Survey Pinpoints 1821 Border between USA and Mexico," Lincoln and Mexico Project, April 11, 2018, https://lincolnandmexicoproject.wordpress.com/2018/04/11/2014-survey-pinpoints-1821-border-between-usa-and-mexico/.

5. In September 2012, candidate Mitt Romney accused President Obama of apologizing for the United States on the basis of a press statement from the Embassy in Cairo appealing for calm from Egyptians protesting a video denigrating Islam circulating in the United States. More detail is related in chapter 10.

6. An additional 11,000 employees are in the civil service, working out of the State Department, mostly in Washington but also in New York and other cities. State's numbers are small compared to the Departments of Justice (100,000), Energy (14,000 federal and 100,000 contract employees), or Veterans Affairs (85,000). These numbers come from a 2009 Office of Personnel Management report, "Agency HR Benchmarking Report." Not included in that report is the size of the Defense Department with an estimated 700,000 civilian staff.

Chapter 2. Mexico

1. José Luis Ruiz, "Monte Albán, Bajo Control de EU," *El Universal,* January 17, 2000, http://www.eluniversal.com.mx/nacion/13006.html.

2. "Albright Hails Good Relations with Mexico," *Daily Courier,* Orlando, January 18, 2000, 2B.

3. Changing names reflects changing circumstances. The war used to be referred to, in the United States, as the Mexican-American War, but perhaps with the large number of Mexican immigrants in the United States, that name makes it sound like a war among Mexican Americans.

4. I use the term "Indian" throughout the text, referring to original inhabitants in the Americas, mostly in order to avoid confusion between the different terms used in Mexico, Canada, and the United States for the Indigenous, First Nation, and Native American inhabitants.

5. Santa Anna was not the only statesman to repudiate a treaty related to this territory. Andrew Jackson claimed the Adams-Onis Treaty to be in error, a treaty that his predecessor had signed with Spain, designating the western boundary of Texas as the Sabine River, hundreds of miles east of the Rio Grande.

6. The incident made front-page news in Mexico the following day. John Ross, a progressive journalist, later used it to investigate the broader role of Mexicans and US Mexicans in the wars. Historian Timothy Henderson also cited it in the introduction to his book, *A Glorious Defeat, Mexico and Its War with the United States* (West Sussex, UK: Wiley-Blackwell, 1988).

7. *Notes for the History of the War,* a history written by a group of fifteen Mexican military veterans, published in 1848. As quoted in Michael Van Wagenen, *Remembering the Forgotten War: The Enduring Legacies of the U.S.-Mexican War* (Amherst: University of Massachusetts Press, 2012), 48.

8. Van Wagenen, *Forgotten War,* 59.

9. Enrique Krauze, "The April Invasion of Veracruz," *New York Times,* April 20, 2014, https://www.nytimes.com/2014/04/21/opinion/krauze-the-april-invasion-of-veracruz.html. In this opinion piece, on the centennial anniversary of the invasion of Veracruz, Krauze appeals for actions of redress, but most of all, "a simple gesture: to remember the dead of April 1914 in the Mexican port of Veracruz."

10. See Andrew Selee's excellent book, *Vanishing Frontiers: Driving Mexico and the United States Together* (New York: Public Affairs, 2018), for both quantitative and qualitative background on the impact of NAFTA.

11. As both candidate and president, Donald Trump had no qualms about throwing aside the hesitancy to reopen NAFTA, calling it "perhaps the worst trade deal ever made." Its replacement, the US-Mexico-Canada Agreement, took three years to negotiate and implement. According to the US Congres-

sional Research Service, the new deal, "composed of 34 chapters and 12 side letters, retains most of NAFTA's chapters, making notable changes to market access provisions for autos and agriculture products, to rules such as investment, government procurement, and intellectual property rights (IPR), and to labor and the environment. New issues, such as digital trade, state-owned enterprises, and currency misalignment are also addressed."

12. Van Wagenen, *Forgotten War,* 245.

Chapter 3. Canada

1. K. M. Tiro, "Now You See It, Now You Don't: The War of 1812 in Canada and the United States in 2012," *Public Historian* 35, no. 1 (February 2013): 87.

2. "McCain Defends Napolitano, Insists 9/11 Perpetrators Came from Canada," CBC News, April 24, 2009, https://www.cbc.ca/news/world/mccain-defends-napolitano-insists-9–11-perpetrators-came-from-canada-1.830149.

3. Alan Taylor, a US scholar and two-time Pulitzer Prize winner, wrote one of only a few books on the war, on either side of the border, timed to the bicentennial. His account, *The Civil War of 1812,* devotes but one mention to Laura Secord, and Charles de Salaberry is mentioned on just two pages of the book.

4. Alan Taylor, *The Civil War of 1812: American Citizens, British Subjects, Irish Rebels, and Indian Allies* (New York: Alfred A. Knopf, 2010), 266.

5. Daniel Victor, "No, Mr. Trump, Canada Did Not Burn the White House Down in the War of 1812," *New York Times,* June 6, 2018, https://www.nytimes.com/2018/06/06/us/politics/war-of-1812-history-facts.html.

6. The SPP with all its color coded lists was scrapped at the end of the Bush administration, and Canada was finally able to persuade President Obama to separate policies along the two land borders by announcing with great fanfare the Beyond the Border project, openly agreeing to securing a North American perimeter, language Canada had eschewed after 9/11. This, too, had its own action plan with a long list of policies and commitments to be negotiated. The Trump administration brought an end to that initiative.

Chapter 4. Nigeria and South Africa

1. Malcolm X, "Letter from Accra," April 1964, http://www.malcolm-x.org/docs/let_laac.htm.

2. Malcolm X, "Letter from Nigeria," April 1964, http://www.malcolm-x.org/docs/let_laac.htm.

3. Malcolm X, "Letter from Accra."

4. The dispersal of African populations outside the continent is due

largely, but not exclusively, to the slave trade. More than one hundred million people in the Western Hemisphere can claim African descent, with smaller numbers in Europe, Asia, and the Middle East. Roughly 10 percent of people who claim African descent live outside the continent. "Sub-Saharan Africa: Total Population from 2009 to 2019," Statista, July 29, 2020, https://www.statista.com/statistics/805605/total-population-sub-saharan-africa/.

5. Juan Williams, "A Black Ambassador to Apartheid South Africa," National Public Radio, October 24, 2006, http://www.npr.org/templates/story/story.php?storyId=6369450.

6. See, for example, Martin Delaney and Robert Campbell's account from their travels to Liberia and the Bight of Benin region in 1859–1860. M. R. Delaney and Joseph Campbell, *Search for a Place, Black Separatism and Africa 1860* (Ann Arbor: University of Michigan Press, 1969).

7. Henry Louis Gates Jr., "Africa, to Me," in *The Henry Louis Gates, Jr. Reader* (New York: Basic Civitas Books, 2012), 415.

8. Association for Diplomatic Studies and Training, "Being Black in a Lily White State Department," accessed September 13, 2020, http://adst.org/oral-history/fascinating-figures/being-black-in-a-lily-white-state-department/.

9. Williams, "Black Ambassador."

10. Robert F. Kennedy, "Day of Affirmation Address, University of Capetown, Capetown, South Africa" June 6, 1966, https://www.jfklibrary.org/learn/about-jfk/the-kennedy-family/robert-f-kennedy/robert-f-kennedy-speeches/day-of-affirmation-address-university-of-capetown-capetown-south-africa-june-6-1966.

11. Williams, "Black Ambassador."

12. The terms to describe racial categories in South Africa are, unsurprisingly, politically charged. Apartheid laws used the term "natives" when referring to Black Africans. During my assignment, the term "Africans" was commonly used to refer to the majority population. Whites in South Africa held the view that they were also African, citing a heritage dating back to their settlement on the southern tip of the continent three centuries earlier. Nevertheless, I use the term white South Africans in describing this racial group.

13. John Higginson, "Privileging the Machines: American Engineers, Indentured Chinese and White Workers in South Africa's Deep-Level Gold Mines, 1902–1907," *International Review of Social History* 52, no. 1 (2007): 7.

14. ISL Leaflet, quoted in Julie Frederikse, *The Unbreakable Thread: Non-Racialism in South Africa* (Bloomington: Indiana University Press, 1990), 8.

15. Walter Sisulu, quoted in Frederikse, *Unbreakable Thread*, 80.

16. Frederikse, *Unbreakable Thread*, 80.

17. "The Freedom Charter, Adopted at the Congress of the People at Kliptown, Johannesburg, on June 25 and 26, 1955," accessed September 13, 2020, http://www.historicalpapers.wits.ac.za/inventories/inv_pdf0/AD1137 /AD1137-Ea6-1-001-jpeg.pdf.

18. National Action Council, "Call to the Congress of the People," 1954, quoted in Frederikse, *Unbreakable Thread*, 62.

19. "Nelson Mandela's Speech on His Release from Prison," February 11, 1990, accessed September 13, 2020, https://allafrica.com/download/resource /main/main/idatcs/00010797:daf2fae771c79dec3c21da5d5cd7e366.pdf.

20. Robert Sobukwe, quoted in Frederikse, *Unbreakable Thread*, 75.

21. Frederikse, *Unbreakable Thread*, 107.

22. Frederikse, 109.

23. Nelson Mandela, "I Am Prepared to Die," statement at the Rivonia Trial, April 20, 1964, in David Mermelstein, ed., *The Anti-Apartheid Reader* (New York, Grove Press, 1987), 232.

24. The rift between the US government and the ANC in the early 1960s has helped fuel rumors that in 1962 the CIA helped the South African government locate Mandela after he and the ANC leadership had adopted the armed struggle and gone underground. The unconfirmed report is the subject of a Freedom of Information Act lawsuit to seek official documents related to Mandela's arrest.

25. Nelson Mandela, quoted in Frederikse, *Unbreakable Thread*, 89.

Chapter 5. Summit of the Americas

1. "Statement by the President on the Shooting in Charleston, South Carolina," White House, June 18, 2015,

https://obamawhitehouse.archives.gov/the-press-office/2015/06/18/state ment-president-shooting-charleston-south-carolina.

2. The actual number may be in the thousands, typical for a presidential visit outside the country. A few years earlier, in Monterrey, Mexico, George W. Bush reportedly passed a motorcade and asked who was driving in the opposite direction. He was told it was still his motorcade, some seventy-five cars long, just catching up after the front of the line of cars had taken a U-turn to get to an exit on the other side of the highway.

3. "Eduardo Galeano," Goodreads, accessed , http://www.goodreads.com /author/show/5822041.Eduardo_Galeano.

4. Eduardo Galeano, *The Open Veins of Latin America* (New York, Monthly Review Press, 1973) 77.

5. Galeano, *Open Veins*, 73.

6. Galeano, 18.

7. Galeano, 115.

8. Galeano, 175.

9. Galeano, 275.

10. Larry Rohter, "Author Changes His Mind on '70s Manifesto," *New York Times*, May 24, 2014, C1.

11. "Remarks by the President at the Summit of the Americas Opening Ceremony," The White House, April 17, 2009, https://obamawhitehouse .archives.gov/the-press-office/remarks-president-summit-americas-open ing-ceremony.

12. "Chávez Creates Overnight Bestseller with Book Gift to Obama," Andrew Clark, *Guardian*, April 19, 2009, https://www.theguardian.com /world/2009/apr/19/obama-Chávez-book-gift-latin-america.

Chapter 6. Haiti

1. The numbers also vary widely and are hard to determine accurately given the extent of the damage and the inaccuracy of pre-earthquake statistics. See "Haiti Reconstruction: USAID Has Achieved Mixed Results and Should Enhance Sustainability Planning," US GAO Report, June 2015, https://www.gao.gov/assets/680/670616.pdf, and Reginald DesRoches, Mary Comerio, Marc Eberhard, Walter Mooney, and Glenn J. Rix, "Overview of the 2010 Haiti Earthquake," Earthquake Science Center, January 23, 2011, https://escweb.wr.usgs.gov/share/mooney/142.pdf.

2. Laurent Dubois, *Haiti: The Aftershocks of History* (New York: Metropolitan Books, 2010), 139.

3. Abraham Lincoln, First Message to Congress, December 3, 1861, accessed October 24, 2020, https://millercenter.org/the-presidency/presidential -speeches/december-3-1861-first-annual-message.

4. Dubois, 224.

5. Daniels was, coincidentally, the cabinet officer who ordered the invasion and occupation of Veracruz, Mexico, in 1914. Franklin Delano Roosevelt, who was Daniel's assistant secretary of the navy, suffered from his own history shock, when the Mexicans protested FDR's appointment of Daniels as ambassador there years later. See Joseph L. Morrison, "Josephus Daniels-Simpatico," *Journal of Inter-American Studies* 5, no. 2 (1963): 277–289, https://www.jstor.org/stable/164815.

6. Dubois, *Aftershocks*, 254.

7. Dubois, 240.

8. Smedley D. Butler, *War Is a Racket: The Antiwar Classic by America's Most Decorated Soldier* (New York: Skyhorse Publishing, 2016), 17.

9. James Weldon Johnson, "The Truth about Haiti: An NAACP Investi-

gation," *Crisis Magazine* 5 (September 1920): 217–224, http://historymatters
.gmu.edu/d/5018/.

10. Mary A. Renda, *Taking Haiti: Military Occupation and the Culture of
U.S. Imperialism 1915–1940* (Chapel Hill: University of North Carolina Press,
2004), 11.

11. Dubois, *Aftershocks*, 366.

12. Magdalena Carmelita Douby Guillaume, "Cultural Conservation: A
Source of Dignity," in Richard Kurin, *Saving Haiti's Heritage, Cultural Recovery after the Earthquake* (Washington, DC: Smithsonian Institution, 2011), 218.

13. Kurin, *Haiti's Heritage*, 43.

Chapter 7. Peru

1. Department of the Treasury, "Archaeological and Ethnological Material
from Peru," *Federal Register* 62, no. 112 (June 11, 1997), https://eca.state.gov
/files/bureau/pe1997dlfrn_o.pdf.

2. Hiram Bingham, quoted in Mark Adams, *Turn Right at Machu Picchu:
Rediscovering the Lost City One Step at a Time* (New York: Dutton, 2011), 252.

3. Hiram Bingham, "In the Wonderland of Peru," *National Geographic
Magazine*, April 1913, 473.

4. Bingham, "Wonderland," 428.

5. Bingham, 421.

6. Ricardo Salvatore, *Disciplinary Conquest: U.S. Scholars in South America,
1900–1945* (Durham, NC: Duke University Press, 2016), 85.

7. Salvatore, *Disciplinary Conquest*, 251.

8. Adams, *Turn Right at Machu Picchu*, 208.

9. Roger Atwood, *Stealing History: Tomb Raiders, Smugglers, and the Looting of the Ancient World* (New York: St. Marten's Press, 2004), 25.

10. Atwood, *Stealing History*, 46.

11. Walter Alva, "Discovering the Tomb of a Moche Lord," *National Geographic*, October 1988, 518.

12. Department of the Treasury. "Import Restrictions Imposed on Significant Archaeological Artifacts from Peru," *Federal Register* 55, no. 88 (May 7,
1990), https://eca.state.gov/files/bureau/pe1990eafrn_o.pdf.

13. Adams, *Stealing History*, 211.

14. Treasury, "Import Restrictions," 1.

15. Fujimori's rise to the presidency of Peru offered yet another example
of history shock. International attention focused on the anomaly of a Peruvian of Japanese heritage winning the presidency. What surprised me was
learning that the United States was not alone in claiming to be a nation of
immigrants. All over Latin America, one finds names of English, German,
Italian, and Irish origin. Japanese migrants arrived in Peru in the late 1800s

to work on the coastal cotton and sugar plantations. Eventually, they made their way to cities to work as street vendors and from there to own small businesses, such as grocery stores, barber shops, and restaurants. The United States connects to Peru's history of Japanese migration first when it curtailed its own intake from Japan in 1907. That resulted in increasing the flows of Japanese heading to other countries in the hemisphere, such as Peru and Brazil, which today have the largest population of people of Japanese origin in Latin America. Second, during World War II, the United States convinced Peruvian authorities to deport 1,800 Japanese to serve in the notorious internment camps alongside Japanese Americans. Fujimori grew up in this environment of an insular ethnic minority, at times facing outright hostility from Peru's majority population. He earned his first degree in agricultural engineering and a second one in mathematics from the University of Wisconsin-Madison. After returning to Peru, he taught at university levels and went on to become rector of the National Agricultural University. From that platform, he ran for president, largely as an unknown, and was able to garner votes from beyond his own ethnic minority as an outsider candidate, appealing to the large indigenous population against his well-known, but elite, rival, the author Mario Vargas Llosa. See Ayumi Takenaka, "The Japanese in Peru: History of Immigration, Settlement, and Racialization," *Latin American Perspectives* 31, no. 3 (May 2004): 77–98.

Chapter 8. Mexico

1. Manuel Gamio, as quoted in Timothy Henderson, *Beyond Borders: A History of Mexican Migration to the United States* (West Sussex, UK: Wiley-Blackwell, 2011), 28.

2. Tadeo Ortiz de Ayala, a Mexican writer, as quoted in José Angel Hernández, *Mexican-American Colonization during the Nineteenth Century: A History of the U.S.-Mexico Borderlands* (New York: Cambridge University Press, 2012), 53.

3. Hernández, *Mexican-American Colonization*, 57.

4. Alexis de Tocqueville, *Democracy in America*, quoted in William C. Davis, *Three Roads to the Alamo: The Lives and Fortunes of David Crockett, James Bowie, and William Barret Travis* (New York: Harper Perennial, 1999), 274.

5. Hernández, *Mexican-American Colonization*, 74–75.

6. Hernández, 46.

7. Henderson, *Beyond Borders*, 19.

8. Henderson, 46.

9. Hernández, *Mexican-American Colonization*, 9–10.

10. Henderson, *Beyond Borders*, 28.

11. Kitty Calavita, *Inside the State: The Bracero Program, Immigration, and the I.N.S.* (New Orleans: Quid Pro Books, 2010), 20.

12. Calavita, *Inside the State*, 28.

13. Commissioner Swing letter to Assistant Secretary of State Henry F. Holland, August 1955, quoted in Calavita, 104.

14. Calavita, 181.

15. Multiple visa categories allowed then—and still do—Mexicans to enter the United States to work legally. The temporary worker program, known as the H2A visa for seasonal agricultural workers, which became the legal option following the Bracero program, has no limit on participants from Mexico. The total number of those visas approved for 2004 was only 28,683, which is small considering an estimated 300,000 crossed into the United States without documents. By 2013, the number of agricultural visas issued to Mexicans had increased, but only to 69,787. Outside of agriculture, another 52,556 Mexicans were able to work temporarily in the United States in 2004. That number fell to 41,883 by 2013. That universe expands when other Mexicans eligible to work in the United States are included. In 2004, the United States issued 44,835 immigrant visas, which climbed to 91,637 in 2008 before falling back to 61,268 in 2013. The numbers skyrocket when green card holders, or legal permanent residents, an estimated 3,300,000 in 2012, are included. See Bureau of Consular Affairs, US State Department, "Non-Immigrant Visa Statistics," accessed November 10, 2014, http://travel.state.gov/content/visas/english/law-and-policy /statistics/non-immigrant-visas.html, and Nancy Rytine, "Estimates of the Legal Permanent Resident Population in 2012," Department of Homeland Security, accessed November 10, 2014, http://www.dhs.gov/sites/default /files/publications/ois_lpr_pe_2012.pdf.

Chapter 9. Cuba

1. "Statement by the President on Cuba Policy Changes," White House, December 17, 2014, https://obamawhitehouse.archives.gov/the-press-office /2014/12/17/statement-president-cuba-policy-changes.

2. Ann Louise Bardach, *Without Fidel: A Death Foretold in Miami, Havana and Washington* (New York: Scribner, 2009), 90.

3. See Dan Fisk, "Cuba and American Public Opinion," *Cuba in Transition* 9, Papers and Proceedings of the Ninth Annual Meeting, August 12–14, 1999, Association for the Study of the Cuban Economy, 311, accessed October 28, 2020, https://www.ascecuba.org/asce_proceedings/comments-by -rene-perez-lopez-on-cuba-and-american-public-opinion-by-fisk/; Institute for Public Opinion Research, Florida International University, Brookings

Institution, Cuba Study Group "2008 Cuba/US Transition Poll Institute for Public Opinion Research," accessed September 24, 2020, https://cri.fiu.edu /research/cuba-poll/2008-cuba-poll.pdf; also Gallup Polls on Cuba, accessed September 24, 2020, http://www.gallup.com/poll/1630/cuba.aspx.

4. Associated Press, "Guatemala Apologizes to Cuba for Allowing CIA to Train Exiles for Bay of Pigs Invasion," Fox News, February 17, 2009, https:// www.foxnews.com/story/guatemala-apologizes-to-cuba-for-allowing-cia -to-train-exiles-for-bay-of-pigs-invasion.

5. US Department of State, "Summary of Speeches Made at October 26, 1959 Mass Demonstration," cable, LANIC, November 11, 1959, http://lanic .utexas.edu/project/castro/db/1959/19591026-2.html.

6. Painted on a roll of linen cloth, the mural was intended as one piece in a traveling exhibit sent to Eastern Europe, before it became lost. It was rediscovered fifty years later, rolled up in the Pushkin Museum, and found its way back to Mexico and then on to Guatemala for exhibits in those two countries. President Álvaro Colom attended the opening of art exhibit in Guatemala in 2010. Colom, who we have seen apologized to Castro, said that the day Árbenz left office "changed Guatemala and we have not recuperated from it yet. It was a crime to Guatemalan society and it was an act of aggression to a government starting its democratic spring." See Mark Vallen, "A New Look at Rivera's 'Glorious Victory,'" Art for a Change, February 8, 2016, http://art-for-a-change.com/blog/2016/02/a-new-look-at-riveras-glo riosa-victoria.html.

7. Quoted in Volker Skierka, *Fidel Castro: A Biography* (Malden MA: Polity Press, 2004), 105.

8. Hugh Thomas, *Cuba, or the Pursuit of Freedom* (London: Eyre & Spottiswoode, 1971), 1302.

9. Jim Rasenberger, *The Brilliant Disaster, JFK, Castro, and America's Doomed Invasion of Cuba's Bay of Pigs* (New York: Scribner, 2011), 219–226.

10. "Cuba: Political, Diplomatic and Economic Problems," Schlesinger Memorandum, Bay of Pigs Invasion Documents, accessed September 24, 2020, http://www.tep-online.info/laku/usa/cuba/baydocs.htm.

11. "Cuba" memorandum.

12. Fidel Castro, "Fidel Castro Speaks to Citizens of Santiago," LANIC, January 3, 1959, accessed September 24, 2020, http://lanic.utexas.edu/project /castro/db/1959/19590103.html.

13. William Randolph Hearst, quoted in Thomas, *Cuba*, 340.

14. William McKinley, quoted in Thomas, *Cuba*, 436.

15. Fidel Castro, "Castro Delivers Speech at Presidential Palace," January 17, 1959, LANIC, accessed September 24, 2020, http://lanic.utexas.edu/proj ect/castro/db/1959/19590117-1.html.

16. Executive Order 12323, "Presidential Commission on Broadcasting to Cuba," September 22, 1981, https://www.presidency.ucsb.edu/documents/ex ecutive-order-12323-presidential-commission-broadcasting-cuba.

17. Teresa Casuso, *Cuba and Castro* (New York: Random House, 1961), 103.

18. Fidel Castro, quoted in Thomas, *Cuba*, 1051.

19. Fidel Castro, "Castro Proclaims Socialist Cuba," May 2, 1961, LANIC, accessed September 24, 2020, http://lanic.utexas.edu/project/castro/db/1961 /19610502.html.

20. José Martí, "Letter to Manuel Mercado" and "To Cuba," quoted in Alfred López, *José Martí: A Revolutionary Life* (Austin: University of Texas Press, 2014), 272, 316.

21. José Martí, "Our America," quoted in López, *José Martí*, 246.

22. José Martí, "Letter to Máximo Gómez," quoted in López, 225.

23. José Martí and Máximo Gómez, *Montechristi Manifesto*, 1895, "Modern Latin America: Web Supplement for 8th Edition," Brown University Library, accessed, https://library.brown.edu/create/modernlatinamerica/chapters/chap ter-4-cuba/primary-documents-w-accompanying-discussion-questions/doc ument-8-montecristi-manifesto-jose-marti-and-maximo-gomez-1895/.

24. "National Poll of Cubans, March 17–25, 2015," conducted by Bendixen and Amandi International and *Washington Post*, April 2015, http://apps .washingtonpost.com/g/page/politics/national-poll-of-cubans-march-17-25 -2015/1661/.

Chapter 10. Choosing to Remember

1. M. Todd Bennett, "Time to Heal the Wounds: America's Bicenten- nial and U.S.- Sweden Normalization in 1976," in *Reasserting America in the 1970s: U.S. Public Diplomacy and the Rebuilding of America's Image Abroad*, ed. Hallvard Notaker, Giles Scott-Smith, and David J. Snyder (Manchester, UK: Manchester University Press, 2016).

2. Walter Thurston, as quoted in Michael Scott Van Wagenen, *Remem- bering the Forgotten War: The Enduring Legacies of the U.S./Mexican War* (Am- herst: University of Massachusetts Press, 2012), 163.

3. Van Wagenen, *Forgotten War*, 163.

4. Sam Dillon, "On Clinton Itinerary: Mexico City Counterpart of the Alamo," *New York Times*, May 6, 1997, http://www.nytimes.com/1997/05/06 /world/on-clinton-itinerary-mexico-city-counterpart-of-the-alamo.html.

5. Dillon, "Clinton Itinerary."

6. Van Wagenen, *Forgotten War*, 224.

7. Nicholas Trist, quoted in Amy Greenberg, *A Wicked War: Polk, Clay, Lincoln, and the 1846 U.S. Invasion of Mexico* (New York: Knopf, 2012), 223.

8. Harry S. Truman, "Address in Mexico City," March 3, 1947, Truman

Public Library, accessed October 8, 2018, https://www.trumanlibrary.org /publicpapers/index.php?pid=2194.

9. Harry S. Truman, "Letter on the Dropping of the Atomic Bomb," August 5, 1963, accessed October 8, 2018, http://www.nuclearfiles.org/menu /library/correspondence/truman-harry/corr_truman_1963-08-05.htm.

10. Summarized in Edwin L. Battistella, *Sorry about That: The Language of Public Apology* (New York: Oxford University Press, 2014), 3.

11. Elise Hu, "Obama Makes Historic Visit to Hiroshima Memorial Peace Park," National Public Radio, May 27, 2016, http://www.npr.org/sections /thetwo-way/2016/05/27/479691439/president-obama-arrives-in-hiroshima -the-first-sitting-commander-in-chief-to-vis.

12. Gerald M. Boyd, "Bush, a Cautious Front-Runner Again, Avoids Attacks and Personal Campaigning," *New York Times*, February 27, 1988, http:// www.nytimes.com/1988/02/27/us/bush-a-cautious-front-runner-again -avoids-attacks-and-personal-campaigning.html.

13. George H. W. Bush, quoted in Battistella, *Sorry about That*, 146.

14. Fox Butterfield, "Iran Falls Short in Drive at U.N. to Condemn U.S. in Airbus Case," *New York Times*, July 15, 1988, http://www.nytimes .com/1988/07/15/world/iran-falls-short-in-drive-at-un-to-condemn-us-in -airbus-case.html.

15. Mitt Romney, *No Apology: The Case for American Greatness* (New York: St. Martin's Press, 2010) 293.

16. Glenn Kessler, "Obama's Apology Tour," The Fact Checker, *Washington Post*, February 22, 2011, http://voices.washingtonpost.com/fact -checker/2011/02/obamas_apology_tour.html.

17. Lawrence Sellin, "How the Cairo Video Became the Benghazi Video," *Accuracy in Media*, May 9, 2014, accessed November 11, 2017, http://www.aim .org/guest-column/how-the-cairo-video-became-the-benghazi-video/.

18. "Transcript And Audio: Second Presidential Debate," National Public Radio, October 16, 2012, https://www.npr.org/2012/10/16/163050988/tran script-obama-romney-2nd-presidential-debate.

19. Battistella, *Sorry about That, 3*.

20. Battistella, 63.

21. Battistella, 64.

22. Battistella, 64.

23. Battistella, 64.

24. Jennifer Lind, *Sorry States: Apologies in International Politics* (Ithaca, NY: Cornell University Press, 2011), 159, 8.

25. Lind, *Sorry States*, 4.

26. Stephen Kinzer, *Overthrow: America's Century of Regime Change from Hawaii to Iraq* (New York: Henry Holt, 2006), 88.

27. Mark Danner, *The Massacre at El Mozote* (New York: Vintage Books, 1994), 262–263.

28. The figure of 200 victims comes from the report of the Commission on the Truth for El Salvador, "From Madness to Hope: The 12-Year War in El Salvador," March 15, 1993, 112. The *New York Times* journalist reported from El Mozote, citing figures from villagers and the national human rights commission ranging from 735 to 926: Raymond Bonner, *New York Times*, January 27, 1982, https://www.nytimes.com/1982/01/27/world/massacre-of-hundreds-reported-in-salvador-village.html. The discrepancy may result from victims from the actual village being reported by the Truth Commission and larger figures including nearby villages.

29. George Vest et al., "Report of the US Secretary of State's Panel on El Salvador," cited in Danner, *El Mozote*, 278.

30. George W. Bush, "On U.S. and Canada Relations and the War on Terrorism," December 1, 2004, American Rhetoric Online Speech Bank, http://www.americanrhetoric.com/speeches/gwbushhalifax.htm. Bush's reference to Prime Minister Paul Martin mentioning the Canadian reaction on 9/11 shows how much this weighed on Canada's mind.

31. David Wilkins, "Open Letter to Canada," Canadian Content, September 12, 2005, http://forums.canadiancontent.net/news/39831-open-letter -canada-u-s.html.

32. "U.S. Embassy, Ontario, 9/11 Memorial Plaque," Memorial Mapping: Transnational 9/11 Memorials, accessed September 25, 2020, http://www.me morialmapping.com/memorials/us-embassy-ontario-9-11-memo rial-plaque.

33. Lind, *Sorry States*, 8.

34. Robert Weyeneth, "The Power of Apology and the Process of Historical Reconciliation," *Public Historian* 23, no. 3 (Summer 2001): 32.

Chapter 11. Connecting the Dots

1. Gore Vidal, "State of the Union 2004," *Nation*, September 13, 2004, 23. In that article, Vidal uses the phrase "United States of Amnesia" principally related to domestic issues, but in the 2005 film *Why We Fight*, he uses the same phrase in reference to foreign conflicts.

2. Mohsin Hamid, *The Reluctant Fundamentalist* (New York: Harcourt Publishing, 2007), 130. Kindle.

3. *Time Magazine* 158, no. 16 (October 15, 2001), cover, accessed October 30, 2020, http://content.time.com/time/magazine/0,9263,7601011015,00.html.

4. Michael H. Hunt, *Ideology and U.S. Foreign Policy* (New Haven, CT: Yale University Press, 1987), 3.

5. William J. Burns, *The Back Channel: A Memoir of American Diplomacy and the Case for Its Renewal* (New York: Random House, 2019), 28.

6. Woodrow Wilson National Fellowship Foundation, "National Survey Finds Just 1 in 3 Americans Would Pass Citizenship Test," October 3, 2018, https://woodrow.org/news/national-survey-finds-just-1-in-3-americans -would-pass-citizenship-test/.

7. Daniel Ellsberg, *Secrets: A Memoir of Vietnam and the Pentagon Papers* (New York: Viking Adult, 2001) 250.

8. Ellsberg, *Secrets*, 347.

9. George Ball, quoted in Mark Lawrence, "Policymaking and the Uses of the Vietnam War," in *The Power of the Past: History and Statecraft*, ed. Hal Brand and Jeremi Suri (Washington, DC: Brookings Institution Press, 2016), 64.

10. Richard E. Neustadt and Ernest R. May, *Thinking in Time: The Uses of History for Decision Makers* (New York: The Free Press, Simon & Schuster, 1988), 111.

11. Thomas Paine, quoted in Hunt, *Ideology and U.S. Foreign Policy*, 20.

12. David Lowenthal, *The Past Is a Foreign Country* (Cambridge: Cambridge University Press, 1985), 108.

13. Ellsberg, *Secrets*, 347.

14. Barack Obama, "Remarks to the Summit of the Americas in Port of Spain, Trinidad and Tobago," April 17, 2009, accessed December 13, 2017, https://www.gpo.gov/fdsys/pkg/PPP-2009-book1/pdf/PPP-2009-book1 -Doc-pg511.pdf.

15. Obama, "Summit of the Americas."

16. John Winthrop, "A Model of Christian Charity," accessed October 30, 2020, https://history.hanover.edu/texts/winthmod.html.

17. Thomas Shannon, "Reimagining the Future of American Leadership," *Foreign Service Journal* 95, no. 1 (January–February 2018): 53–55.

18. Several essays compiled in *The Power of the Past: History and Statecraft*, edited by Brand and Suri, analyze the analogies of Munich and Vietnam that continue to guide US political debate over foreign policy.

19. Kenneth Adelman, "Stronger Voice for U.S.," *New York Times*, August 1, 1980, quoted in Lowenthal, *Foreign Country*, 346.

20. V. S. Naipaul, *A Bend in the River*, cited in Lowenthal, *Foreign Country*, 67.

21. Hubert Bauch, "FAST Cards Will Likely Meet WHTI Requirements: Wilkins," *Montreal Gazette*, November 7, 2006, https://www.pressreader .com/canada/montreal-gazette/20061107/281715495115647.

22. Jennifer M. Lind, *Sorry States: Apologies in International Politics* (Ithaca, NY: Cornell University Press, 2008), 8

23. Herman Melville, *White Jacket, or, the World in a Man-of-War* (London: Richard Bentley, 1850), 238–239.

24. Jimmy Carter, "Crisis of Confidence," American Experience, PBS, July 15, 1979, http://www.pbs.org/wgbh/americanexperience/features/primary-resources/carter-crisis.

25. Stephen Kinzer, *Overthrow: America's Century of Regime Change from Hawaii to Iraq* (New York: Times Books/Henry Holt, 2006), 293.

26. David Brion Davis, *Inhuman Bondage: The Rise and Fall of Slavery in the New World* (New York: Oxford University Press, 2006), 176.

27. *Oxford Dictionary*, Oxford University Press, s.v. "trope," https://en.oxforddictionaries.com/definition/us/trope.

28. Benedict Anderson, *Imagined Communities: Reflections on the Origin and Spread of Nationalism* (London: Verso, 1983)

29. Michael Scott Van Wagenen, *Remembering the Forgotten War: The Enduring Legacies of the U.S./Mexican War* (Amherst : University of Massachusetts Press, 2012), 4.

30. Richard Nixon, *Beyond Peace*, 30, quoted in Walter Russell Mead, *Special Providence, American Foreign Policy and How It Changed the World* (New York: Alfred A. Knopf, 2001), 6.

31. Theodore Roosevelt, quoted in Mathew Frye Jacobson, *Barbarian Virtues: The United States Encounters Foreign Peoples at Home and Abroad, 1876–1917* (New York: Hill and Wang, 2000), 45.

32. Kinzer, *Overthrow*, 316.

33. Robert Kagan, *Dangerous Nation: America's Place in the World from Its Earliest Days to the Dawn of the Twentieth Century* (New York: Alfred A. Knopf, 2006), 5.

34. *Baltimore American*, quoted in Kinzer, *Overthrow*, 54.

35. Kinzer, 55.

36. H. W. Brands, "Neither Munich nor Vietnam, The Gulf War of 1991," in Brands and Suri, *Power of the Past*, 74.

37. Alan Taylor, *Civil War of 1812: American Citizens, British Subjects, Irish Rebels, and Indian Allies* (New York: Alfred A. Knopf, 2010), 10.

38. Van Wagenen, *Forgotten War*, 6.

39. Mary A. Renda, *Taking Haiti: Military Occupation and the Culture of U.S. Imperialism, 1915–1940* (Chapel Hill: University of North Carolina Press, 2001), 11.

40. Richard E. Neustadt and Ernest May, *Thinking in Time: The Uses of History for Decision Makers* (New York: Free Press, New York, 1986). See also the excellent essays in Hal Brands and Jeremi Suri, eds., *The Power of the Past, History and Statecraft of the Past* (Washington, DC: Brookings Institution Press, 2016).

41. Peter Feaver and William Imboden, "Looking Forward through the Past: The Role of History in Bush White House National Security Policymaking," in Brands and Suri, *Power of the Past*, 267.

42. Brands and Suri, *Power of the Past*, 15.

43. David Remnick, "Going the Distance," *New Yorker*, January 27, 2014, 55.

Index